The Complete Book of Personal Legal Forms

(+ CD-ROM)

Mark Warda
James C. Ray

Attorneys at Law

SPHINX® PUBLISHING
AN IMPRINT OF SOURCEBOOKS, INC.®
NAPERVILLE, ILLINOIS
www.SphinxLegal.com

First Edition: 2005

Published by: **Sphinx® Publishing, An Imprint of Sourcebooks, Inc.®**

<u>Naperville Office</u>
P.O. Box 4410
Naperville, Illinois 60567-4410
630-961-3900
Fax: 630-961-2168
www.sourcebooks.com
www.SphinxLegal.com

This publication is designed to provide accurate and authoritative information in regard to the subject matter covered. It is sold with the understanding that the publisher is not engaged in rendering legal, accounting, or other professional service. If legal advice or other expert assistance is required, the services of a competent professional person should be sought.

From a Declaration of Principles Jointly Adopted by a Committee of the
American Bar Association and a Committee of Publishers and Associations

This product is not a substitute for legal advice.

Disclaimer required by Texas statutes.

Library of Congress Cataloging-in-Publication Data
Warda, Mark.
  The complete book of personal legal forms : plus CD-ROM / Mark Warda and James C. Ray.
     p. cm.
  Includes index.
  ISBN 1-57248-499-3 (pbk. : alk. paper)
  1. Forms (Law)--United States. I. Ray, James C., 1945- II. Title.
  KF170.W366 2005
  347.73'55--dc22
                                                    2005009074

Printed and bound in the United States of America.

SB — 10 9 8 7 6

Contents

> *Forms in Chapter:*
> • **Contract**
> • **Addendum to Contract**
> • **Amendment to Contract**
> • **Assignment of Contract**
> • **Termination of Contract**

Types of Legal Forms
Contracts
    Mutual Agreement
    Oral Contracts
    Statute of Frauds
Sample Simple Contract
    Addendum to Contract
Sample Addendum to Contract
    Amending a Contract
Sample Amendment to Contract
    Assigning a Contract

Forms in Chapter:
- **Cohabitation Agreement**
- **Family Contract of Adult Child Living with Parents**
- **Premarital Agreement**
- **Marital Agreement**
- **Notice of Name Change**
- **Separation Agreement**
- **Divorce Settlement**
- **Delegation of Parental Responsibility**

> • **Child Authorization**
> • **Authorization for Child to Travel**
> • **Pet Care Agreement**
> • **Official Mail Forwarding Change of Address Order**
> • **Address Change Notice to Contacts**
> • **Change of Address Notice (to IRS)**
> • **Birth or Death Certificate Request**
> • **Application for U.S. Passport**
> • **Passport Renewal (Application for U.S. Passport by Mail)**
> • **Application for Social Security Card**

Chapter 3: Forms for Estate Planning

> *Forms in Chapter:*
> • **Asset and Beneficiary List**
> • **Will—Spouse and Children**
> • **Will—Spouse and No Children**
> • **Will—Children and No Spouse**
> • **Will—No Spouse and No Children**
> • **Will—Codicil**
> • **Living Trust**
> • **Living Trust—Schedule of Assets**
> • **Declaration of Joint Property**
> • **Declaration of Separate Property**
> • **Living Trust—Amendment**

> • **Request for Forbearance on Loan**
> • **Request for Consolidation of Loans**
> • **Notice of Death of Debtor**

Receipt
Sample Receipt
Promissory Note
    Amortization
    Interest
    Negotiability
    Guarantee
Sample Guarantee
    Security
Forms for Credit Matters
    Credit Report
Sample Request for Correction of Credit Report
    Dealing with Debts
    Judgments
    Credit Cards
    Identity Theft
    Loans
    Social Security

> *Forms in Chapter:*
>   • **Request for Quotation**
>   • **Bill of Sale—with Warranty**
>   • **Bill of Sale**
>   • **Chattel Mortgage**
>   • **UCC-1 Financing Statement**
>   • **UCC-3 Financing Statement Amendment**
>   • **Receipt for Personal Property**

Placing an Order
Sample Request for Quotation
Buying and Selling
Sample Bill of Sale
Installment Sales
    Forms
Loaning Property

Chapter 6: Real Estate Forms 219

Forms in Chapter:
- Real Estate Sales Contract
- Warranty Deed
- Quitclaim Deed
- Assignment of Mortgage
- Satisfaction of Mortgage
- Option Agreement
- Exercise of Option
- Rental Application
- Inspection Report
- Disclosure of Information on Lead-Based Paint (Rental)
- House Lease—Set Term
- House Lease—Month-to-Month
- Apartment Rental Agreement—Set Term
- Apartment Rental Agreement—Month-to-Month
- Pet Agreement
- Amendment to Lease Agreement
- Lease Assignment
- Consent to Sublease
- Roommate Agreement
- Notice to Landlord to Make Repairs
- Annual Letter—Continuation of Tenancy
- Letter to Vacating Tenant
- Notice of Intent to Vacate at End of Lease
- Demand for Return of Security Deposit
- Waiver and Assumption of Risk
- Declaration of Homestead

Buying and Selling Real Estate
    Real Estate Contract
Sample Real Estate Sales Contract
    Real Estate Deed
Financing Real Estate
    Mortgage or Deed of Trust
    Real Estate Options
Leasing and Renting Real Estate
    Rental Application
    Property Inspections
    Lead-Based Paint
    Lease Agreement

Chapter 7: Employment Forms 297

Forms in Chapter:
- **Application for Employment**
- **Authorization to Release Employment Information**
- **Verification of Education**
- **Verification of Licensure**
- **Employment Eligibility Verification (I-9)**
- **Application for Employer Identification Number (SS-4)**
- **Employee's Withholding Allowance Certificate (W-4)**
- **Household Help Agreement**
- **Determination of Worker Status (SS-8)**
- **Independent Contractor Agreement**
- **Modification of Independent Contractor Agreement**
- **Termination of Independent Contractor Agreement**

> *Forms in Chapter:*
> - **Affidavit**
> - **Arbitration Agreement**
> - **Mediation Agreement**
> - **Covenant Not to Sue**
> - **Accident Worksheet**
> - **General Release**
> - **Specific Release**
> - **Mutual Release**
> - **Request for Information under the Freedom of Information Act**
> - **Mailing List Name Removal**
> - **Request to Stop Telephone Solicitations**

Table of Forms

Chapter 6: Real Estate Forms

- Real Estate Sales Contract
- Warranty Deed
- Quitclaim Deed
- Assignment of Mortgage
- Satisfaction of Mortgage
- Option Agreement
- Exercise of Option
- Rental Application
- Inspection Report
- Disclosure of Information on Lead-Based Paint (Rental)
- House Lease—Set Term
- House Lease—Month-to-Month
- Apartment Rental Agreement—Set Term
- Apartment Rental Agreement—Month-to-Month
- Pet Agreement
- Amendment to Lease Agreement
- Lease Assignment
- Consent to Sublease
- Roommate Agreement
- Notice to Landlord to Make Repairs
- Annual Letter—Continuation of Tenancy
- Letter to Vacating Tenant
- Notice of Intent to Vacate at End of Lease
- Demand for Return of Security Deposit
- Waiver and Assumption of Risk
- Declaration of Homestead

Chapter 7: Employment Forms

- Application for Employment
- Authorization to Release Employment Information
- Verification of Education
- Verification of Licensure
- Employment Eligibility Verification (I-9)
- Application for Employer Identification Number (SS-4)
- Employee's Withholding Allowance Certificate (W-4)
- Household Help Agreement
- Determination of Worker Status (SS-8)
- Independent Contractor Agreement
- Modification of Independent Contractor Agreement
- Termination of Independent Contractor Agreement

Chapter 8: Miscellaneous Forms

- **Affidavit**
- **Arbitration Agreement**
- **Mediation Agreement**
- **Covenant Not to Sue**
- **Accident Worksheet**
- **General Release**
- **Specific Release**
- **Mutual Release**
- **Request for Information under the Freedom of Information Act**
- **Mailing List Name Removal**
- **Request to Stop Telephone Solicitations**

How to Use
the CD-ROM

Thank you for purchasing *The Complete Book of Personal Legal Forms (+ CD-ROM)*. In this book, we have worked hard to compile exactly what you need to negotiate any number of legal situations, from the commonplace to the critical. Whether a change of address or a living will, we have gathered the most important forms and documents you need to protect yourself, your family, and your assets. To make this material even more useful, we have included every document in the book on the CD-ROM that is attached to the inside back cover of the book.

Use the list at the end of this section for help finding the form you are looking for. You can use these forms just as you would the forms in the book. Print them out, fill them in, and use them however you need. You can also fill in the forms directly on your computer. Just identify the form you need, open it, click on the space where the information should go, and input your information. Customize each form for your particular needs. Use them over and over again.

The CD-ROM is compatible with both PC and Mac operating systems. (While it should work with either operating system, we cannot guarantee that it will work with your particular system and we cannot provide technical assistance.) To use the forms on your computer, you will need to use Acrobat® Reader®. The CD-ROM does not contain this program. You can download this program from Adobe's website at **www.adobe.com**. Click on the "Get Acrobat® Reader®" icon to begin the download process and follow the instructions.

Once you have Acrobat® Reader® installed, insert the CD-ROM into your computer. Double click on the icon representing the disc on your desktop or go through your hard drive to identify the drive that contains the disc and click on it.

Once opened, you will see the files contained on the CD-ROM listed as "Form #: [Form Title]." Open the file you need through Acrobat® Reader®. You may print the form to fill it out manually at this point or you can use the "Hand Tool" and click on the appropriate line to fill it in using your computer.

Any time you see bracketed information [ ] on the form, you can click on it and delete the bracketed information from your final form. This information is only a reference guide to assist you in filling in the forms and should be removed from your final version. Once all your information is filled in, you can print your filled-in form.

NOTE: *Acrobat® Reader® does not allow you to save the PDF with the boxes filled in.*

• • • • • • • •

Purchasers of this book are granted a license to use the forms contained in it for their own personal use. By purchasing this book, you have also purchased a limited license to use all forms on the accompanying CD-ROM. The license limits you to personal use only and all other copyright laws must be adhered. No claim of copyright is made in any government form reproduced in the book or on the CD-ROM. You are free to modify the forms and tailor them to your specific situation.

The author and publisher have attempted to provide the most current and up-to-date information available. However, the courts, Congress, and your state's legislatures review, modify, and change laws on an ongoing basis, as well as create new laws from time to time. By the very nature of the information and due to the continual changes in our legal system, to be sure that you have the current and best information for your situation, you should consult a local attorney or research the current laws yourself.

• • • • • • • •

This publication is designed to provide accurate and authoritative information in regard to the subject matter covered. It is sold with the understanding that the publisher is not engaged in rendering legal, accounting, or other professional service. If legal advice or other expert assistance is required, the services of a competent professional person should be sought.
    —*From a Declaration of Principles Jointly Adopted by a Committee of the American Bar Association and a Committee of Publishers and Associations*

This product is not a substitute for legal advice.
    —*Disclaimer required by Texas statutes*

Using Self-Help Law Books

Before using a self-help law book, you should realize the advantages and disadvantages of doing your own legal work and understand the challenges and diligence that this requires.

The Growing Trend

Rest assured that you won't be the first or only person handling your own legal matter. For example, in some states, more than seventy-five percent of the people in divorces and other cases represent themselves. Because of the high cost of legal services, this is a major trend and many courts are struggling to make it easier for people to represent themselves. However, some courts are not happy with people who do not use attorneys and refuse to help them in any way. For some, the attitude is, "Go to the law library and figure it out for yourself."

We write and publish self-help law books to give people an alternative to the often complicated and confusing legal books found in most law libraries. We have made the explanations of the law as simple and easy to understand as possible. Of course, unlike an attorney advising an individual client, we cannot cover every conceivable possibility.

Cost/Value Analysis

Whenever you shop for a product or service, you are faced with various levels of quality and price. In deciding what product or service to buy, you make a cost/value analysis on the basis of your willingness to pay and the quality you desire.

When buying a car, you decide whether you want transportation, comfort, status, or sex appeal. Accordingly, you decide among such choices as a Neon, a Lincoln, a Rolls Royce, or a Porsche. Before making a decision, you usually weigh the merits of each option against the cost.

When you get a headache, you can take a pain reliever (such as aspirin) or visit a medical specialist for a neurological examination. Given this choice, most people, of course, take a pain reliever, since it costs only pennies; whereas a medical examination costs hundreds of dollars and takes a lot of time. This is usually a logical choice because it is rare to need anything more than a pain reliever for a headache. But in some cases, a headache may indicate a brain tumor and failing to see a specialist right away can result in complications. Should everyone with a headache go to a specialist? Of course not, but people treating their own illnesses must realize that they are betting on the basis of their cost/value analysis of the situation. They are taking the most logical option.

The same cost/value analysis must be made when deciding to do one's own legal work. Many legal situations are very straight forward, requiring a simple form and no complicated analysis. Anyone with a little intelligence and a book of instructions can handle the matter without outside help.

But there is always the chance that complications are involved that only an attorney would notice. To simplify the law into a book like this, several legal cases often must be condensed into a single sentence or paragraph. Otherwise, the book would be several hundred pages long and too complicated for most people. However, this simplification necessarily leaves out many details and nuances that would apply to special or unusual situations. Also, there are many ways to interpret most legal questions. Your case may come before a judge who disagrees with the analysis of our authors.

Therefore, in deciding to use a self-help law book and to do your own legal work, you must realize that you are making a cost/value analysis. You have decided that the money you will save in doing it yourself outweighs the chance that your case will not turn out to your satisfaction. Most people handling their own simple legal matters never have a problem, but occasionally people find that it ended up costing them more to have an attorney straighten out the situation than it would have if they had hired an attorney in the beginning. Keep this in mind while handling your case, and be sure to consult an attorney if you feel you might need further guidance.

Local Rules

The next thing to remember is that a book which covers the law for the entire nation, or even for an entire state, cannot possibly include every procedural difference of every jurisdiction. Whenever possible, we provide the exact form needed; however, in some areas, each county, or even each judge, may require unique forms and procedures. In our state books, our forms usually cover the majority of counties in the state, or provide examples of the type of form which will be required. In our national books, our forms are sometimes even more general in nature but are designed to give a good idea of the type of form that will be needed in most locations.

Nonetheless, keep in mind that your state, county, or judge may have a requirement, or use a form, that is not included in this book.

You should not necessarily expect to be able to get all of the information and resources you need solely from within the pages of this book. This book will serve as your guide, giving you specific information whenever possible and helping you to find out what else you will need to know. This is just like if you decided to build your own backyard deck. You might purchase a book on how to build decks. However, such a book would not include the building codes and permit requirements of every city, town, county, and township in the nation; nor would it include the lumber, nails, saws, hammers, and other materials and tools you would need to actually build the deck. You would use the book as your guide, and then do some work and research involving such matters as whether you need a permit of some kind, what type and grade of wood is available in your area, whether to use hand tools or power tools, and how to use those tools.

Changes in the Law

Before using the forms in a book like this, you should check with your court clerk to see if there are any local rules of which you should be aware, or local forms you will need to use. Often, such forms will require the same information as the forms in the book but are merely laid out differently or use slightly different language. They will sometimes require additional information.

Besides being subject to local rules and practices, the law is subject to change at any time. The courts and the legislatures of all fifty states are constantly revising the laws. It is possible that while you are reading this book, some aspect of the law is being changed.

In most cases, the change will be of minimal significance. A form will be redesigned, additional information will be required, or a waiting period will be extended. As a result, you might need to revise a form, file an extra form, or wait out a longer time period; these types of changes will not usually affect the outcome of your case. On the other hand, sometimes a major part of the law is changed, the entire law in a particular area is rewritten, or a case that was the basis of a central legal point is overruled. In such instances, your entire ability to pursue your case may be impaired.

Again, you should weigh the value of your case against the cost of an attorney and make a decision as to what you believe is in your best interest.

Introduction

A book of this type, covering the most common legal situations a family faces, cannot possibly include or explain every possible legal situation. In most situations, the forms are basic and simple; but occasionally, legal relationships are more complicated. If, in using this book, you find that your facts do not fit into the explanations or forms, you should seek further guidance. For most subjects, such as wills, trusts, real estate, and getting a divorce, *Sphinx Publishing*, an imprint of Sourcebooks, Inc., offers a detailed book on the subject. These books go into much deeper analysis and offer a wider variety of forms than this book.

Hopefully this book will make fewer the occasions in which you will need a lawyer. At a minimum, it will help you be a wiser consumer of legal services and understand more of what a lawyer is doing for you. It will have served its purpose if it helps you recognize when you do need a lawyer and helps you use your lawyer more efficiently.

If, in reading this book, you discover that what you want to do is more complicated than you imagined or involves a large sum of money, then get a lawyer. If all goes well, you can complain about paying for something you did not need after all. That is better than not hiring a lawyer and having something more serious to complain about.

Some clients believe that, having turned a matter over to the lawyers, they are released from all further responsibility. Such clients think that if they pay a large amount of money for their lawyer to draft a contract, they should not have to bore themselves by reading it, since it is the lawyer's job to make sure it is right.

This thinking makes the lawyer's job nearly impossible. You know your situation and what is important to you. Use this book to know what to expect from your lawyer and why. Then read and understand the work your lawyer does for you. Make sure it works for you.

The forms in this book have been limited to those that are usable in the most common situations in most states. There are other forms books on the market that claim to be comprehensive, but include many forms that may not comply with state law.

The forms in this book will work in most situations, but you should check local requirements for certain documents—such as deeds—that may need a certain portion left blank for recording information. Keep in mind that laws also change, so you should check with the clerk of any office where a form will be filed to see if there are special requirements before bringing yours in for recording.

Organization of This Book

The first chapter of the book deals with some general principles of contract law and using legal forms. The subsequent chapters apply those principles to specific situations. Before you use any of the contract forms in this book, pay careful attention to the first chapter, especially the information about the proper execution (signing) of contracts. Depending on the form you are using and who the parties are, you will need to insert the proper signature format to make sure the proper party executes the contract correctly.

Chapters 2 through 7 cover specific situations, including family relationships, financial matters, real estate, personal property, hiring services, and wills. The final chapter has some miscellaneous forms that do not fit into the previous categories, but may be useful. Each chapter is followed with the blank forms discussed within the chapter.

The sample forms in the main part of the book are presented with information filled in for fictional situations. The forms may be abbreviated or otherwise slightly different from the blank forms provided. The forms at the end of the chapters are designed to be used in most cases as is, although you may need to modify them to meet your specific needs. As stated, the forms are designed for general use.

Applicable Laws

This book is intended to be used throughout the United States, and the laws of no specific jurisdiction are cited or relied upon in this text. While the laws of the various states vary significantly, general principles of contract and agency apply in every state. However, it may be that your specific circumstances raise a legal issue unique to your jurisdiction. For that reason and others, competent legal advice is always desirable—especially in the areas where the need for a lawyer is explicitly mentioned.

Every form in the book is also included on the accompanying CD-ROM. You can fill in the forms on your computer, then just print and sign. You can now reuse the form over and over again as you need it. Plus, since no form is truly *one size fits all*, you can add, delete, or otherwise modify the information on the form to make it better suited for your particular situation.

If you want to use the forms provided in the text, you certainly can. Tear them out and fill them in legibly by hand or with a typewriter. Be sure to make a copy of the form BEFORE you mark on it, so you will always have a fresh, blank form for future use.

Chapter 1:
Basics of Legal Forms

This chapter explains the types of documents contained in this book and what the basics are to make them legal. The following chapters explain how these types of legal forms are used in family, finances, wills and trusts, personal property, real estate, hired help, and dispute resolution situations. The forms used in all of these situations will fall into the three categories discussed in this chapter.

> ### _Forms in Chapter:_
> - **Contract**
> - **Addendum to Contract**
> - **Amendment to Contract**
> - **Assignment of Contract**
> - **Termination of Contract**

Types of Legal Forms

There are several types of legal forms that people can execute. Some are contracts that must be agreed upon by two or more parties. Others are authorization forms and title transfer forms that only one person must sign. Some forms must have the signatures of witnesses or a notary in order to be legally effective. Others only need your signature.

Before using the forms in this book, be sure that you understand the legal ramifications of each form as explained. You should also understand how to complete and execute any form you use to be sure that it is legally enforceable.

Contracts

A *contract* is an agreement between two or more people. One of the first things taught in law school is that to be legal, a contract must have three elements: an *offer*; an *acceptance* of that offer; and, some *consideration*. Consideration is a legal term that means something of value that is exchanged between the parties.

If you go over to your neighbor and say, "Would you like to go fishing with me Saturday?" and he says, "Sure," you have an offer and acceptance, but you do not have a legal contract because there is no legal consideration. But if you say to him, "I'll give you $25 to mow my yard," and he agrees and then does it, you do have a contract that the law would enforce (though it would not be worth getting a court involved for such a small amount).

There are many types of legal contracts that you are involved with in your daily life, though you probably do not realize that they are contracts. You are usually creating legal contracts when you take your clothes to a dry cleaner; sell your lawn mower at a garage sale; hire someone to clean your carpets; or, move in with a friend to share expenses.

The important thing to know about these contracts is that unless you set the *terms* to them, the terms will be set for you. The terms are either set by state law or by the forms provided by the party you are dealing with.

For example, in some states, if you hire others to do work on your house, you may be liable if they injure themselves or are accidentally killed. However, you can avoid this risk by having a written agreement with them in which they agree to be responsible for their own safety. The benefit of knowing the rules of contracts and using your own forms is that you can protect yourself from unexpected *liability*.

In some situations, you may not be able to get the other party to go along with your terms. For example, if you store your property in a self-storage locker, the owner probably will not agree to be responsible for your property if the building burns down. Most likely, the contract the facility uses protects it and makes clear that you should obtain insurance to protect your property.

Sometimes you can protect yourself even if the other party has forms of its own and refuses to use yours. If you understand each clause of the contracts you are asked to sign, you can sometimes cross out something that would be risky to you.

Often, business contracts are full of this standard, *boilerplate* language to protect the company from anything that might happen. The contracts are usually prepared by the company's lawyer, and the business owner does not always know why all the clauses are in there or what they mean.

If a company is very eager to get your business, you may be able to cross out things in its contract and still have them accept it. For example, if you are paying a company to fix your roof and its standard contract says the work is guaranteed for six months, you might be able to cross that off and put in "one year," and have the company still do the job.

Mutual Agreement

Contracts require two parties to agree to the same thing. If they do not, there is no legal contract. What happens in a situation where you change "six months" to "one year," sign the contract, and then they take it to their office, change it back to "six months," and they sign it? In this example, the company would need to return the contract to you for you to sign or initial where they changed it back to "six months" before they had a binding contract.

What if they do not, and they do the job assuming that the six months applies while you assume that it is one year? That depends. If they called you and discussed it with you and you agreed to the change, it would probably be valid even if you did not sign it. If they just did the job without telling you, then the terms of your agreement would be *ambiguous*. Whether you had a six-month or a one-year guarantee would have to be decided by a court, looking at all the facts of the case and using state law to determine who is correct.

Oral Contracts

Contrary to popular belief, contracts do not always have to be in writing to be legally enforceable. Verbal agreements can constitute legally binding contracts in many situations. The problem with verbal contracts is how to convince a court that one really existed and what the terms were. For this reason, you should try to always get your agreements in writing.

Statute of Frauds

In some matters, contracts are required by law to be in writing. Every state has what is called *statute of frauds* that explain which contracts must be in writing. For example, a typical statute of frauds might state that all sales of goods over $1,000, all leases over one year, and all sales of real estate must be in writing. This means that if your neighbor agrees to sell you his house but at the last minute changes his mind, the courts will not help you because the law clearly says that verbal agreements for sale of real estate are not enforceable.

Exceptions

There are many exceptions to the statute of frauds. If you get into a situation in which the statute of frauds affects your rights, either check with a lawyer or do some legal research yourself.

For example, *partial performance* of a contract may make it enforceable, even if it violates the statute of frauds. If you agree to buy your neighbor's house, and you move into it and pay him $1,000 a month for several months, a court might rule that the verbal agreement to sell it is enforceable. However, the court would have to be convinced that there really was an agreement to sell the house to you. If the neighbor said you were only renting it and you had no proof otherwise, you would probably lose. But if the insurance was changed over to your name and you were given the tax bill (that you paid), then you would be more likely to win.

Another way a *verbal agreement* might be enforceable—even if it violates the statute of frauds—is if there is written proof of the agreement signed by the person trying to disclaim the agreement. For example, if someone verbally agrees to sell you their car for $5,000, it would not be enforceable in a state where sales of that amount have to be in writing. But if you gave them a deposit and they signed a receipt that said "deposit on Ford," then you might be able to go to court and force them to complete the sale.

Again, you have the problem of proving to a court what the terms were. What if the seller says the price was $6,000, but you remember it was $5,000? If there is no evidence, you might not win. The purpose of the statute of frauds is to avoid enforcing agreements where the terms are not known.

As you can see, when coming to an agreement with someone, you should spell out as many details as possible so that there is no misunderstanding. (see form 1, p.19.) Below is a sample of a SIMPLE CONTRACT.

Sample: **Simple Contract**

CONTRACT

THIS AGREEMENT is entered into by and between _____ Bob Jones _____ and _____ Jon Dough _____. In consideration of the mutual promises made in this agreement and other valuable consideration, the receipt and sufficiency of which is acknowledged, the parties agree as follows:

Bob Jones will mow Jon Dough's front and backyards once a week during June, July, and August, 2006, while Jon Dough is at Oxford studying Sanskrit.

The following addenda, dated the same date as this agreement, are incorporated in, and made a part of, this agreement:

❏ None.

This agreement shall be governed by the laws of _____ Georgia _____.

Addendum to Contract

An **ADDENDUM TO CONTRACT** is used to add lengthy details that would not easily fit into the contract form. (see form 2, p.21.) For example, if you were buying someone's collection of plants, you would probably want to list each one on an addendum, as in the example below.

Sample: **Addendum to Contract**

ADDENDUM TO CONTRACT

The following terms are a part of the contract dated _____ June 6, 2006 _____, between _____ Marvin Gardene _____ and _____ Jon Dough _____

1 Ficus, 5 feet high
2 Ficus, 3 feet high
1 African Violet
5 Bonsai trees
6 Venus Flytraps
1 Oak tree in 24" pot
3 Ferns in hanging baskets
2 Poison ivy in pots
2 Marigolds in pots

Amending a Contract

Sometimes the parties to a contract will come to the conclusion that the contract no longer reflects their agreement and needs to be modified, or *amended*. Unless otherwise agreed to in the original contract, the modification of a contract is a contract in its own right, and must contain all the elements described earlier in this chapter, including consideration. (see form 3, p.23.) A sample **AMENDMENT TO CONTRACT** follows.

Sample: **Amendment to Contract**

For valuable consideration, the receipt and sufficiency of which is acknowledged by each of the parties, this agreement amends a contract dated _____ May 1, 2006 _____, between _____ Jon Dough _____ and _____ Fred Farkle _____ relating to _____ 1956 Chevrolet Belair ID #6J123456 _____. This contract amendment is hereby incorporated into the contract.
Because the car needs a new clutch, the price will be lowered by $500, so the balance due will be $1,500.

Assigning a Contract

The right to performance under a contract is a property right like any other and ordinarily can be bought and sold. Courts distinguish between the *assignment* of a right to receive performance from the other party and the *delegation* of your duty to perform. Because performance can vary from person to person, courts are less likely to allow an assignment of a duty to perform unless it is allowed in the contract. For example, if you hire a famous artist to paint a mural on your building, the artist could not assign the contract to an unknown painter. However, you could sell the building and assign the right to have the mural painted by the artist. (Unless, for some reason, the artist only agreed to do it because you were the building's owner.)

The law of assignment of contracts varies by state. In some states, some contracts may be assigned unless they specifically state that they cannot be assigned. In other states, some contracts cannot be assigned unless they specifically state that they can. Be sure that the contracts you sign state whether or not you want them to be assignable. Even if a contract says that it may not be assigned, if all parties agree to an assignment, then the original contract is considered amended and the assignment is valid. An **ASSIGNMENT OF CONTRACT** can be used to accomplish this. (see form 4, p.25.) If you wish to assign a contract and the other party will not agree to it, and the contract does not spell out whether you have the right to assign it, you should check with an attorney to be sure you have the legal right to do so.

Many people use the term *contract assignment* to mean both the *assignment of rights* and the *delegation of duties*. However, if you intend to delegate a duty, it is better to be specific. If you wish to rid yourself of the possibility of ever having to perform the duty, you must be released from that duty by the person entitled to receive the performance.

Having assigned a contract, it is important to notify the person expecting to receive the performance that the assignment has been made. Suppose the assigned contract is an agreement to move one hundred cases of wine from warehouse A to warehouse B. Quick Moving Company assigns the moving contract to Fast Movers, Inc. (the *assignee*), which promptly does the job, but Quick Moving neglects to notify the owner of the wine that the contract has been assigned. The owner arrives at warehouse B, discovers the job complete, and sends a check for the moving job to Quick Moving Company. Fast Movers then asks to be paid. Fast Movers cannot recover its fee from the owner, because the owner has performed its part of the contract—paying for the completed job—as required by the terms of the agreement. Fast Movers will have to hope it can recover the fee from Quick Moving. If Fast Movers had promptly notified the owner of the assignment, then the owner would have paid Fast Movers directly.

On the next page is an example of the type of letter that may be used to notify someone that the assignee of a contract has assumed the duty to perform some service for the person notified, and that payment should therefore be sent to the assignee. Frequently, the contract being assigned is the right to receive payment for a debt.

Sample Letter: **Notice of Assignment of a Contract**

Jon Dough
8321 S. Main Street, Fort Worth, TX 76011
804-555-4441

June 8, 2006

Fred Jackson, President
Fred's Lawn Service
842 US Hwy. 81
Fort Worth, TX 76012

Dear Mr. Jackson:

This letter is to inform you that we have sold our home at 1254 Purgatory Lane to William McClenaghan. The lawn service contract that we signed with your company has been assigned to him, and he has agreed to be responsible for it. All further bills should be directed to him at the same address. If you have any questions, feel free to call.

Sincerely,

Jon Dough

Jon Dough

Terminating a Contract

Contracts are *terminated* for different reasons and under different circumstances. One reason is to make sure that all the parties to a contract have completely performed the duties they had to perform according to its terms. But suppose that before the parties completely perform their duties, they decide to call it off. For example, suppose you hire a contractor to build a second story on your house, and then both of you find out that the zoning prohibits second stories in your area. If you signed a contract with the contractor, the easiest way to indicate termination of it is to tear it up. If there were duplicate copies, be sure all copies are destroyed. Another way would be to sign an *agreement of termination*. A **TERMINATION OF CONTRACT** could be used to do this. (see form 5, p.27.) This also could be a simple letter, a copy of which is signed by the recipient and returned.

The following sample letter is the basic language for an agreement between two parties to terminate a contract and release each other from all duties to be performed.

Sample Letter: **Agreement to Terminate**

Jon Dough

8321 S. Main Street, Fort Worth, TX 76011

804-555-4441

April 4, 2006

Bob Jones
Jones Construction
222 US Hwy. 20
Fort Worth, TX 76012

Dear Mr. Jones:

This letter is to confirm our agreement to terminate our contract for you to build a second story on my home due to the fact that second stories are not permitted by law in this area.

This will further confirm that the $1,000 deposit that we paid you on that contract will be used toward our new contract to build a swimming pool in our back yard.

Sincerely,

Jon Dough

Jon Dough

Agreed:

Jones Construction

By: *Bob Jones* _____

Bob Jones, President

Termination for Breach

Another way to terminate a contract is for one or more parties to *breach* the agreement so completely that the other parties are relieved of their duties to perform. For example, if you contract to have your house painted and the painter completely fails to perform the job, then you are relieved of your promise to pay. However, this does not necessarily mean that the contract is terminated. If the contract required the job to be done by a certain day, but it has been raining all week, the painter could show up next week to do the job. You will be required to pay under the contract. If, because the first painter did not show up (due to rain) you then hired a second painter, you could end up having to pay both painters to paint your house.

For this reason, contracts should spell out as precisely as possible what is required of the parties. If something must be done by a certain date, the contract should say that if it is not done by that date, the contract will terminate. A legal phrase that is used to signify that deadlines are important is:

Time is of the essence.

Without wording such as this, the law will usually give a person a *reasonable* amount of time to perform under a contract. What is reasonable is always a gray area of law. It depends on what the situation is and who is making the determination.

If you have entered into a contract with someone and they have clearly violated the terms, you can terminate the contract. You should do so in writing. The following sample letter is a notice given by one party to another that the latter has violated a contract and it is being terminated.

Sample Letter: **Notice of Breach**

Jon Dough

8321 S. Main Street, Fort Worth, TX 76011

804-555-4441

August 12, 2006

Fred Jackson, President
Fred's Lawn Service
842 US Hwy. 81
Fort Worth, TX 76012

Dear Mr. Jackson:

This letter is to inform you that you have breached our contract to provide lawn service to my property by failing to show up since the middle of June, despite numerous phone calls requesting you to show and provide the service.

Because of your failure to perform as agreed, I consider our contract terminated and have hired another service to handle the mowing.

Sincerely,

Jon Dough

Jon Dough

Most breaches are not so clear-cut, of course. Usually, if one party believes the other is not living up to its duties, the party in default will be notified of its shortcomings, and a period of negotiation and compromise will follow.

Be very careful about terminating a contract without the other person's consent—especially if he or she has begun performance. If you have a legal contract and you attempt to terminate it without giving the other side a reasonable chance to perform, you may have to pay them even after you terminated the contract. When in doubt, ask an attorney what your rights are. Realize that because this is a gray area of law, even an attorney can be wrong when deciding whether a contract can be terminated.

Right of Rescission

One common misunderstanding with contracts is the thinking that there is always a *right of rescission* of, for example, a week. This perceived *right* to cancel the contract is the *exception* rather than the rule.

In some states, where there have been abuses in certain industries—such as with health club memberships or door-to-door sales—laws have been passed allowing a right to cancel the contract. Also, in some consumer loan transactions, there is a legal right to change your mind by signing a rescission notice within a certain number of days. However, unless there is a law specifically giving a right of rescission, you are legally obligated the moment you sign.

Keep in mind—you can add a right of rescission to any agreement. If you are considering leasing an apartment and the owner insists that you sign a lease before leaving so he or she can do a credit check, you can agree only if you have three days to rescind and he or she accepts this condition.

Title Transfer and Acknowledgment

When transferring the ownership of property, such as with a deed, bill of sale, or will, the person receiving the property usually does not have to sign. Only the one doing the transferring signs. In many cases, these documents need to have one or two witnesses, and sometimes they need to be notarized.

The legal effect of a title transfer document usually does not occur until it has been physically given to the recipient. For example, if you make a deed of your house to your children, it would be valid the moment you handed it to them. It would not be valid if it was found in your safe deposit box after your death.

NOTE: *Although a deed kept in your safe deposit box might not be valid under the law, in many cases, the issue would not come up. If there was no one contesting the validity of the deed, it might work fine. But, if the deed was to one child and there was another who was unhappy about it, he or she could go to court and claim the deed was invalid since it was not delivered.*

Title transfers and acknowledgments are very broad areas of legal documents. Specific examples of title transfers and acknowledgments are discussed in later chapters, such as **WILLS** (Chapter 3), **BILLS OF SALE** (Chapter 5), and **DEEDS** (Chapter 6).

Authorization

Authorization forms usually only need to be signed by one party. For example, if you give a school permission to take your child on a trip or if you give your neighbor permission to pick up your car from a mechanic, no one else has to sign. You are granting something (permission) without asking anything in return.

Suppose you want to receive something in return. For example, if you allow your child to go on a school trip only if the school promises to have six teachers accompany the group, then you usually need the other party to sign an *acceptance* of the terms. In such case, you would have a contract—not an authorization.

Alternatively, if the school gave you an authorization form that said six teachers would accompany the group, it might be construed as a binding contract. But it could go either way. If your child was hurt and you sued the school saying they breached an agreement to have six teachers along, they could argue that six was a tentative number and that it was not a material part of your agreement. The only way to beat such an argument would be to write on the form something like "my child only has permission if six teachers accompany the group" and then get an agent of the school to sign it.

There are many different types of authorizations. For examples of specific authorizations, see **CHILD AUTHORIZATION** (Chapter 2), **AUTHORIZATION TO CHECK CREDIT** (Chapter 4), and **AUTHORIZATION TO RELEASE EMPLOYMENT INFORMATION** (Chapter 7).

Components of Legal Forms

Legal forms have various parts. Not all forms require the same parts, but each legal form has its own requirements that make the form binding. For example, while a contract requires signatures of the people who are contracting but not witnesses, a will requires witnesses. Form components are what make the documents legal in nature.

Duplicate Copies

It is usually wise to make at least one duplicate copy of your legal forms in case the original is lost or destroyed. Contrary to popular belief, a contract does not need to have original signatures to be enforceable in court. A photocopy can be just as enforceable under the right circumstances.

Duplicate Originals

A *duplicate original* of a legal document is a copy with original signatures of the parties. For some types of legal forms, such as contracts, there should be two original copies that are signed by all parties. This way, each party has a copy with everyone's original signature. The next best thing is for each party to have a copy with the other party's original signature, so they can add their own. But in some cases you do not even need your own signature, as long as you have the signature of the person against whom you wish to enforce the contract.

You should *not* make duplicate originals of documents that transfer title, such as deeds and wills, or of promissory notes. If you sign a duplicate of a promissory note, you may have to pay twice. And if you make a duplicate original of your will and later wish to revoke it by destroying it, your revocation may not be effective if someone else has the duplicate original and files it after your death. For documents like these, make photocopies of the signed originals and make them as copies, but do not sign originals again.

Seals

In the past, when few people could write, a seal was added to a legal document to make it valid. This was a wax seal or merely a hand-drawn one. Today, seals are in most cases obsolete, but in some states they are necessary to make certain types of documents, such as deeds, valid. In some states, they may give a party more legal rights, such as a longer time period in which to sue. In some cases, it is important to put the word "seal" next to the signature line. When you are unsure what your state law provides, it does not hurt to include it. Some of the forms in this book include the word "seal" for this reason.

Signatures

In nearly all cases, a legal document must have a signature to be valid. Just as important, the signature must be done properly or the document might not be legal. For example, if both spouses do not sign a document, or if the wrong officer of a company signs a document, it might not be valid.

Spouses

For some types of legal documents, it is necessary to have both spouses' signatures. For example, in some states, a deed of the home is not valid unless both spouses sign it, even if a home is owned by one spouse alone. Even if a spouse's signature is not required, it can be a good idea to include it. For example, if you loan money to someone and have them sign a promissory note, you may not be able to collect if all of their property is owned jointly with their spouse. Or, if you rent an apartment to a couple and only one signs the lease, you might not be able to hold the other spouse responsible for the rent.

For this reason, when you are getting someone to sign an obligation, you should usually get the spouse to sign as well. If *you* are signing an obligation, you should try to avoid having your spouse sign.

Sole Proprietorships

The signature of a *sole proprietorship* is really the same as an individual's signature, because the owner of the business operates it as an individual rather than as a separate entity. If the business is conducted under a trade name (or a *fictitious* or *assumed* name), confusion may result. The following sample makes it clear that the signature is that of a sole proprietor rather than a corporation or some other business organization.

Sample: **Signature of a Sole Proprietor of Business**

> *Henry Hardy*   (Seal)
> Henry Hardy, a sole proprietor
> d/b/a Scrupulous Enterprises

The letters "d/b/a" stand for "doing business as." You may instead sometimes see "t/a" for "transacting as."

Corporations

Like individuals, corporations can sign documents either under seal or not. The corporate seal usually carries somewhat more meaning than an individual's. In addition to the effects of an individual's seal, the corporate seal entitles other parties to the agreement to presume that the signer acted under the appropriate authorization of the corporation's board of directors.

Corporate seals are usually rubber stamps or embossers, but anything the corporation's board of directors adopts by resolution as the corporate seal will do. The first sample shows the signature of a corporation not under seal. The next sample shows that of a corporation under seal. Note that the secretary of the corporation is the custodian of the seal and is responsible for *attesting* that the president or vice president's signature is affixed by the board's authority.

Sample: **Corporate Signature (one officer)**

Scrupulous Corporation

By: _Henry Hardy_
Henry Hardy, President

Sample: **Corporate Signature (under seal)**

Scrupulous Corporation

By: _Henry Hardy_
Henry Hardy, President

Attest: _Calvin Collier_
Calvin Collier, Secretary

General Partnerships

It may be helpful to think of a *partnership* as a group of sole proprietors in business together, with each member of the group acting as the agent of all the others. It is fundamental to partnership law that each partner is bound by the acts of the others in furtherance of the business, and that each partner is liable for the debts of the partnership.

It used to be that the law refused to recognize the partnership as an entity separate from the partners. This meant, for example, that a real estate deed for partnership property had to be signed by all of the partners.

The modern rule follows the *Uniform Partnership Act*, the *Revised Uniform Partnership Act* (one of these two has been enacted in all states except Louisiana), or the *Louisiana Partnership Act*. Each of these acts recognize the separate existence of the partnership and hold that one partner, acting within his or her authority, can bind the rest of the partners on most contracts—including deeds. Many states do not require general partnerships to publish lists of partners or explanations of the limits of their authority.

It is not always possible to tell who is a partner or what limits there may be on a signer's authority. For this reason, persons entering into agreements with general partners should take precautions to make sure the person signing has adequate authority. Sometimes all the partners will be asked to sign a document, even though it may not be required by law to make a contract enforceable.

The following sample shows the signature of a partnership where one of the general partners has signed for the partnership.

Sample: **General Partnership Signature**

Scrupulous Associates, a general partnership

By: _____*Henry Hardy*_____ (Seal)
Henry Hardy, General Partner

Limited Liability Partnerships

You may see the initials "LLP" after the name of a partnership. It means that the partnership is a *limited liability partnership,* which is not the same as a *limited partnership* described later. A partner in a LLP is not liable for certain damages caused by his or her partner. For example, a lawyer in a law firm organized as an LLP will not be liable for the legal malpractice committed by another partner in the firm, unless the malpractice was committed under the supervision of the first lawyer.

Limited Partnerships

A limited partnership is much like a general partnership, with one major difference. In addition to general partners, it has a special category of *limited partners* who do not participate in management of the business and are not liable for the debts and liabilities of the business beyond the amount of their investment or *contribution.* A limited partnership is created under a special state statute, usually the *Uniform Limited Partnership Act,* and will have the words "limited partnership" as part of its name.

Only a general partner (there may be one or more) will have the authority to sign contracts. Limited partners usually have no authority to sign contracts for, or otherwise represent, the limited partnership. An example of a limited partnership signature follows.

Sample: **Limited Partnership Signature**

Scrupulous Hardy Enterprises, a limited partnership

By: _____*Henry Hardy*_____ (Seal)
Henry Hardy, General Partner

Limited Liability Companies

A *limited liability company* is a relatively new form of business organization. It has the limited liability of a corporation, but is usually taxed like a partnership. It is also allowed to have just one member or can have several. Usually, any member can sign for a limited liability company, but it can be set up so that only a manager or a managing member can sign.

Sample: **Limited Liability Company Signature**

Smith Enterprises, LLC

By: _____*Michael Smith*_____ (Seal)
             Member

Witnesses

For some types of legal documents, *witnesses* are required. Without them, the document has no legal validity. For example, in most states, wills and deeds of real estate must have two witnesses. In some states, leases of longer than one year must also have witnesses.

For other types of forms and agreements, witnesses are superfluous. They are helpful in the occasional court case, if one party denies he or she signed a document. But even then, a handwriting expert can usually substantiate the legitimacy of a signature enough to win in court.

Notaries and Acknowledgments

Some people think that having a document notarized makes it *legal*. It does not. A contract signed by two people without a notary is—in most cases—perfectly legal.

A *notary public* is empowered by the state to administer various oaths and to testify to the genuineness of signatures. The term *acknowledgment* refers to a signer's statement that he or she truly is that person, intends to sign the document, and that (in the case of a corporate officer) he or she holds the corporate office claimed. The notary will verify the identity of the signer and affirm—in writing—that the person signing the document is who he or she claims. The next two samples are what an acknowledgment by a notary looks like.

Sample: **Acknowledgment by an Individual**

STATE OF   Texas   )
COUNTY OF   Hockley   )

I certify that _____Mary Smith_____, who ❑ is personally known to me to be the person whose name is subscribed to the foregoing instrument ☒ produced ___a state driver's license_____ as identification, personally appeared before me on ___March 5, 2006_____, and ☒ acknowledged the execution of the foregoing instrument ~~❑ acknowledged that (s)he is (Assistant) Secretary of _____, and that by authority duly given and as the act of the corporation, the foregoing instrument was signed in its name by its (Vice) President, sealed with its corporate seal and attested by him/her as its (Assistant) Secretary.~~

Jon Dough
Notary Public, State of _Texas_____
My commission expires: April 15, 2007

Sample: **Acknowledgment by a Corporation**

STATE OF   Texas   )
COUNTY OF   Hockley   )

I certify that _____Mary Smith_____, who ❑ is personally known to me to be the person whose name is subscribed to the foregoing instrument ☒ produced __passport_____ as identification, personally appeared before me on ___March 5, 2006_____, and ❑ acknowledged the execution of the foregoing instrument ☒ acknowledged that (s)he is (Assistant) Secretary of _Scrupulous, Inc_____, and that by authority duly given and as the act of the corporation, the foregoing instrument was signed in its name by its (Vice) President, sealed with its corporate seal and attested by him/her as its (Assistant) Secretary.

Jon Dough
Notary Public, State of _Texas_____
My commission expires: April 15, 2007

Facsimile and Email Acceptance

Legally, there is no problem accepting an agreement by fax. Someone can fax you an agreement and, you can sign it and fax it back. The only possible risk would be if a person tried to deny signing the document. For this reason, businesses such as banks do not like to accept documents by fax, though they may initially, if the original will be sent to them shortly.

Most states have passed laws specifically allowing signatures by fax. Even some secretaries of state are accepting corporate filings by fax, so this type of signature is becoming more common.

Signatures by email is the subject of pending legislation as this book is being written. While the Internet has allowed instant transmission of data, it has been slower in finding an efficient way to transmit signatures. Some companies, like the United States Postal Service, are setting up systems that would offer signature guarantees for email.

For the present, you cannot be sure that an agreement made solely by email is legally enforceable. To be sure, you can have the recipients print out the email and then mail or fax it back with a real signature on the copy.

CONTRACT

THIS AGREEMENT is entered into by and between _____ and _____. In consideration of the mutual promises made in this Agreement and other valuable consideration, the receipt and sufficiency of which is acknowledged, the parties agree as follows:

The following addenda, dated the same date as this Agreement, are incorporated in, and made a part of, this Agreement:

❑ _____

❑ _____

❑ _____

❑ None.

This Agreement shall be governed by the laws of _____.

If any part of this Agreement is adjudged invalid, illegal, or unenforceable, the remaining parts shall not be affected and shall remain in full force and effect.

This Agreement shall be binding upon the parties, and upon their heirs, executors, personal representatives, administrators, and assigns. No person shall have a right or cause of action arising out of or resulting from this Agreement, except those who are parties to it and their successors in interest.

This instrument, including any attached exhibits and addenda, constitutes the entire Agreement of the parties. No representations or promises have been made except those that are set out in this Agreement. This Agreement may not be modified except in writing signed by all the parties.

IN WITNESS WHEREOF the parties have signed this Agreement under seal on _____, 20_____.

_____   _____

_____   _____

This page intentionally left blank.

ADDENDUM TO CONTRACT

Addendum No. _____

The following terms are a part of the Contract, dated _____, 20_____, by and between
_____ and _____:

_____   _____

_____   _____

This page intentionally left blank.

AMENDMENT TO CONTRACT

For valuable consideration, the receipt and sufficiency of which is acknowledged by each of the parties, this agreement amends a Contract dated _____, 20_____, between _____ and _____ , relating to _____ _____. This contract amendment is hereby incorporated into the Contract.

Except as changed by this amendment, the Contract shall continue in effect according to its terms. The amendments herein shall be effective on the date this document is executed by all parties.

IN WITNESS WHEREOF the parties have signed this agreement under seal on _____, 20_____.

_____   _____

_____   _____

This page intentionally left blank.

ASSIGNMENT OF CONTRACT

FOR VALUE RECEIVED, the undersigned (the "Assignor") hereby assigns, transfers, and conveys to _____ (the "Assignee") all the Assignor's rights, title, and interests in and to a contract (the "Contract") dated _____, 20____, between _____ and _____.

The Assignor hereby warrants and represents that the Contract is in full force and effect and is fully assignable.

The Assignee hereby assumes the duties and obligations of the Assignor under the Contract, and agrees to hold the Assignor harmless from any claim or demand thereunder.

The date of this assignment is _____, 20_____.

IN WITNESS WHEREOF the parties have signed this agreement under seal on _____, 20_____.

Assignor: Assignee:

_____   _____

_____   _____

This page intentionally left blank.

TERMINATION OF CONTRACT

For valuable consideration, the receipt and sufficiency of which is acknowledged by each of the parties to that certain Contract, dated _____, 20_____, between _____ and _____, relating to _____ hereby agree that said contract shall be terminated by mutual agreement, and that each party releases the other from any and all claims thereunder.

IN WITNESS WHEREOF the parties have signed this agreement under seal on _____, 20_____.

_____   _____

_____   _____

Chapter 2:
Family Legal Forms

Although family living arrangements are rarely thought of as being legal agreements, they are. Most people do not realize that if they do not write up a legal agreement between themselves and their spouse or partner, the state and its judges can provide a legal agreement, based upon statutes and other cases.

Whether you are married, living together, or having a child on your own, your legal rights and those of others involved can either be decided by you in advance, or by the courts when a dispute comes up. If you wish to ensure that your desires are met, you should come to an agreement with your partner and put it into writing.

To be sure that all issues are covered and that you have adequately protected yourself, you should either consult an attorney or a book that analyzes each issue in detail. However, forms are included in this book to help you understand all of the issues and for your use in an emergency situation. For example, if your spouse announces that he or she is leaving for good, sitting down and filling out a property settlement agreement would be much better than trying to locate him or her two years later through a divorce case.

Forms in Chapter:
- **Cohabitation Agreement**
- **Family Contract of Adult Child Living with Parents**
- **Premarital Agreement**
- **Marital Agreement**
- **Notice of Name Change**
- **Separation Agreement**

- Divorce Settlement
- Delegation of Parental Responsibility
- Child Authorization
- Authorization for Child to Travel
- Pet Care Agreement
- Official Mail Forwarding Change of Address Order
- Address Change Notice to Contacts
- Change of Address (to IRS)
- Birth or Death Certificate Request
- Application for U.S. Passport
- Passport Renewal (Application for U.S. Passport by Mail)
- Application for Social Security Card

Living Together

Not many legal issues come up while a couple is happily living together. The trouble arises when one of them dies or they decide to split up. Usually, the trouble involves who owns what property and who is responsible for which debts. If they have a child, custody and support become issues as well.

Often, a person has conflicting desires in a situation like this. On the one hand, you may want your partner to inherit the property you were using jointly if anything happens to you. On the other hand, if you split up, you do not want him or her claiming any interest in what you consider your property.

The best way to protect both of your interests is to have a *cohabitation agreement* stating what property is separate. Other documents can be useful as well. A will can distribute your property as you wish. You may also want a trust or declaration of joint property to clarify your wishes and direct your property. (Wills and trusts are discussed in Chapter 3.)

Cohabitation Agreement

A COHABITATION AGREEMENT usually lists what property each party claims as separate and what is joint. (see form 6, p.39.) It can also spell out who will pay which expense during the relationship, and even list household duties if the parties think this will be an issue. To list out your property, simply attach additional sheets of paper to the agreement marked "Exhibit" and list each person's property. (Make sure you clearly distinguish whose is whose.)

This agreement can also protect either of you from *palimony* claims. These are cases in which one cohabitant claims that his or her partner agreed to support him or her forever. The cohabitation agreement could state that neither party promises to support the other in the event of separation and that any changes to this agreement must be in writing.

NOTE: *Two people who are merely sharing a house or apartment, without a relationship or shared funds, would more likely need a roommate agreement. (see Chapter 6.)*

Family Contracts

A century ago, entire families of three or more generations lived together in the same house or apartment. In the 20th century, as people preferred their own places, children moved out as soon as they could afford the rent of an apartment and the older generation got their own condo.

Today, for some families, the trend is reversing. Children who are not married by their 30s or 40s sometimes move back with their parents, and elderly parents sometimes move in with their children.

While a harmonious family relationship is ideal, the stress of living together for adults who are used to being independent sometimes results in problems. Occasionally, it results in legal problems.

While a legal agreement between family members may seem odd, a simple statement of what is expected of each party can help avoid tension and bitter fights. A form is included that can help families define their relationship and expectations. The **FAMILY CONTRACT OF ADULT CHILD LIVING WITH PARENTS** can easily be rewritten to cover an elderly parent living with adult children. (see form 7, p.43.)

If you do not want to sign a formal agreement, you can use the following simple checklist to discuss your expectations with each other.

❏   How long will this arrangement last? Will it be open-ended or until some future date or event?

❏   Will the child be using all areas of the house/basement/attic/garage, or only designated areas?

❏   Will the child be expected to hold a job or stay in school?

❏   Will the child be expected to contribute financially to the family?

❏   Will the child be expected to provide any food or other household supplies?

❏   Will the child be expected to do certain chores around the house?

❏   Is the child allowed to have daytime or overnight guests?

❏   Is smoking allowed in the house or any areas of it?

❏   Are there rules regarding alcohol or drug use?

❏   Is the child allowed to have one or more pets?

❏   Where should the child park his or her car?

Premarital Agreements

A *premarital agreement* (also called an *ante-nuptial agreement*) is an agreement that spells out the legal rights of the parties during and after a marriage. It can cover how property will be divided in the event of divorce and how property may be distributed in the event of death. In most states, a spouse is entitled to a certain percentage of a deceased spouse's property, regardless of what the deceased spouse's will states. A premarital agreement can overrule those laws.

Some people even try to spell out—in detail—their rights during marriage, such as how often the parties will go out to dinner or have sex! However, not all things a couple agrees to are enforceable in court. Courts have been slow to accept premarital agreements. Such agreements were thought to encourage divorce by discussing the subject even before marriage, and so were held illegal. But that has changed in most states.

The legality of premarital agreements is determined by state law, and what is acceptable varies from state to state. In some states, such an agreement is not valid unless both parties make full disclosure of their assets. Some cases have held that such agreements are not enforceable if they were not fairly obtained. For example, if a premarital agreement was presented minutes before a wedding ceremony with the ultimatum, "sign it or the wedding's off," it would be held by a judge to be void. There were similar results when one party was intoxicated or unable to consult a lawyer.

Because premarital agreements often cover large amounts of property and effect important rights, it is best to consult a lawyer to be sure your agreement is legal in your state. At a minimum, you should do some research into your state's laws.

In addition to the **PREMARITAL AGREEMENT** form included (see form 8, p.45), you will need to prepare the following exhibits.

Exhibit A: A financial statement for the husband.

Exhibit B: A financial statement for the wife.

Exhibit C: A list of the property that will be the separate property of the husband.

Exhibit D: A list of the property that will be the separate property of the wife.

If your assets are limited, you can make your own financial statement listing all of them and their estimated value. If your assets are substantial, you should have your accountant prepare a financial statement.

Marital Agreements

Marital agreements are like premarital agreements, but they are signed by couples who are already married. The usual reason is that they are having some friction and want to spell out in detail their rights. The longer a marriage lasts, the more property the less wealthy spouse can usually get in a divorce. A marital agreement is sometimes offered as an alternative to a divorce. The wealthier spouse says, "I want a divorce now, but if you sign this, we can wait and see if things work out."

The big difference between a premarital and a marital agreement is that people who are married already have legal rights, while unmarried people do not. In the event of divorce, the formula in most states is that each spouse gets one-half of all *joint property* and one-half of the property the other spouse accumulated during the marriage.

So, if one spouse built up a big pension plan or accumulated a lot of wealth during a marriage—even if the marriage was short—the other spouse could be giving up half of that by signing a marital agreement that waives property rights. For this reason, it is absolutely necessary that both spouses give complete financial disclosure before signing a marital agreement. If the disclosure is incomplete or false, the agreement can be held void.

A **MARITAL AGREEMENT** is included at the end of the chapter. (see form 9, p.51.) Because of the important legal rights that are involved, you should not sign such an agreement before you fully understand the legal consequences. Consider consulting an attorney if there is a considerable amount of property at stake.

When your name changes, either by marriage or through court action, it can be convenient to have a standard form you send to everyone who needs to know. Some businesses or government agencies may have their own form that they require you to submit. But for those who do not, a NOTICE OF CHANGE OF NAME would be acceptable. (see form 10, p.57.)

Separation Agreements

A *separation agreement* is signed by parties who are married, but wish to live apart. In some states, you cannot get a divorce until you have lived apart for a certain period, such as six months or a year.

Separation agreements usually cover matters such as who will be entitled to what marital property, who will pay each of the existing debts, whether there will be child support paid, and who will have custody of any minor children. (It is very similar to a divorce settlement agreement.) Other things that may be covered are agreements that each party waives a right to the other's estate and agrees not to harass the other.

A SEPARATION AGREEMENT is included on page 59. (see form 11.) Again, these forms determine important legal rights, so they should not be signed until you understand all your legal rights.

Divorce Settlements

When a couple gets a divorce, it is usually necessary to come to an agreement regarding who will get the joint property and who will be responsible for the joint debts. This is usually called a DIVORCE SETTLEMENT AGREEMENT. (see form 12, p.63.) In some states it will be called a MARITAL SETTLEMENT AGREEMENT. The only time it would not be necessary is if the parties had no property, debts, or children.

A couple divorcing has two choices. They can decide between themselves how they will divide their property and handle issues such as child custody and support, or they can hire two separate lawyers to argue to a judge what is best and let the judge decide.

If you can work these matters out with your spouse, you will come out ahead both financially and emotionally. Marital property is usually split 50/50, and child support is determined by income. There is not much advantage to fighting over the issue unless one spouse is being dishonest and hiding income and assets.

There are a lot of legal issues involved in a divorce. For example, *alimony* is tax deductible to the payer and taxable to the recipient, while child support and property settlements are not. Rights to each other's pension plans can be complicated. Therefore, if you and your spouse have any more than just minimal property, you should either do some research or consult an attorney. Some attorneys will give you a consultation for a fixed fee, for example $75 or $150, and answer all of your questions about whether you have any rights to be concerned with or if your divorce can be simple.

Care of Children

Because you are not always present with your children, you may need to delegate your parental responsibility to someone in whose care you have entrusted your children. This will allow that person to authorize necessary medical care and to have the right to discipline them when needed. For this purpose, use a **DELEGATION OF PARENTAL RESPONSIBILITY**. (see form 13, p.67.)

When your child is in an activity with a school or other organization, you will usually be asked to sign an authorization. Less formal groups may not have a form, or the form used by your group may not cover all of the conditions you wish to impose upon the activity. For these instances, a **CHILD AUTHORIZATION** form can be used. (see form 14, p.69.)

With many children being involved in custody disputes and a rising numbers of missing children taken by noncustodial parents, border crossings with children can be delayed if there are any suspicions by authorities. Written authorization by the other parent could save time and smooth the crossing. The **AUTHORIZATION FOR CHILD TO TRAVEL** form can be used for this purpose. If the child is traveling with a nonparent, both parents should sign; otherwise, only the one not traveling needs to sign. (see form 15, p.71.)

Care of Pets

If you leave your pet with a professional boarder, they will most likely have their own contract. But if you hire someone who is not a professional to care for your pet, you should have your own **PET CARE AGREEMENT** to cover his or her duties and obligations. (see form 16, p.73.)

Address Change

To be sure that you do not miss any of your mail when you move, you should be sure to notify both the post office and your important contacts. The post office does not forward certain types of mail (catalogs, for example), and it only forwards other mail for a limited time. After that, it is returned to sender. The OFFICIAL MAIL FORWARDING CHANGE OF ADDRESS ORDER to the post office is included to notify the post office. An ADDRESS CHANGE NOTICE TO CONTACTS is included for notifying other people, such as doctors and other professionals, magazines, newspapers, friends, banks, credit card companies, and anyone else with whom you have an ongoing relationship. (see forms 17 and 18, p.75–77.)

A separate form is included for notifying the IRS of your change of address. (see form 19, p.79.)

Your address can also be changed online at:

http://moversguide.usps.com

Birth and Death Certificates

To obtain copies of birth and death certificates, you need to contact the department that keeps *vital statistics* for your state. Sometimes you can get their number in your local phone book. If not, get the address, phone number, and fees from the following website:

www.cdc.gov/nchs/howto/w2w/w2welcom.htm

If you do not have access to a computer, you can obtain it from:

U.S. DEPARTMENT OF HEALTH AND HUMAN SERVICES
Centers for Disease Control and Prevention
National Center for Health Statistics
3311 Toledo Road
Hyattsville, MD 20782
301-458-4000
866-441-NCHS *(toll-free)*

Form 20 can be used to make a BIRTH OR DEATH CERTIFICATE REQUEST. (see p.81.)

Passport Application

While you used to be able to visit countries like Canada and Mexico with just your driver's license and birth certificate, due to changes with security, you may want to carry a passport. You must have a passport before visiting most other countries of the world. If you never had a passport, you must apply in person at a passport agency. They are usually located in federal buildings or courthouses. Look in the government pages of your phone book. They could be under the federal, state, or county listings. Call first to see if you need an appointment. If you need to renew a passport, this can be done by mail. An **APPLICATION FOR U.S. PASSPORT (NEW)** and **APPLICATION FOR U.S. PASSPORT BY MAIL (RENEWAL)** are included. (see form 21, p.83 and form 21A, p.87.)

Social Security Number

When you give birth to or adopt a child, you will need to obtain a Social Security number for that child if you want to take advantage of the tax deduction. A Social Security number is also helpful if the child is a designated beneficiary of a 529 College Savings Plan. To obtain a Social Security number, you should use **FORM SS-5 APPLICATION FOR A SOCIAL SECURITY CARD.** (see form 22, p.91.)

COHABITATION AGREEMENT

This agreement is entered into on _____, 20_____ by and between
_____ and _____, as follows:

1. PURPOSE. The parties to this agreement wish to live together in an unmarried state. The parties intend to provide in this agreement for their property and other rights that may arise because of their living together. Both parties currently own assets, and anticipate acquiring additional assets, that they wish to continue to control, and they are entering into this agreement to determine their respective rights and duties while living together.

2. DISCLOSURE. The parties have revealed to each other full financial information regarding their net worth, assets, holdings, income, and liabilities not only by their discussions with each other, but also through copies of their current financial statements, copies of which are attached hereto as Exhibits A and B. Both parties acknowledge that they had sufficient time to review the other's financial statement, are familiar with and understand the other's financial statement, had any questions satisfactorily answered, and are satisfied that full and complete financial disclosure has been made by the other.

3. LEGAL ADVICE. Each party had legal and financial advice, or had the opportunity to consult independent legal and financial counsel, prior to executing this agreement. Either party's failure to so consult legal and financial counsel constitutes a waiver of such right. By signing this agreement, each party acknowledges that he or she understands the facts of this agreement, and is aware of his or her legal rights and obligations under this agreement, or arising because of their living together in an unmarried state.

4. CONSIDERATION. The parties acknowledge that each of them would not continue living together in an unmarried state except for the execution of this agreement in its present form.

5. EFFECTIVE DATE. This Agreement shall become effective and binding as of _____, 20____ , and shall continue until they no longer live together or until the death of either party.

6. DEFINITIONS. As used in this agreement, the following terms shall have the following meanings:

   (a) "Joint Property" means property held and owned by the parties together. Such ownership shall be as tenants by the entirety in jurisdictions where such a tenancy is permitted. If such jurisdiction does not recognize or permit a tenancy by the entirety, then ownership shall be as joint tenants with rights of survivorship. The intention of the parties is to hold joint property as tenants by the entirety whenever possible.

   (b) "Joint Tenancy" means tenancy by the entirety in jurisdictions where such a tenancy is permitted, and joint tenancy with rights of survivorship if tenancy by the entirety is not recognized or permitted. The intention of the parties is to hold joint property as tenants by the entirety whenever possible.

7. SEPARATE PROPERTY. _____ is the owner of certain property, which is listed in Exhibit A, attached hereto and made a part hereof, which he intends to keep as his nonmarital, separate, sole, and individual property. All income, rents, profits, interest, dividends, stock splits, gains, and appreciation in value relating to any such separate property shall also be deemed separate property.

_____ is the owner of certain property, which is listed in Exhibit B, attached hereto and made a part hereof, which she intends to keep as her nonmarital, separate, sole, and individual property. All income, rents, profits, interest, dividends, stock splits, gains, and appreciation in value relating to any such separate property shall also be deemed separate property.

8. JOINT PROPERTY. The parties intend that certain property shall, from the effective date of this agreement, be joint property with full rights of survivorship. This property is listed and described in Exhibit C, attached hereto and made a part hereof.

9. PROPERTY ACQUIRED WHILE LIVING TOGETHER. The parties recognize that either or both of them may acquire property during the time they are living together. The parties agree that the the ownership of such property shall be determined by the source of the funds used to acquire it. If joint funds are used, it shall be jointly owned property with full rights of survivorship. If separate funds are used, it shall be separately owned property, unless it is added to Exhibit C by the purchaser.

10. BANK ACCOUNTS. Any funds deposited in either party's separate bank accounts shall be deemed that party's separate property. Any funds deposited in a bank account held by the parties jointly shall be deemed joint property.

11. PAYMENT OF EXPENSES. The parties agree that their expenses shall be paid as follows:

_____

_____

_____

_____

_____

12. DISPOSITION OF PROPERTY. Each party retains the management and control of the property belonging to that party and may encumber, sell, or dispose of the property without the consent of the other party. Each party shall execute any instrument necessary to effectuate this paragraph on the request of the other party. If a party does not join in or execute an instrument required by this paragraph, the other party may sue for specific performance or for damages, and the defaulting party shall be responsible for the other party's costs, expenses, and attorney's fees. This paragraph shall not require a party to execute a promissory note or other evidence of debt for the other party. If a party executes a promissory note or other evidence of debt for the other party, that other party shall indemnify the party executing the note or other evidence of debt from any claims or demands arising from the execution of the instrument. Execution of an instrument shall not give the executing party any right or interest in the property or the party requesting execution.

13. PROPERTY DIVISION UPON SEPARATION. In the event of separation of the parties, they agree that the terms and provisions of this agreement shall govern all of their rights as to property, property settlement, rights of community property, and equitable distribution against the other. Each party releases and waives any claims for special equity in the other party's separate property or in jointly owned property.

14. EFFECT OF SEPARATION OR DEATH. Each of the parties waives the right to be supported by the other after their separation or after the death of either party.

15. DEBTS. Neither party shall assume or become responsible for the payment of any preexisting debts or obligations of the other party. Neither party shall do anything that would cause the debt or obligation of one of them to be a claim, demand, lien, or encumbrance against the property of the other party without the other party's written consent. If a debt or obligation of one party is asserted as a claim or demand against the property of the other without such written consent, the party who is responsible for the debt or obligation shall indemnify the other from the claim or demand, including the indemnified party's costs, expenses, and attorneys' fees.

16. FREE AND VOLUNTARY ACT. The parties acknowledge that executing this agreement is a free and voluntary act, and has not been entered into for any reason other than the desire for the furtherance of their relationship in living together. Each party acknowledges that he or she had adequate time to fully consider the consequences of signing this agreement, and has not been pressured, threatened, coerced, or unduly influenced to sign this agreement.

17. SEVERABILITY. If any part of this agreement is adjudged invalid, illegal, or unenforceable, the remaining parts shall not be affected and shall remain in full force and effect.

18. FURTHER ASSURANCE. Each party shall execute any instruments or documents at any time requested by the other party that are necessary or proper to effectuate this agreement.

19. BINDING EFFECT. This agreement shall be binding upon the parties, and upon their heirs, executors, personal representatives, administrators, successors, and assigns.

20. NO OTHER BENEFICIARY. No person shall have a right or cause of action arising out of or resulting from this agreement, except those who are parties to it and their successors in interest.

21. RELEASE. Except as otherwise provided in this agreement, each party releases all claims or demands to the property or estate of the other, however and whenever acquired, including acquisitions in the future.

22. ENTIRE AGREEMENT. This instrument, including any attached exhibits, constitutes the entire agreement of the parties. No representations or promises have been made except those that are set out in this agreement. This agreement may not be modified or terminated except in writing signed by the parties.

23. PARAGRAPH HEADINGS. The headings of the paragraphs contained in this agreement are for convenience only, and are not to be considered a part of this agreement or used in determining its content or context.

24. ATTORNEYS' FEES IN ENFORCEMENT. A party who fails to comply with any provision or obligation contained in this agreement shall pay the other party's attorneys' fees, costs, and other expenses reasonably incurred in enforcing this agreement and resulting from the noncompliance.

25. SIGNATURES AND INITIALS OF PARTIES. The signatures of the parties on this document, and their initials on each page, indicate that each party has read, and agrees with, this entire Cohabitation Agreement, including any and all exhibits attached hereto.

26. ❑ OTHER PROVISIONS. Additional provisions are contained in the Addendum, attached hereto and made a part hereof.

_____   _____
(Signature of male)   (Signature of female)

STATE OF   )
COUNTY OF   )

The foregoing Agreement, consisting of _____ pages and Exhibits _____ through _____, was acknowledged before me this _____ day of _____, 20_____, by _____
_____, who are personally known to me or who have produced _____ as identification.

_____
Signature

_____
(Typed Name of Acknowledger)

NOTARY PUBLIC

Commission Number: _____

My Commission Expires:

FAMILY CONTRACT OF ADULT CHILD LIVING WITH PARENTS

This agreement is made between _____ (Parent) and
_____ (Child) to cover the understandings between the
parties during the time that the Child will be living with the Parent.

While the Child is legally an adult and able to conduct his or her life in any way desired while living independently, it is understood that the right of an adult to continue to live under the roof of the Parent includes the duty to follow any conditions required by the Parent.

The Child is free at any time to move out and to live under any rules, or lack thereof, that he or she desires.

As long as the Child is living with the parents, he or she agrees to the following conditions:

1. This agreement is initially intended to last until _____. This agreement may be extended or either party may end this agreement at any time.

2. As long as the Child is living with Parent, Child will ❏ work ❏ attend school, ❏ full time ❏ part time.

3. Child will contribute $_____ per _____ to the family expenses.

4. Child will help around the house by _____
_____

5. Child can have no more than _____ guests at a time during the day and _____ overnight.

6. Smoking ❏ is ❏ is not allowed in the house in _____

7. Child is allowed to have the following pets: _____

8. No controlled substances, illegal drugs, or drug paraphernalia shall be allowed in the house at any time.

9. Alcoholic beverages ❏ are ❏ are not allowed in the house.

10. Child's car can be parked _____ and should not be parked
_____.

11. Child may store his or her possessions in _____ but not
_____.

12. Child will, at all times, keep his or her living area clean and neat, and not create any health, electrical, or other hazards.

Agreed to:

_____   _____
Parent   Child

Date: _____, 20____   Date: _____, 20____

This page intentionally left blank.

PREMARITAL AGREEMENT

This Agreement is entered into on _____, 20_____, by and between _____ (hereafter referred to as the Husband) and _____ (hereafter referred to as the Wife), who agree that:

1. MARRIAGE. The parties plan to marry each other, and intend to provide in this agreement for their property and other rights that may arise because of their contemplated marriage.

2. PURPOSE OF AGREEMENT. Both parties currently own assets, and anticipate acquiring additional assets, that they wish to continue to control, and they are executing this Agreement to fix and determine their respective rights and duties during the marriage, in the event of a divorce or dissolution of the marriage or on the death of one of the parties.

3. FINANCIAL DISCLOSURE. The parties have revealed to each other full financial information regarding their net worth, assets, holdings, income, and liabilities; not only by their discussions with each other, but also through copies of their current financial statements, copies of which are attached hereto as Exhibits A and Exhibit B. Both parties acknowledge that they had sufficient time to review the other's financial statement, are familiar with and understand the other's financial statement, had any questions satisfactorily answered, and are satisfied that full and complete financial disclosure has been made by the other.

4. ADVICE OF COUNSEL. Each party had legal and financial advice, or had the opportunity to consult independent legal and financial counsel, prior to executing this agreement. Either party's failure to consult legal and financial counsel constitutes a waiver of such right. By signing this agreement, each party acknowledges that he or she understands the facts of this agreement, and is aware of his or her legal rights and obligations under this agreement or arising because of their contemplated marriage.

5. CONSIDERATION. The parties acknowledge that each of them would not enter into the contemplated marriage except for the execution of this agreement in its present form.

6. EFFECTIVE DATE. This Agreement shall become effective and binding upon the marriage of the parties. In the event the marriage does not take place, this agreement shall be null and void.

7. DEFINITIONS. As used in this agreement, the following terms shall have the following meanings:

  (a) "Joint Property" means property held and owned by the parties together. Such ownership shall be as tenants by the entirety in jurisdictions where such a tenancy is permitted. If such jurisdiction does not recognize or permit a tenancy by the entirety, then ownership shall be as joint tenants with rights of survivorship. The intention of the parties is to hold joint property as tenants by the entirety whenever possible.

  (b) "Joint Tenancy" means tenancy by the entirety in jurisdictions where such a tenancy is permitted, and joint tenancy with rights of survivorship if tenancy by the entirety is not recognized or permitted. The intention of the parties is to hold joint property as tenants by the entirety whenever possible.

8. HUSBAND'S SEPARATE PROPERTY. The Husband is the owner of certain property, which is set forth and described in Exhibit A, attached hereto and made a part hereof, that he intends to keep as his nonmarital, separate, sole, and individual property. All income, rents, profits, interest, dividends, stock splits, gains, and appreciation in value, relating to any such separate property shall also be deemed separate property.

9. WIFE'S SEPARATE PROPERTY. The Wife is the owner of certain property, which is set forth and described in Exhibit B, attached hereto and made a part hereof, that she intends to keep as her nonmarital, separate, sole, and individual property. All income, rents, profits, interest, dividends, stock splits, gains, and appreciation in value, relating to any such separate property shall also be deemed separate property.

10. JOINT OR COMMUNITY PROPERTY. The parties intend that certain property shall, from the beginning of the marriage, be marital, joint, or community property, which is set forth and described in Exhibit C, attached hereto and made a part hereof.

11. PROPERTY ACQUIRED DURING MARRIAGE. The parties recognize that either or both of them may acquire property during the marriage. The parties agree that the manner in which such property is titled during the marriage shall control such property's ownership and distribution in the event of any divorce, dissolution of marriage, separation, or death of either party. Such property shall be held as provided in the instrument conveying or evidencing title to such property. If the instrument does not specify or if there is no instrument, the property shall be held as a tenancy by the entirety, or as a joint tenancy with rights of survivorship in the event tenancy by the entirety is not recognized by the court having jurisdiction over the distribution of such property. Any property acquired that does not normally have a title or ownership certificate shall be considered as joint property unless otherwise specified by the parties in writing. All wedding gifts shall be deemed joint property, unless specified as separate property in either Exhibit A or B.

12. BANK ACCOUNTS. Any funds deposited in either party's separate bank accounts shall be deemed that party's separate property. Any funds deposited in a bank account held by the parties jointly shall be deemed joint property.

13. PAYMENT OF EXPENSES. The parties agree that their expenses shall be paid as set forth in Exhibit F, attached hereto and made a part hereof.

14. DISPOSITION OF PROPERTY. Each party retains the management and control of the property belonging to that party and may encumber, sell, or dispose of the property without the consent of the other party. Each party shall execute any instrument necessary to effectuate this paragraph on the request of the other party. If a party does not join in or execute an instrument required by this paragraph, the other party may sue for specific performance or for damages, regardless of the doctrine of spousal immunity, and the defaulting party shall be responsible for the other party's costs, expenses, and attorney's fees. This paragraph shall not require a party to execute a promissory note or other evidence of debt for the other party. If a party executes a promissory note or other evidence of debt for the other party, that other party shall indemnify the party executing the note or other evidence of debt from any claims or demands arising from the execution of the instrument. Execution of an instrument shall not give the executing party any right or interest in the property or the party requesting execution.

15. PROPERTY DIVISION UPON DIVORCE, DISSOLUTION OF MARRIAGE, OR SEPARATION. In the event of divorce, dissolution of marriage, or separation proceedings being filed and pursued by either party, the parties agree that the terms and provisions of this agreement shall govern all of their rights as to property, alimony including permanent periodic, rehabilitative, and lump sum, property settlement, rights of community property, and equitable distribution against the other. Each party releases and waives any claims for special equity in the other party's separate property or in jointly owned property. If either party files for divorce, dissolution, alimony, or spousal support unconnected with divorce, separation, or separate maintenance, the parties agree that either shall, in the filing of said proceedings, ask the court to follow the provisions and terms of this premarital agreement, and be bound by the terms of this agreement.

16. ALIMONY. In the event of divorce or dissolution of marriage proceedings being filed by either party in any state or country, each party forever waives any right to claim or seek any form of alimony or spousal support, attorneys' fees, and costs from the other. Any rights concerning distribution of property are otherwise covered by this agreement, and any rights to community property or claims of special equity are waived and released. In the event that a final judgment, decree of divorce, or dissolution of marriage is entered for whatever reason, the parties agree that the provisions of this agreement are in complete settlement of all rights to claim or seek any form of financial support, except child support for any living minor children of the parties, from the other.

17. DISPOSITION UPON DEATH. Each party consents that his or her estate, or the estate of the other, may be disposed of by will, codicil, or trust, or in the absence of any such instrument, according to the laws of descent and distribution and intestate succession as if the marriage of the parties had not taken place. In either event, the estate shall be free of any claim or demand of inheritance, dower, curtesy, elective share, family allowance, homestead election, right to serve as executor, administrator, or personal representative, or any spousal or other claim given by law, irrespective of the marriage and any law to the contrary. Neither party intends by this agreement to limit or restrict the right to give to, or receive from, the other an inter vivos or testamentary gift. Neither party intends by this agreement to release, waive, or relinquish any devise or bequest left to either by specific provision in the will or codicil of the other, any property voluntarily transferred by the other, any joint tenancy created by the other, or any right to serve as executor or personal representative of the other's estate if specifically nominated in the other's will or codicil.

18. DEBTS. Neither party shall assume or become responsible for the payment of any preexisting debts or obligations of the other party because of the marriage. Neither party shall do anything that would cause the debt or obligation of one of them to be a claim, demand, lien, or encumbrance against the property of the other party without the other party's written consent. If a debt or obligation of one party is asserted as a claim or demand against the property of the other without such written consent, the party who is responsible for the debt or obligation shall indemnify the other from the claim or demand, including the indemnified party's costs, expenses, and attorneys' fees.

19. HOMESTEAD. Each party releases any claim, demand, right, or interest that the party may acquire because of the marriage in any real property of the other because of the homestead property provisions of the laws of any state concerning the descent of the property as homestead.

20. FREE AND VOLUNTARY ACT. The parties acknowledge that executing this agreement is a free and voluntary act, and has not been entered into for any reason other than the desire for the furtherance of their relationship in

marriage. Each party acknowledges that he or she has had adequate time to fully consider the consequences of signing this agreement, and has not been pressured, threatened, coerced, or unduly influenced to sign this agreement.

21. GOVERNING LAW. This agreement shall be governed by the laws of _____.

22. SEVERABILITY. If any part of this agreement is adjudged invalid, illegal, or unenforceable, the remaining parts shall not be affected, and shall remain in full force and effect.

23. FURTHER ASSURANCE. Each party shall execute any instruments or documents at any time requested by the other party that are necessary or proper to effectuate this agreement.

24. BINDING EFFECT. This agreement shall be binding upon the parties, and upon their heirs, executors, personal representatives, administrators, successors, and assigns.

25. NO OTHER BENEFICIARY. No person shall have a right or cause of action arising out of or resulting from this agreement, except those who are parties to it and their successors in interest.

26. RELEASE. Except as otherwise provided in this agreement, each party releases all claims or demands to the property or estate of the other, however and whenever acquired, including acquisitions in the future.

27. ENTIRE AGREEMENT. This instrument, including any attached exhibits, constitutes the entire agreement of the parties. No representations or promises have been made except those that are set out in this agreement. This agreement may not be modified or terminated except in writing signed by the parties.

28. PARAGRAPH HEADINGS. The headings of the paragraphs contained in this agreement are for convenience only, and are not to be considered a part of this agreement or used in determining its content or context.

29. ATTORNEYS' FEES IN ENFORCEMENT. A party who fails to comply with any provision or obligation contained in this agreement shall pay the other party's attorneys' fees, costs, and other expenses reasonably incurred in enforcing this agreement and resulting from the noncompliance.

30. SIGNATURES AND INITIALS OF PARTIES. The signatures of the parties on this document, and their initials on each page, indicate that each party has read, and agrees with, this entire Premarital Agreement, including any and all exhibits attached hereto.

31. ❑ OTHER PROVISIONS. Additional provisions are contained in the Addendum to Premarital Agreement, attached hereto and made a part hereof.

_____   _____
Husband   Wife

Executed in the presence of:

_____   _____

Name: _____   Name: _____

Address: _____   Address: _____

_____   _____

STATE OF   )
COUNTY OF   )

The foregoing Agreement, consisting of _____ pages and Exhibits _____ through _____, was acknowledged before me this _____ day of _____, 20_____, by _____ _____, who are personally known to me or who have produced _____ as identification.

_____
Signature

_____
(Typed Name of Acknowledger)

NOTARY PUBLIC

Commission Number: _____

My Commission Expires:

This page intentionally left blank.

MARITAL AGREEMENT

This Agreement is entered into on _____, 20_____, by and between _____ (hereafter referred to as the Husband) and _____ (hereafter referred to as the Wife), who agree that:

1. MARRIAGE. The parties were married on _____.

2. PURPOSE OF AGREEMENT. Both parties currently own assets, and anticipate acquiring additional assets, that they wish to continue to control, and they are executing this Agreement to fix and determine their respective rights and duties during the marriage, in the event of a divorce or dissolution of the marriage, or on the death of one of the parties.

3. FINANCIAL DISCLOSURE. The parties have revealed to each other full financial information regarding their net worth, assets, holdings, income, and liabilities; not only by their discussions with each other, but also through copies of their current financial statements, copies of which are attached hereto as Exhibits A and Exhibit B. Both parties acknowledge that they had sufficient time to review the other's financial statement, are familiar with and understand the other's financial statement, had any questions satisfactorily answered, and are satisfied that full and complete financial disclosure has been made by the other.

4. ADVICE OF COUNSEL. Each party had legal and financial advice, or had the opportunity to consult independent legal and financial counsel, prior to executing this Agreement. Either party's failure to so consult legal and financial counsel constitutes a waiver of such right. By signing this Agreement, each party acknowledges that he or she understands the facts of this Agreement, and is aware of his or her legal rights and obligations under this Agreement, or arising because of their contemplated marriage.

5. CONSIDERATION. The parties acknowledge that the mutual promises and covenants of this Agreement are the consideration for their acceptance.

6. EFFECTIVE DATE. This Agreement shall become effective and binding upon execution.

7. DEFINITIONS. As used in this Agreement, the following terms shall have the following meanings:

   (a) "Joint Property" means property held and owned by the parties together. Such ownership shall be as tenants by the entirety in jurisdictions where such a tenancy is permitted. If such jurisdiction does not recognize or permit a tenancy by the entirety, then ownership shall be as joint tenants with rights of survivorship. The intention of the parties is to hold joint property as tenants by the entirety whenever possible.

   (b) "Joint Tenancy" means tenancy by the entirety in jurisdictions where such a tenancy is permitted, and joint tenancy with rights of survivorship if tenancy by the entirety is not recognized or permitted. The intention of the parties is to hold joint property as tenants by the entirety whenever possible.

8. HUSBAND'S SEPARATE PROPERTY. The Husband is the owner of certain property, which is set forth and described in Exhibit A, attached hereto and made a part hereof, that he intends to keep as his nonmarital, separate,

sole, and individual property. All income, rents, profits, interest, dividends, stock splits, gains, and appreciation in value, relating to any such separate property shall also be deemed separate property.

9. WIFE'S SEPARATE PROPERTY. The Wife is the owner of certain property, which is set forth and described in Exhibit B, attached hereto and made a part hereof, that she intends to keep as her nonmarital, separate, sole, and individual property. All income, rents, profits, interest, dividends, stock splits, gains, and appreciation in value, relating to any such separate property shall also be deemed separate property.

10. JOINT OR COMMUNITY PROPERTY. The parties intend that certain property shall, from the beginning of the marriage, be marital, joint, or community property, which is set forth and described in Exhibit C, attached hereto and made a part hereof.

11. PROPERTY ACQUIRED DURING MARRIAGE. The parties recognize that either or both of them may acquire property during the marriage. The parties agree that the manner in which such property is titled during the marriage shall control such property's ownership and distribution in the event of any divorce, dissolution of marriage, separation, or death of either party. Such property shall be held as provided in the instrument conveying or evidencing title to such property. If the instrument does not specify or if there is no instrument, the property shall be held as a tenancy by the entirety, or as a joint tenancy with rights of survivorship in the event tenancy by the entirety is not recognized by the court having jurisdiction over the distribution of such property. Any property acquired that does not normally have a title or ownership certificate shall be considered as joint property unless otherwise specified by the parties in writing. All wedding gifts shall be deemed joint property, unless specified as separate property in either Exhibit A or B.

12. BANK ACCOUNTS. Any funds deposited in either party's separate bank accounts shall be deemed that party's separate property. Any funds deposited in a bank account held by the parties jointly shall be deemed joint property.

13. PAYMENT OF EXPENSES. The parties agree that their expenses shall be paid as set forth in Exhibit D, attached hereto and made a part hereof.

14. DISPOSITION OF PROPERTY. Each party retains the management and control of the property belonging to that party, and may encumber, sell, or dispose of the property without the consent of the other party. Each party shall execute any instrument necessary to effectuate this paragraph on the request of the other party. If a party does not join in or execute an instrument required by this paragraph, the other party may sue for specific performance or for damages, regardless of the doctrine of spousal immunity, and the defaulting party shall be responsible for the other party's costs, expenses, and attorney's fees. This paragraph shall not require a party to execute a promissory note or other evidence of debt for the other party. If a party executes a promissory note or other evidence of debt for the other party, that other party shall indemnify the party executing the note or other evidence of debt from any claims or demands arising from the execution of the instrument. Execution of an instrument shall not give the executing party any right or interest in the property, or the party requesting execution.

15. PROPERTY DIVISION UPON DIVORCE, DISSOLUTION OF MARRIAGE, OR SEPARATION. In the event of divorce, dissolution of marriage, or separation proceedings being filed and pursued by either party, the parties agree

that the terms and provisions of this agreement shall govern all of their rights as to property; alimony, including permanent periodic, rehabilitative, and lump sum; property settlement; rights of community property; and, equitable distribution against the other. Each party releases and waives any claims for special equity in the other party's separate property or in jointly owned property. If either party files for divorce, dissolution, alimony, or spousal support unconnected with divorce, separation, or separate maintenance, the parties agree that either shall, in the filing of said proceedings, ask the court to follow the provisions and terms of this Marital Agreement and be bound by the terms of this Agreement.

16. ALIMONY. In the event of divorce or dissolution of marriage proceedings being filed by either party in any state or country, each party forever waives any right to claim or seek any form of alimony or spousal support, attorneys' fees, and costs from the other. Any rights concerning distribution of property are otherwise covered by this Agreement, and any rights to community property or claims of special equity are waived and released. In the event that a final judgment or decree of divorce or dissolution of marriage is entered for whatever reason, the parties agree that the provisions of this agreement are in complete settlement of all rights to claim or seek any form of financial support, except child support for any living minor children of the parties, from the other.

17. DISPOSITION UPON DEATH. Each party consents that his or her estate, or the estate of the other, may be disposed of by will, codicil, or trust, or in the absence of any such instrument, according to the laws of descent and distribution and intestate succession as if the marriage of the parties had not taken place. In either event, the estate shall be free of any claim or demand of inheritance, dower, curtesy, elective share, family allowance, homestead election, right to serve as executor, administrator, or personal representative, or any spousal or other claim given by law, irrespective of the marriage and any law to the contrary. Neither party intends by this agreement to limit or restrict the right to give to, or receive from, the other an inter vivos or testamentary gift. Neither party intends by this agreement to release, waive, or relinquish any devise or bequest left to either by specific provision in the will or codicil of the other, any property voluntarily transferred by the other, any joint tenancy created by the other, or any right to serve as executor or personal representative of the other's estate if specifically nominated in the other's will or codicil.

18. DEBTS. Neither party shall assume or become responsible for the payment of any preexisting debts or obligations of the other party because of the marriage. Neither party shall do anything that would cause the debt or obligation of one of them to be a claim, demand, lien, or encumbrance against the property of the other party without the other party's written consent. If a debt or obligation of one party is asserted as a claim or demand against the property of the other without such written consent, the party who is responsible for the debt or obligation shall indemnify the other from the claim or demand, including the indemnified party's costs, expenses, and attorneys' fees.

19. HOMESTEAD. Each party releases any claim, demand, right, or interest that the party may acquire because of the marriage in any real property of the other because of the homestead property provisions of the laws of any state concerning the descent of the property as homestead.

20. FREE AND VOLUNTARY ACT. The parties acknowledge that executing this agreement is a free and voluntary act, and has not been entered into for any reason other than the desire for the furtherance of their relationship in

marriage. Each party acknowledges that he or she has had adequate time to fully consider the consequences of signing this agreement, and has not been pressured, threatened, coerced, or unduly influenced to sign this agreement.

21. GOVERNING LAW. This Agreement shall be governed by the laws of _____.

22. SEVERABILITY. If any part of this Agreement is adjudged invalid, illegal, or unenforceable, the remaining parts shall not be affected and shall remain in full force and effect.

23. FURTHER ASSURANCE. Each party shall execute any instruments or documents at any time requested by the other party that are necessary or proper to effectuate this Agreement.

24. BINDING EFFECT. This Agreement shall be binding upon the parties, and upon their heirs, executors, personal representatives, administrators, successors, and assigns.

25. NO OTHER BENEFICIARY. No person shall have a right or cause of action arising out of or resulting from this Agreement except those who are parties to it and their successors in interest.

26. RELEASE. Except as otherwise provided in this Agreement, each party releases all claims or demands to the property or estate of the other, however and whenever acquired, including acquisitions in the future.

27. ENTIRE AGREEMENT. This instrument, including any attached exhibits, constitutes the entire agreement of the parties. No representations or promises have been made except those that are set out in this Agreement. This Agreement may not be modified or terminated except in writing signed by the parties.

28. PARAGRAPH HEADINGS. The headings of the paragraphs contained in this Agreement are for convenience only, and are not to be considered a part of this Agreement or used in determining its content or context.

29. ATTORNEYS' FEES IN ENFORCEMENT. A party who fails to comply with any provision or obligation contained in this agreement shall pay the other party's attorneys' fees, costs, and other expenses reasonably incurred in enforcing this Agreement and resulting from the noncompliance.

30. SIGNATURES AND INITIALS OF PARTIES. The signatures of the parties on this document, and their initials on each page, indicate that each party has read, and agrees with, this entire Marital Agreement, including any and all exhibits attached hereto.

31.❏ OTHER PROVISIONS. Additional provisions are contained in the Addendum to Marital Agreement, attached hereto and made a part hereof.

_____   _____
Husband   Wife

Executed in the presence of:

_____   _____

Name: _____   Name: _____

Address: _____   Address: _____

_____   _____

STATE OF   )
COUNTY OF   )

The foregoing Agreement, consisting of _____ pages and Exhibits _____ through _____, was acknowledged before me this _____ day of _____, 20_____, by _____ _____, who are personally known to me or who have produced _____ as identification.

_____

Signature

_____

(Typed Name of Acknowledger)

NOTARY PUBLIC

Commission Number: _____

My Commission Expires:

This page intentionally left blank.

NOTICE OF NAME CHANGE

Notice is hereby given that I, _____, have changed my

legal name and shall hereafter be known as _____.

This change was made by:

_____ Marriage on _____, 20_____

_____ Court Order issued on _____, 20_____ in case no. _____, in

_____ Court.

Date: _____, 20_____

_____

Signature, New Name

This page intentionally left blank.

SEPARATION AGREEMENT

This Agreement is entered into on _____, 20_____, by and between
_____ and _____.

The parties were married on _____, _____.

As a result of disputes and serious differences, they have separated and are now living separate and apart, and wish to continue living apart. They intend to settle by this agreement their marital matters, including child custody, child support, division of property and debts, and their rights to alimony.

For these reasons and in consideration of the mutual promises contained in this Agreement, Husband and Wife agree as follows:

1. LIVING SEPARATE. Husband and Wife will live separate and apart from each other, as if they were single and unmarried.

2. NO HARASSMENT OR INTERFERENCE. Neither party will in any manner harass, annoy, or interfere with the other.

3. CHILD CUSTODY

❑   There are no minor children.

❑   The parties will share in parenting responsibilities; however, physical custody of the minor child(ren), _____ shall be awarded to the _____, and the _____ shall have reasonable and liberal visitation rights.

❑   Other:
_____
_____
_____

4. CHILD SUPPORT

❑   There are no minor children.

❑   The _____ shall pay the sum of $ _____ per _____ as support and maintenance for the minor child(ren) in the physical custody of the other parent.

❑   The _____ shall maintain health insurance coverage for the minor child(ren) as long as such insurance is available at a reasonable group rate.

❑   Other:

_____

_____

_____

5. DIVISION OF PROPERTY

The Husband transfers to the Wife as her sole and separate property:

_____

_____

_____

_____

_____

❑   Continued on Additional Sheet.

The Wife transfers to the Husband as his sole and separate property:

_____

_____

_____

_____

_____

❑   Continued on Additional Sheet.

6. DIVISION OF DEBTS

The Husband shall pay, and will not at any time hold the Wife responsible for, the following debts:

_____

_____

_____

_____

❑   Continued on Additional Sheet.

The Wife shall pay, and will not at any time hold the Husband responsible for, the following debts:

_____
_____
_____
_____
_____

❑   Continued on Additional Sheet.

7. ALIMONY

The ❑ Husband ❑ Wife shall pay alimony in the sum of $ _____ per _____, for a period of _____; or until the ❑ Husband ❑ Wife dies or remarries, whichever occurs first.

❑   Other:

_____
_____
_____

8. EFFECT OF DIVORCE OR DISSOLUTION OF MARRIAGE. In the event of a divorce or dissolution of marriage, this Separation Agreement shall, if the court approves, be merged with, incorporated into, and become a part of any subsequent decree or judgment for divorce or dissolution of marriage.

9. FINANCIAL DISCLOSURE. The parties have revealed to each other full financial information regarding their net worth, assets, holdings, income, and liabilities; not only by their discussions with each other, but also through copies of their current financial statements, copies of which are attached hereto as Exhibits A and B. Both parties acknowledge that they had sufficient time to review the other's financial statement, are familiar with and understand the other's financial statement, had any questions satisfactorily answered, and are satisfied that full and complete financial disclosure has been made by the other.

10. WAIVER OF ESTATE. Both parties to this agreement agree to waive any and all right to the estate of the other, including dower, curtesy, elective share, community property rights, or rights of intestacy. Each party shall be allowed to pass his or her property freely by will.

11. INDEPENDENT REPRESENTATION BY COUNSEL. Each party has the right to representation by independent counsel. Each party fully understands his or her rights and considers the terms of this agreement to be fair and reasonable.

12. EXECUTION OF NECESSARY INSTRUMENTS. The parties will execute and deliver any other instruments and documents that may be necessary and convenient to carry out all of the terms of this Agreement.

13. ENTIRE AGREEMENT. This instrument, including any attached exhibits, constitutes the entire agreement of the parties. No representations or promises have been made except those that are set out in this Agreement. This agreement may not be modified or terminated except in writing signed by the parties.

14. GOVERNING LAW. This Agreement shall be governed by the laws of _____.

15. BINDING EFFECT. This agreement shall be binding upon the parties, and upon their heirs, executors, personal representatives, administrators, successors, and assigns.

_____   _____
Husband's Signature   Wife's Signature

STATE OF _____)
COUNTY OF _____)

The foregoing Agreement, consisting of _____ pages and Exhibits _____ through _____, was acknowledged before me this _____ day of _____, 20____, by _____ _____, who are personally known to me or who have produced _____ as identification.

_____
Signature

_____
(Typed Name of Acknowledger)

NOTARY PUBLIC

Commission Number: _____

My Commission Expires:

DIVORCE SETTLEMENT
(MARITAL SETTLEMENT AGREEMENT)

This Agreement is entered into on _____, 20_____, by and between _____ (Husband) and _____ (Wife) whose address are as follows:

_____   _____
(Address)   (Address)

_____   _____
(City)   (County)   (State)   (City)   (County)   (State)

The parties were married on _____, _____.

As a result of disputes and serious differences, they have separated and are now living separate and apart, and wish to continue living permanently apart. They intend to settle by this agreement their marital matters, including child custody, child support, division of property and debts, and their rights to alimony.

For these reasons and in consideration of the mutual promises contained in this agreement, Husband and Wife agree as follows:

1. LIVING SEPARATE. Husband and Wife will live separate and apart from each other, as if they were single and unmarried.

2. NO HARASSMENT OR INTERFERENCE. Neither party will, in any manner, harass, annoy or interfere with the other.

3. CHILD CUSTODY.

❏   The parties will share in parenting responsibilities; however, physical custody of the minor child(ren), _____ shall be awarded to the Wife and the Husband shall have reasonable and liberal visitation rights.

❏   The parties will share in parenting responsibilities; however, physical custody of the minor child(ren), _____ shall be awarded to the Husband and the Wife shall have reasonable and liberal visitation rights.

❏   Other:

_____

_____

❏ The ❏ Husband ❏ Wife shall pay the sum of $ _____ per _____ as support and maintenance for the minor child(ren) in the physical custody of the other parent.

❏ The ❏ Husband ❏ Wife shall maintain health insurance coverage for the minor child(ren), as long as such insurance is available at a reasonable group rate.

❏ Other:

_____

_____

_____

5. DIVISION OF PROPERTY

The Husband transfers to the Wife as her sole and separate property:

_____

_____

_____

_____

_____

❏ Continued on Additional Sheet.

The Wife transfers to the Husband as his sole and separate property:

_____

_____

_____

_____

_____

❏ Continued on Additional Sheet.

6. DIVISION OF DEBTS

The Husband shall pay, and will not at any time hold the Wife responsible for, the following debts:

_____

_____

_____

_____

_____

❏ Continued on Additional Sheet.

The Wife shall pay, and will not at any time hold the Husband responsible for, the following debts:

_____

_____

_____

_____

_____

❑ Continued on Additional Sheet.

7. ALIMONY

❑ The ❑ Husband ❑ Wife shall pay alimony in the sum of $ _____ per _____, for a period of _____, or until the ❑ Husband ❑ Wife dies or remarries, whichever occurs first.

❑ Other:

8. EFFECT OF DIVORCE OR DISSOLUTION OF MARRIAGE. In the event of a divorce or dissolution of marriage, this Marital Settlement Agreement shall, if the court approves, be merged with, incorporated into, and become a part of any subsequent decree or judgment for divorce or dissolution of marriage.

9. FINANCIAL DISCLOSURE. The parties have revealed to each other full financial information regarding their net worth, assets, holdings, income, and liabilities; not only by their discussions with each other, but also through copies of their current financial statements, copies of which are attached hereto as Exhibits A and B. Both parties acknowledge that they had sufficient time to review the other's financial statement, are familiar with and understand the other's financial statement, had any questions satisfactorily answered, and are satisfied that full and complete financial disclosure has been made by the other.

10. INDEPENDENT REPRESENTATION BY COUNSEL. Each party has the right to representation by independent counsel. Each party fully understands his or her rights, and considers the terms of this agreement to be fair and reasonable.

11. EXECUTION OF NECESSARY INSTRUMENTS. The parties will execute and deliver any other instruments and documents that may be necessary and convenient to carry out all of the terms of this Agreement.

12. ENTIRE AGREEMENT. This instrument, including any attached exhibits, constitutes the entire agreement of the parties. No representations or promises have been made except those that are set out in this Agreement. This Agreement may not be modified or terminated except in writing signed by the parties.

13. GOVERNING LAW. This Agreement shall be governed by the laws of _____.

14. BINDING EFFECT. This Agreement shall be binding upon the parties, and upon their heirs, executors, personal representatives, administrators, successors, and assigns.

_____   _____
(Husband's signature)   (Wife's signature)

Name: _____   Name: _____

Address: _____   Address: _____

        _____   _____

STATE OF   )
COUNTY OF   )

The foregoing Agreement, consisting of _____ pages and Exhibits _____ through _____, was acknowledged before me this _____ day of _____, 20____, by _____ _____, who are personally known to me or who have produced _____ as identification.

_____
Signature

_____
(Typed Name of Acknowledger)

NOTARY PUBLIC

Commission Number: _____

My Commission Expires:

DELEGATION OF PARENTAL RESPONSIBILITY

The undersigned, being the natural parent of _____, a minor, hereby grants to
_____, as Custodian, the following authority over said child:

1. To have custody of the child during the following periods:

2. To discipline said child in a reasonable manner as discussed previously.

3. To authorize any and all emergency medical treatment that is deemed necessary or advisable for any injury or illness while child is in his/her custody.

Custodian agrees to use all reasonable means to protect the child while in his/her custody and to make reasonable effort to reach the undersigned in the event of an emergency. Parent can be reached at:

Cell phone:_____

Beeper: _____

Other phone:_____

Other phone:_____

_____
Parent

_____
Child's Custodian

This page intentionally left blank.

CHILD AUTHORIZATION

To: _____

This is to confirm that my child, _____, is authorized to participate in:
_____ on _____, 20_____
under the following conditions:

If these conditions will not be met, my child may not participate.

During participation, I can be reached at:

      Cell phone:_____

      Beeper: _____

      Other phone:_____

      Other phone:_____

If I cannot be reached in any of these ways, I authorize _____ to consent
to any emergency medical care that may be necessary.

                 _____

                 Parent

                 Accepted by:

                 _____

This page intentionally left blank.

AUTHORIZATION FOR CHILD TO TRAVEL

To whom it may concern:

The undersigned parent(s) authorize my/our child, _____, whose birth date is _____, and whose passport number is _____, to travel with _____ to _____ from _____, 20_____ until _____, 20_____.

I/we affirm that I/we have full legal rights and/or custody of said child and that there are no custody disputes pending in any court.

I/we authorize _____ to make any and all necessary decisions regarding medical care.

Parent's name _____

Address _____

City, state, zip _____

Day phone _____

Evening phone _____

Cell phone _____

Pager _____

Parent's name _____

Address _____

City, state, zip _____

Day phone _____

Evening phone _____

Cell phone _____

Pager _____

72

_____   _____
Signature   Signature

_____
(Typed Name of Acknowledger)

NOTARY PUBLIC

Commission Number: _____

My Commission Expires:

PET CARE AGREEMENT

This is agreement is made between _____, (Owner) as pet owner, and
_____ (Care Giver), who has agreed to care for a pet known as
_____, which is a _____.

The parties agree that Care Giver shall care for Owner's pet from _____ until
_____.

Pet shall be cared for at ❏ Owner's house ❏ Care Giver's house.

Pet shall be fed and given fresh water at least _____ times each day.

Care Giver shall be paid the sum of $ _____ per _____ for said services.

If Owner cannot be reached, Care Giver is authorized to consent to any emergency medical care that may be necessary.

Date: _____

_____
Owner

_____
Care Giver

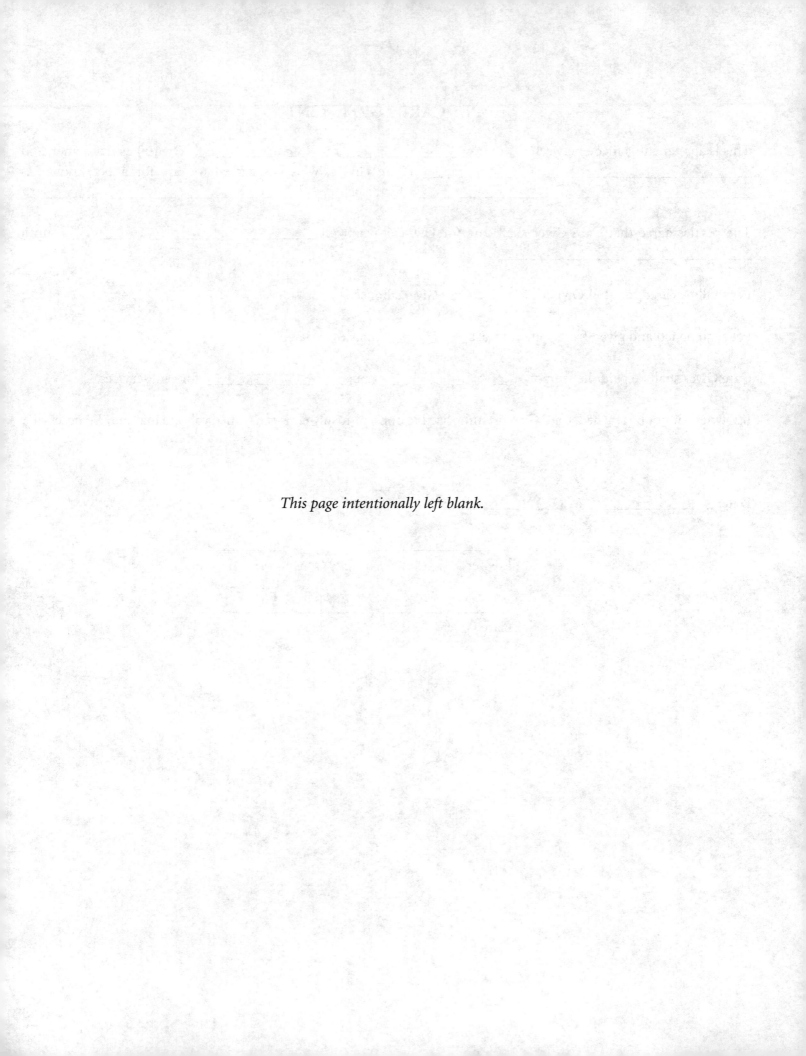

This page intentionally left blank.

OFFICIAL MAIL FORWARDING CHANGE OF ADDRESS ORDER

OFFICIAL USE ONLY

Please PRINT items 1-10 in blue or black ink. Your signature is required in item 9.

Zone/Route ID No.

1. Change of Address for: (Read Attached Instructions)
☐ Individual (#5)   ☐ Entire Family (#5)   ☐ Business (#6)

2. Is This Move Temporary?   ☐ Yes   ☐ No

Date Entered on Form 3982
M M D D Y Y

3. Start Date: (ex. 02/27/05)   M M D D Y Y

4. If TEMPORARY move, print date to discontinue forwarding: (ex. 03/27/05)   M M D D Y Y

Expiration Date
M M D D Y Y

5a. LAST Name & Jr./Sr./etc.

5b. FIRST Name and MI

Clerk/Carrier Endorsement

6. If BUSINESS Move, Print Business Name

PRINT OLD MAILING ADDRESS BELOW: HOUSE/BUILDING NUMBER AND STREET NAME (INCLUDE ST., AVE., CT., ETC.) OR PO BOX

7a. OLD Mailing Address

7a. OLD APT or Suite   **7b. For Puerto Rico Only:** If address is in PR, print urbanization name, if appropriate.

7c. OLD CITY   **7d. State**   **7e. ZIP**

PRINT NEW MAILING ADDRESS BELOW: HOUSE/BUILDING NUMBER AND STREET NAME (INCLUDE ST., AVE., CT., ETC.) OR PO BOX

8a. NEW Mailing Address

8a. NEW APT/Ste or PMB   **8b. For Puerto Rico Only:** If address is in PR, print urbanization name, if appropriate.

8c. NEW CITY   **8d. State**   **8e. ZIP**

9. Print and Sign Name (see conditions on reverse)
Print: _____
► Sign: _____

10. Date Signed: (ex. 01/27/05)   M M D D Y Y

OFFICIAL USE ONLY

PS FORM 3575 January 2005   Visit http://usps.com/moversguide to change your address online.   0015

Instructions

BEFORE YOU FILL OUT THE CHANGE OF ADDRESS FORM (PS FORM 3575), print the City, State and ZIP Code of your old address in the proper spaces on the other side of the form. Then complete items 1 through 10. Remember to sign the form in item 9.

1. WHO'S MOVING?
- If it's just you, check the INDIVIDUAL box.
- If it's some members of your family with the same last name and others are staying, fill out a separate form for each mover and check the INDIVIDUAL box.
- If it's some members of your family with different last names, fill out a separate form for each mover and check the INDIVIDUAL box.
- If it's everyone in your family with the same last name, just fill out one card and check the ENTIRE FAMILY box.
- If it's your business, check the BUSINESS box.

2. IS THIS A TEMPORARY MOVE?
Check YES if you plan to return to your old address within 12 months. Otherwise, check NO.

3. WHEN SHOULD WE BEGIN FORWARDING MAIL?
Fill in the date you want us to begin forwarding your mail to your new address in the START DATE field.

4. RETURN DATE
For a temporary move, indicate the date when you want to stop forwarding mail to the TEMPORARY address. If this date should change, be sure to notify the post office that serves your OLD ADDRESS when to stop forwarding your mail.

5a. LAST NAME OF MOVER
- Fill in only one LAST NAME.
- If anyone with the same last name is moving to a different address, use a separate form for each person.

5b. FIRST NAME OF MOVER
- If you checked INDIVIDUAL, give us your FIRST NAME.
- If you checked ENTIRE FAMILY, print the first name of the head of household and any commonly used middle names or initials.

6. BUSINESS NAME
For a BUSINESS move, print the name of the business. Each business must file a separate form.

7. OLD ADDRESS
Print your complete OLD ADDRESS, including an APARTMENT NUMBER, SUITE or PO BOX NUMBER, if appropriate. Include City, State and ZIP.

8. NEW ADDRESS
Print your complete NEW ADDRESS, including an APARTMENT NUMBER, SUITE or PO BOX NUMBER, if appropriate. Include City, State and ZIP.

9. SIGNATURE
To make this change of address valid, print and sign your name.

10. DATE
Fill in the date you signed this form. Be sure to read the "Note" and "Privacy Notice" statements on the reverse side of the Change of Address Form.

This page intentionally left blank.

ADDRESS CHANGE NOTICE TO CONTACTS

> **Send this card to magazines, businesses, friends and family to let them know you've moved.**

Please send mail to my new address starting: ____ / ____ / ____
                                                              Month   Day   Year

My Name: _____

Old Address:

STREET OR PO BOX	APT/SUITE #
CITY OR POST OFFICE	STATE ZIP+4

New Address:

STREET OR PO BOX	APT/SUITE #
CITY OR POST OFFICE	STATE ZIP+4

UNITED STATES POSTAL SERVICE.

This page intentionally left blank.

Form **8822**
(Rev. December 2004)
Department of the Treasury
Internal Revenue Service

Form 19 **79**

Change of Address

▶ **Please type or print.**

OMB No. 1545-1163

▶ **See instructions on back.** ▶ **Do not attach this form to your return.**

Part I	**Complete This Part To Change Your Home Mailing Address**

Check **all** boxes this change affects:

1 ☐ Individual income tax returns (Forms 1040, 1040A, 1040EZ, TeleFile, 1040NR, etc.)
  ▶ If your last return was a joint return and you are now establishing a residence separate
    from the spouse with whom you filed that return, check here . . . . ▶ ☐

2 ☐ Gift, estate, or generation-skipping transfer tax returns (Forms 706, 709, etc.)
  ▶ For Forms 706 and 706-NA, enter the decedent's name and social security number below.

  ▶ Decedent's name   ▶ Social security number

3a Your name (first name, initial, and last name)	**3b** Your social security number
4a Spouse's name (first name, initial, and last name)	**4b** Spouse's social security number

5 Prior name(s). See instructions.

6a Old address (no., street, city or town, state, and ZIP code). If a P.O. box or foreign address, see instructions.	Apt. no.
6b Spouse's old address, if different from line 6a (no., street, city or town, state, and ZIP code). If a P.O. box or foreign address, see instructions.	Apt. no.
7 New address (no., street, city or town, state, and ZIP code). If a P.O. box or foreign address, see instructions.	Apt. no.

Part II	**Complete This Part To Change Your Business Mailing Address or Business Location**

Check **all** boxes this change affects:

8 ☐ Employment, excise, income, and other business returns (Forms 720, 940, 940-EZ, 941, 990, 1041, 1065, 1120, etc.)
9 ☐ Employee plan returns (Forms 5500, 5500-EZ, etc.)
10 ☐ Business location

11a Business name	**11b** Employer identification number
12 Old mailing address (no., street, city or town, state, and ZIP code). If a P.O. box or foreign address, see instructions.	Room or suite no.
13 New mailing address (no., street, city or town, state, and ZIP code). If a P.O. box or foreign address, see instructions.	Room or suite no.
14 New business location (no., street, city or town, state, and ZIP code). If a foreign address, see instructions.	Room or suite no.

Part III	**Signature**

Daytime telephone number of person to contact (optional) ▶ ( )

**Sign
Here**

▶ _____ _____ ▶ _____
  Your signature   Date   If Part II completed, signature of owner, officer, or representative   Date

▶ _____ _____ ▶ _____
  If joint return, spouse's signature   Date   Title

For Privacy Act and Paperwork Reduction Act Notice, see back of form.   Cat. No. 12081V   Form **8822** (Rev. 12-2004)

Purpose of Form

You can use Form 8822 to notify the Internal Revenue Service if you changed your home or business mailing address or your business location. If this change also affects the mailing address for your children who filed income tax returns, complete and file a separate Form 8822 for each child. If you are a representative signing for the taxpayer, attach to Form 8822 a copy of your power of attorney.

Changing both home and business addresses? If you are, use a separate Form 8822 to show each change.

Prior Name(s)

If you or your spouse changed your name because of marriage, divorce, etc., complete line 5. Also, be sure to notify the Social Security Administration of your new name so that it has the same name in its records that you have on your tax return. This prevents delays in processing your return and issuing refunds. It also safeguards your future social security benefits.

Addresses

Be sure to include any apartment, room, or suite number in the space provided.

P.O. Box

Enter your box number instead of your street address only if your post office does not deliver mail to your street address.

Foreign Address

Enter the information in the following order: city, province or state, and country. Follow the country's practice for entering the postal code. Please do not abbreviate the country name.

Signature

If you are completing Part II, the owner, an officer, or a representative must sign. An officer is the president, vice president, treasurer, chief accounting officer, etc. A representative is a person who has a valid power of attorney to handle tax matters or is otherwise authorized to sign tax returns for the business.

Where To File

Send this form to the Internal Revenue Service Center shown next that applies to you.

 If you checked the box on line 2, see Filers Who Checked the Box on Line 2 or Completed Part II for where to file this form.

Filers Who Checked the Box on Line 1 and Completed Part I

IF your old home mailing address was in . . .	THEN use this address . . .
Alabama, Florida, Georgia, Mississippi, North Carolina, Rhode Island, South Carolina, West Virginia	Atlanta, GA 39901
Arkansas, Colorado, Kentucky, Louisiana, New Mexico, Oklahoma, Tennessee, Texas	Austin, TX 73301
Alaska, Arizona, California, Hawaii, Idaho, Montana, Nevada, Oregon, Utah, Virginia, Washington, Wyoming	Fresno, CA 93888
Maine, Massachusetts, New Hampshire, New York, Vermont	Andover, MA 05501
Connecticut, Delaware, Illinois, Indiana, Iowa, Kansas, Michigan, Minnesota, Missouri, Nebraska, North Dakota, South Dakota, Wisconsin	Kansas City, MO 64999
Ohio*	Memphis, TN 37501
District of Columbia, Maryland, New Jersey, Pennsylvania	Philadelphia, PA 19255
American Samoa	Philadelphia, PA 19255
Guam: Permanent residents	Department of Revenue and Taxation Government of Guam P.O. Box 23607 GMF, GU 96921
Guam: Nonpermanent residents Puerto Rico (or if excluding income under Internal Revenue Code section 933) Virgin Islands: Nonpermanent residents	Philadelphia, PA 19255
Virgin Islands: Permanent residents	V. I. Bureau of Internal Revenue 9601 Estate Thomas Charlotte Amalie St. Thomas, VI 00802
Foreign country: U.S. citizens and those filing Form 2555, Form 2555-EZ, or Form 4563 Dual-status aliens All APO and FPO addresses	Philadelphia, PA 19255

*If you live in Ohio and mail Form 8822 after June 30, 2005, send it to: Internal Revenue Service Center, Fresno, CA 93888.

Filers Who Checked the Box on Line 2 or Completed Part II

IF your old business address was in . . .	THEN use this address . . .
Connecticut, Delaware, District of Columbia, Illinois, Indiana, Kentucky, Maine, Maryland, Massachusetts, Michigan, New Hampshire, New Jersey, New York, North Carolina, Ohio, Pennsylvania, Rhode Island, South Carolina, Vermont, Virginia, West Virginia, Wisconsin	Cincinnati, OH 45999
Alabama, Alaska, Arizona, Arkansas, California, Colorado, Florida, Georgia, Hawaii, Idaho, Iowa, Kansas, Louisiana, Minnesota, Mississippi, Missouri, Montana, Nebraska, Nevada, New Mexico, North Dakota, Oklahoma, Oregon, South Dakota, Tennessee, Texas, Utah, Washington, Wyoming	Ogden, UT 84201
Outside the United States	Philadelphia, PA 19255

Privacy Act and Paperwork Reduction Act Notice. We ask for the information on this form to carry out the Internal Revenue laws of the United States. We may give the information to the Department of Justice and to other Federal agencies, as provided by law. We may give it to cities, states, the District of Columbia, and U.S. commonwealths or possessions to carry out their tax laws. We may also disclose this information to other countries under a tax treaty, to federal and state agencies to enforce federal nontax criminal laws, or to federal law enforcement and intelligence agencies to combat terrorism.

Our legal right to ask for information is Internal Revenue Code sections 6001 and 6011, which require you to file a statement with us for any tax for which you are liable. Section 6109 requires that you provide your social security number on what you file. This is so we know who you are, and can process your form and other papers.

You are not required to provide the information requested on a form that is subject to the Paperwork Reduction Act unless the form displays a valid OMB control number. Books or records relating to a form or its instructions must be retained as long as their contents may become material in the administration of any Internal Revenue law. Generally, tax returns and return information are confidential, as required by section 6103.

The use of this form is voluntary. However, if you fail to provide the Internal Revenue Service with your current mailing address, you may not receive a notice of deficiency or a notice and demand for tax. Despite the failure to receive such notices, penalties and interest will continue to accrue on the tax deficiencies.

The time needed to complete and file this form will vary depending on individual circumstances. The estimated average time is 16 minutes.

If you have comments concerning the accuracy of this time estimate or suggestions for making this form simpler, we would be happy to hear from you. You can write to the Internal Revenue Service, Tax Products Coordinating Committee, SE:W:CAR:MP:T:T:SP, 1111 Constitution Ave. NW, IR-6406, Washington, DC 20224. Do not send the form to this address. Instead, see *Where To File* on this page.

BIRTH OR DEATH CERTIFICATE REQUEST

TO: [Office of Vital Statistics Address]

FROM: [Current name and address]

I request a certified copy of the ❑ birth certificate ❑ death certificate of _____

_____
(Give full name)

DATE OF BIRTH OR DEATH _____

PLACE OF BIRTH OR DEATH _____
(City, town, county, and state)

HOSPITAL: _____

SEX: _____   RACE: _____

NAME OF FATHER: _____

NAME OF MOTHER: _____ (Include maiden name)

The purpose for which this certificate is needed is: _____

_____.

My relationship to the person is ❑ Self ❑ Other: _____

ENCLOSED (Do not send cash)

❑ Certified check for $ _____   ❑ Money order for $ _____

_____

Signature

This page intentionally left blank.

U.S. Department of State
APPLICATION FOR A U.S. PASSPORT OR REGISTRATION
HOW TO APPLY FOR A U.S. PASSPORT

OMB APPROVAL NO. 1405-0004
EXPIRATION DATE: 03/31/2005
ESTIMATED BURDEN: 20 MINUTES
(See Page 4)

PLEASE DETACH AND RETAIN THIS INSTRUCTION SHEET FOR YOUR RECORDS.

I applied: **Place:** _____

Date: _____

FOR INFORMATION, QUESTIONS, AND INQUIRIES: Please visit our website at **travel.state.gov.** In addition, contact the National Passport Information Center (NPIC) toll-free at **1-877-487-2778 (TDD: 1-888-874-7793)** or by email at **NPIC@state.gov.** Customer Service Representatives are available M-F 8AM-8PM EST (excluding federal holidays). Automated information is available 24/7.

U.S. PASSPORTS ARE ISSUED ONLY TO U.S. CITIZENS OR NATIONALS. EACH PERSON MUST OBTAIN HIS OR HER OWN PASSPORT.

APPLICANTS WHO HAVE HAD A PREVIOUS U.S. PASSPORT:

If your most recent passport was issued less than 15 years ago and you were over 16 years old at the time of issuance, you may be eligible to use Form DS-82 (mail-in application). Please inquire about eligibility when you apply or visit our website or contact NPIC. Address any requests for a passport amendment, extension of validity, or the addition of visa pages to a Passport Agency or a U.S. consulate or embassy abroad. In advance of your departure, check visa requirements with consular officials of the countries you will be visiting.

SPECIAL REQUIREMENTS FOR CHILDREN

- **AS DIRECTED BY PUBLIC LAW 106-119:**

  To submit an application for a child under age 14 <u>both parents or the child's legal guardian(s) must appear</u> and present all of the following:
  - Evidence of the child's U.S. citizenship,
  - Evidence of the child's relationship to parents/guardian(s), **AND**
  - Parental identification.

  IF ONLY ONE PARENT APPEARS YOU MUST ALSO SUBMIT ONE OF THE FOLLOWING:
  - Second parent's written statement consenting to passport issuance for the child,
  - Primary evidence of sole authority to apply, **OR**
  - A written statement (made under penalty of perjury) explaining the second parent's unavailability.

- **AS DIRECTED BY REGULATION 22CFR51 Effective February 1, 2004:**

  Each minor child applying for a passport shall appear in person.

FIRST TIME APPLICANTS:

Please complete and submit this application in person. Each application must be accompanied by:
1. PROOF OF U.S. CITIZENSHIP
2. PROOF OF IDENTITY
3. TWO RECENT, IDENTICAL, COLOR PHOTOGRAPHS, **AND**
4. FEES (as explained on reverse of form) to one of the following acceptance agents: a clerk of a Federal or State court of record or a judge or clerk of a probate court accepting applications; a designated municipal or county official; a designated postal employee at an authorized post office; or an agent at a Passport Agency in Boston, Chicago, Honolulu, Houston, Los Angeles, Miami, New Orleans, New York, Norwalk CT, Philadelphia, San Francisco, Seattle, or Washington DC; or a U.S. consular official at a U.S. embassy or consulate, if abroad. To find your nearest acceptance facility, visit our website or contact the National Passport Information Center.

See Reverse Side for Detailed Information.

PLEASE DETACH AND RETAIN THIS INSTRUCTION SHEET FOR YOUR RECORDS

1. PROOF OF U.S. CITIZENSHIP

a. **APPLICANTS BORN IN THE UNITED STATES:** Submit a previous U.S. passport or **certified** birth certificate. A birth certificate must include your given name and surname, date and place of birth, date the birth record was filed, and the seal or other certification of the official custodian of such records.

(1) If the birth certificate was filed more than 1 year after the birth: It is acceptable if it is supported by evidence described in the next paragraph.

(2) If no birth record exists: Submit registrar's notice to that effect. Also submit an early baptismal or circumcision certificate, hospital birth record, early census, school, or family Bible records, newspapers or insurance files, or notarized affidavits of persons having knowledge of your birth (preferably in addition to at least one record listed above). Evidence should include your given name and surname, date and place of birth, and the seal or other certification of the issuing office (if customary) and the signature of the issuing official.

b. **APPLICANTS BORN OUTSIDE THE UNITED STATES:** Submit a previous U.S. passport, Certificate of Naturalization, Certificate of Citizenship, Consular Report of Birth Abroad, or evidence described below.

(1) If You Claim Citizenship Through Naturalization of Parent(s): Submit the Certificate(s) of Naturalization of your parent(s), your foreign birth certificate, **and** proof of your admission to the United States for permanent residence.

(2) If You Claim Citizenship Through Birth Abroad to One U.S. Citizen Parent: Submit a Consular Report of Birth (Form FS-240), Certification of Birth (Form DS-1350 or FS-545), **or** your foreign birth certificate, proof of citizenship of your parent, **and** an affidavit showing all of your U.S. citizen parent's periods and places of residence/physical presence in the United States and abroad before your birth.

(3) If You Claim Citizenship Through Birth Abroad to Two U.S. Citizen Parents: Submit a Consular Report of Birth (Form FS-240), Certification of Birth (Form DS-1350 or FS-545), **or** your foreign birth certificate, parent's marriage certificate, proof of citizenship of your parent(s), **and** an affidavit showing all of your U.S. citizen parent's periods and places of residence/physical presence in the United States and abroad before your birth.

(4) If You Claim Citizenship Through Adoption by a U.S. Citizen Parent(s): Submit evidence of your permanent residence status, full and final adoption, **and** your U.S. citizen parent(s) evidence of legal and physical custody.

2. PROOF OF IDENTITY

You must establish your identity to the acceptance agent. You may submit items such as the following containing your signature AND physical description or photograph that is a good likeness of you: previous U.S. passport, Certificate of Naturalization, Certificate of Citizenship, driver's license (not temporary or learner's license), or government (Federal, State, municipal) employee identification card or pass. Temporary or altered documents are not acceptable.

IF YOU CANNOT PROVE YOUR IDENTITY as stated above, you must appear with an IDENTIFYING WITNESS who is a U.S. citizen or permanent resident alien who has known you for at least 2 years. Your witness must prove his or her identity and complete and sign an Affidavit of Identifying Witness (Form DS-71) before the acceptance agent. You must also submit some identification of your own.

3. TWO RECENT, IDENTICAL, COLOR PHOTOGRAPHS

Submit two color photographs of you alone, sufficiently recent to be a good likeness of you (normally taken within the last six months), and 2x2 inches in size. The image size measured from the bottom of your chin to the top of your head (including hair) should not be less than 1 inch and not more than 1-3/8 inches. The photographs must be color, clear, with full front view of your face, and printed on thin paper with plain light (white or off-white) background. They must be capable of withstanding a mounting temperature of 225 Fahrenheit (107 Celsius). The photographs must be taken in normal street attire, without a hat, head covering, or dark glasses unless a signed statement is submitted by the applicant verifying the item is worn daily for religious purposes or a signed doctor's statement is submitted verifying the item is used daily for medical purposes. Photographs retouched so that your appearance is changed are unacceptable. Snapshots, most vending machine prints, and magazine or full-length photographs are unacceptable. Digitized photos must meet the previously stated qualifications and will be accepted for use at the discretion of Passport Services. (Visit our website for details.)

4. FEES

a. If you are 16 years of age or older: The passport processing fee is $55. In addition, a fee of $30 is charged for the execution of the application. Your passport will be valid for 10 years from the date of issue except where limited by the Secretary of State to a shorter period.

b. If you are 15 years of age or younger: The passport processing fee is $40. In addition, a fee of $30 is charged for the execution of the application. Your passport will be valid for 5 years from the date of issue except where limited by the Secretary of State to a shorter period.

BY LAW, THE PASSPORT PROCESSING AND EXECUTION FEES ARE NON-REFUNDABLE.

● **The passport processing and execution fees may be paid in one of the following forms:** Checks (personal, certified, traveler's), major credit card (Visa, Master Card, American Express, and Discover), bank draft or cashier's check, money order (U.S. Postal, international, currency exchange), or if abroad, the foreign currency equivalent, or a check drawn on a U.S. bank. All fees should be payable to the "U.S. Department of State" (except the $30 execution fee when applying at a designated acceptance facility), or if abroad, the appropriate U.S. embassy or consulate. **[NOTE: Some designated acceptance facilities do not accept credit cards as a form of payment].**

● **For faster processing,** you may request expedited service. Expedited requests will be processed in three workdays from receipt at a passport agency. The additional fee for expedited service is $60. Expedited service is available only in the United States.

● **If you desire SPECIAL POSTAGE SERVICE** (overnight mail, special delivery, etc.), include the appropriate postage fee with your payment.

● An additional $45 fee will be charged when, upon your request, the U.S. Department of State verifies issuance of a previous U.S. passport or Consular Report of Birth Abroad because you are unable to submit evidence of U.S. citizenship.

● For applicants with U.S. Government or military authorization for no-fee passports, **no fees are charged, except the execution fee** when **applying at a designated acceptance facility.**

IMPORTANT NOTICE TO APPLICANTS WHO HAVE LOST OR HAD A PREVIOUS PASSPORT STOLEN

A United States citizen may not normally bear more than one valid or potentially valid U.S. passport at a time. It therefore is necessary to submit a statement with an application for a new U.S. passport when a previous valid or potentially valid U.S. passport cannot be presented with an application for a new passport. Your statement must detail why the previous U.S. passport cannot be presented.

The information you provide regarding your lost or stolen U.S. passport will be placed into our Consular Lost or Stolen Passport System. This system is designed to prevent the misuse of your lost or stolen U.S. passport. Anyone using a passport book reported as lost or stolen may be detained upon entry into the United States. Should you locate your U.S. passport (previously reported lost or stolen) at a later time, report it as found and submit it for cancellation. It has been invalidated. You may not use that passport for travel.

For more information or to report your lost or stolen passport by phone, call NPIC or visit our website: *travel.state.gov*

U.S. Department of State

APPLICATION FOR A ☐ U.S. PASSPORT ☐ REGISTRATION

(Type or print in capital letters using blue or black ink in white areas only.)

1. NAME (First and Middle)

☐☐☐☐☐☐☐☐☐☐☐☐☐☐☐☐☐☐☐☐☐☐☐☐☐

LAST

☐☐☐☐☐☐☐☐☐☐☐☐☐☐☐☐☐☐☐☐☐☐

2. MAIL PASSPORT TO: STREET / RFD # OR P.O. BOX   **APT. #**

☐☐☐☐☐☐☐☐☐☐☐☐☐☐☐☐☐☐☐☐☐☐

CITY   **STATE**

☐☐☐☐☐☐☐☐☐☐☐☐☐☐☐☐☐☐☐☐☐

ZIP CODE   **COUNTRY / IN CARE OF** *(if applicable)*

☐☐☐☐☐☐☐☐☐☐☐☐☐☐☐☐☐☐☐☐☐☐☐

☐ 5 Yr.   ☐ 10 Yr.   Issue Date _____

☐ R ☐ D ☐ O ☐ DP

End. # _____ Exp. _____

3. SEX	4. PLACE OF BIRTH (City & State OR City & Country)	5. DATE OF BIRTH Month Day Year	6. SOCIAL SECURITY NUMBER (SEE FEDERAL TAX LAW NOTICE ON PAGE 4)
☐ M ☐ F			

7. HEIGHT Feet Inches	8. HAIR COLOR	9. EYE COLOR	10. HOME TELEPHONE	11. BUSINESS TELEPHONE	12. OCCUPATION

13. PERMANENT ADDRESS (DO NOT LIST P.O. BOX) STREET/R.F.D.#   CITY   STATE   ZIP CODE

14. FATHER'S FULL NAME Last First	BIRTHPLACE	BIRTHDATE	U.S. CITIZEN ☐ Yes ☐ No	15. MOTHER'S FULL MAIDEN NAME Last First	BIRTHPLACE	BIRTHDATE	U.S. CITIZEN ☐ Yes ☐ No

16. HAVE YOU EVER BEEN MARRIED? ☐ Yes ☐ No	SPOUSE'S OR FORMER SPOUSE'S FULL NAME AT BIRTH	BIRTHPLACE	BIRTHDATE	U.S. CITIZEN ☐ Yes ☐ No

DATE OF MOST RECENT MARRIAGE Month Day Year	WIDOWED/DIVORCED? ☐ Yes Give Date ☐ No Month Day Year	17. OTHER NAMES YOU HAVE USED (1) (2)

18. HAVE YOU EVER BEEN ISSUED A U.S. PASSPORT? ☐ Yes ☐ No   IF YES, COMPLETE NEXT LINE AND SUBMIT PASSPORT IF AVAILABLE.   **DISPOSITION**

NAME IN WHICH ISSUED   MOST RECENT PASSPORT NUMBER   APPROXIMATE ISSUE DATE Month Day Year   ☐ Submitted ☐ Stolen ☐ Lost ☐ Other _____

STAPLE   STAPLE

2" × 2"

STAPLE   STAPLE

SUBMIT TWO RECENT, IDENTICAL, COLOR PHOTOGRAPHS

It is necessary to submit a statement with an application for a new passport when a previous valid or potentially valid passport cannot be presented. The statement must set forth in detail why the previous passport cannot be presented. Use Form DS-64.

19. EMERGENCY CONTACT. If you wish, you may supply the name, address and telephone number of a person not traveling with you to be contacted in case of emergency.

NAME

STREET

CITY   STATE   ZIP CODE   TELEPHONE

20. TRAVEL PLANS *(not mandatory)* Month Day Year

Date of Trip

Length of Trip

COUNTRIES TO BE VISITED:

21. STOP! DO NOT SIGN APPLICATION UNTIL REQUESTED TO DO SO BY PERSON ADMINISTERING OATH.

I have not, since acquiring United States citizenship, performed any of the acts listed under "Acts or Conditions" on the reverse of this application form (unless explanatory statement is attached). I solemnly swear (or affirm) that the statements made on this application are true and the photograph attached is a true likeness of me.

X _____ Applicant's Signature - age 14 or older

X _____ Father's/Legal Guardian's Signature (if identifying minor)

X _____ Mother's/Legal Guardian's Signature (if identifying minor)

22. FOR ACCEPTANCE AGENT'S USE

Month Day Year (SEAL)

☐ Clerk of Court; Location _____
☐ PASSPORT Agent
☐ Postal Employee
☐ (Vice) Consul USA

(Signature of person authorized to accept application)

23a. Applicant's or Father's Identifying Documents

☐ Driver's License ☐ Passport ☐ Other (Specify) _____

Issue Date: Expiration Date: Place of Issue: _____

Name _____ ID No. _____

23b. Mother's Identifying Documents

☐ Driver's License ☐ Passport ☐ Other (Specify) _____

Issue Date: Expiration Date: Place of Issue: _____

Name _____ ID No. _____

24. FOR ISSUING OFFICE USE ONLY (Applicant's evidence of citizenship)

☐ Birth Certificate ☐ SR ☐ CR ☐ City Filed/Issued: _____
☐ Passport Bearer's Name: _____
☐ Report of Birth:
☐ Naturalization/Citizenship Cert. No./Issued: _____
☐ Other:
☐ Seen & Returned:
☐ Attached:

APPLICATION APPROVAL

25. FEE _____ EXEC. _____ EF _____ OTHER _____

DS-11   OMB No. 1405-0004 Expires: 03/31/2005 Estimated Burden - 20 Minutes   Page 3 of 4

U.S. Department of State
APPLICATION FOR U.S. PASSPORT OR REGISTRATION

FEDERAL TAX LAW

26 U.S.C. 6039E (Internal Revenue Code) requires a passport applicant to provide his or her name and social security number. If you have not been issued a social security number, enter zeros in box #6. The U.S. Department of State must provide this information to the Internal Revenue Service routinely. Any applicant who fails to provide the required information is subject to a $500 penalty enforced by the IRS. All questions on this matter should be referred to the nearest IRS office.

ACTS OR CONDITIONS

(If any of the below-mentioned acts or conditions has been performed by or apply to the applicant, the portion which applies should be lined out, and a supplementary explanatory statement under oath (or affirmation) by the applicant should be attached and made a part of this application.) I have not, since acquiring United States citizenship, been naturalized as a citizen of a foreign state; taken an oath or made an affirmation or other formal declaration of allegiance to a foreign state; entered or served in the armed forces of a foreign state; accepted or performed the duties of any office, post, or employment under the government of a foreign state or political subdivision thereof; made a formal renunciation of nationality either in the United States, or before a diplomatic or consular officer of the United States in a foreign state; or been convicted by a court or court martial of competent jurisdiction of committing any act of treason against, or attempting by force to overthrow, or bearing arms against, the United States, or conspiring to overthrow, put down, or to destroy by force, the Government of the United States.

WARNING: False statements made knowingly and willfully in passport applications or in affidavits or other supporting documents submitted therewith are punishable by fine and/or imprisonment under provisions of 18 U.S.C. 1001 and/or 18 U.S.C. 1542. Alteration or mutilation of a passport issued pursuant to this application is punishable by fine and/or imprisonment under the provisions of 18 U.S.C. 1543. The use of a passport in violation of the restrictions contained therein or of the passport regulations is punishable by fine and/or imprisonment under 18 U.S.C. 1544. All statements and documents submitted are subject to verification.

PRIVACY ACT AND PAPERWORK REDUCTION ACT STATEMENTS

AUTHORITIES: The information solicited on this form is requested pursuant to provisions in Titles 8, 18, and 22 of the United States Code, whether or not codified, including specifically 22 U.S.C. 211a, 212, 213, and all regulations issued pursuant to Executive Order 11295 (August 5, 1966), including Part 51, Title 22, Code of Federal Regulations (CFR). Also, as noted, 26 U.S.C. 6039E.

PURPOSE: The primary purpose for soliciting the information is to establish citizenship, identity, and entitlement to issuance of a U.S. passport. The information may also be used in connection with issuing other travel documents or evidence of citizenship, and in furtherance of the Secretary's responsibility for the protection of U.S. nationals abroad.

ROUTINE USES: The information solicited on this form may be made available as a routine use to other government agencies, to assist the U.S. Department of State in adjudicating passport applications, and for law enforcement and administration purposes. It may also be disclosed pursuant to court order. The information may be made available to foreign government agencies to fulfill passport control and immigration duties or to investigate or prosecute violations of law. The information may also be made available to private U.S. citizen 'wardens' designated by U.S. embassies and consulates.

Failure to provide the information requested on this form may result in the denial of a United States passport, related document, or service to the individual seeking such passport, document, or service.

Public reporting burden for this collection of information is estimated to average 20 minutes per response, including time required for searching existing data sources, gathering the necessary data, providing the information required, and reviewing the final collection. You do not have to provide the information unless this collection displays a currently valid OMB number. Send comments on the accuracy of this estimate of the burden and recommendations for reducing it to: U.S. Department of State (A/RPS/DIR) Washington, DC 20520.

U.S. Department of State
APPLICATION FOR A U.S. PASSPORT BY MAIL

PLEASE DETACH AND RETAIN THIS INSTRUCTION SHEET FOR YOUR RECORDS.

Date of Application:

CAN I USE THIS FORM?
Complete this checklist to determine your eligibility to use this form.

1. I can submit my most recent U.S. passport. ☐ Yes ☐ No

2. I was at least 16 years old when my most recent U.S. passport was issued. ☐ Yes ☐ No

3. I was issued my most recent U.S. passport less than 15 years ago. ☐ Yes ☐ No

4. I use the same name as on my most recent U.S. passport. ☐ Yes ☐ No
   -- OR --
   I have had my name changed by marriage or court order and can submit proper documentation to reflect my name change.

If you answered NO to any of the four statements above, <u>STOP</u> - You cannot use this form!!!
You must apply on application form DS-11 by making a personal appearance before a passport agent, postal clerk or clerk of court authorized to accept passport applications.

CAREFULLY FOLLOW THE INSTRUCTIONS ON THE REVERSE OF THIS PAGE
INCOMPLETE OR UNACCEPTABLE APPLICATIONS WILL DELAY THE ISSUANCE OF YOUR PASSPORT.

FOR INFORMATION, QUESTIONS, AND INQUIRIES: Please visit our website at *travel.state.gov.* In addition, contact the National Passport Information Center (NPIC) toll-free at 1-877-487-2778 (TDD: 1-888-874-7793) or by e-mail at NPIC@state.gov. Customer Service Representatives are available M-F 8AM-8PM EST (excluding federal holidays). Automated information is available 24/7.

WHAT DO I NEED TO SEND WITH THE APPLICATION FORM?

1. **Your most recent U.S. passport**
2. **A marriage certificate or court order if your name has changed**
3. **Passport processing fee of $55**
4. **Two recent, color, identical photographs**

For detailed information on the items to be included, see below.

1. **YOUR MOST RECENT U.S. PASSPORT.** Issued at age 16 or older in your current name (or see item #2 below) and issued within the past 15 years. If your passport is damaged, you must apply on the DS-11 application form as specified below.

2. **A MARRIAGE CERTIFICATE OR COURT ORDER.** If the name you are currently using differs from the name on your most recent passport, you must submit a marriage certificate or court order showing the change of name. The name change document MUST bear the official seal of the issuing authority. Uncertified copies or notarized documents cannot be accepted. All documents will be returned to you with your passport. If you are unable to document your name change in this manner, you must apply on the DS-11 application form by making a personal appearance at (1) a passport agency; (2) any clerk of a Federal or State court of record or judge or clerk of a probate court accepting passport applications; or (3) a designated municipal or county official, or a designated postal employee at an authorized post office.

3. **THE PASSPORT PROCESSING FEE OF $55.** Enclose the $55 passport processing fee in the form of a personal check or money order. **MAKE CHECKS PAYABLE TO "U.S. DEPARTMENT OF STATE". THE FULL NAME AND DATE OF BIRTH OF THE APPLICANT MUST BE TYPED OR PRINTED ON THE FRONT OF THE CHECK. DO NOT SEND CASH.** Passport services cannot be responsible for cash sent through the mail. By law, the passport processing fee is non-refundable.

    For faster processing, you may request expedited service. Expedited requests will be processed in three workdays from receipt at a passport agency. The additional fee for expedited service is $60. Expedited service is available only in the United States.

    If you desire SPECIAL POSTAGE SERVICE (overnight, special delivery, etc.), include the appropriate postage fee on the check or include a pre-paid envelope.

4. **TWO RECENT, IDENTICAL, COLOR PHOTOGRAPHS.** Submit two color photographs of you alone, sufficiently recent to be a good likeness of you (normally taken within the last six months), and 2x2 inches in size. The image size measured from the bottom of the chin to the top of your head (including hair) should not be less than 1 inch and not more than 1-3/8 inches. The photographs must be color, clear, with a full front view of your face, and printed on thin paper with plain light (white or off-white) background. They must be capable of withstanding a mounting temperature of 225 Fahrenheit (107 Celsius). The photographs must be taken in normal street attire, without a hat, head covering, or dark glasses unless a signed statement is submitted by the applicant verifying the item is worn daily for religious purposes or a signed doctor's statement is submitted verifying the item is used daily for medical purposes. Photographs retouched so that your appearance is changed are unacceptable. Snapshots, most vending machine prints, and magazine or full-length photographs are unacceptable. Digitized photos must meet the previously stated qualifications and will be accepted for use at the discretion of Passport Services. (Visit our website for details.)

MAIL THIS FORM TO:	**DELIVERY - Other Than U.S. Postal Service**	**FOR INQUIRIES CONTACT:**
National Passport Center P.O. Box 371971 Pittsburgh, PA 15250-7971	Passport Services Lockbox Attn: Passport Supervisor, 371971 500 Ross Street, Room 154-0670 Pittsburgh, PA 15262-0001	National Passport Information Center 1-877-487-2778 For TDD: 1-888-874-7793 E-mail: NPIC@state.gov Website: *travel.state.gov*

NOTICE TO APPLICANTS RESIDING ABROAD
United States citizens residing abroad CANNOT submit this form to the Passport Facility listed above. Such applicants should contact the nearest United States embassy or consulate for procedures to be followed when applying overseas.

NOTICE TO APPLICANTS FOR OFFICIAL, DIPLOMATIC, OR NO-FEE PASSPORTS
You may use this application if you meet all of the provisions listed above. Submit your U.S. Government or military authorization for a no-fee passport with your application in lieu of the passport fee. CONSULT YOUR SPONSORING AGENCY FOR INSTRUCTIONS ON PROPER ROUTING PROCEDURES BEFORE FORWARDING THIS APPLICATION. Your completed passport will be released to your sponsoring agency for forwarding to you.

IMPORTANT NOTICE TO APPLICANTS REGARDING LOST AND STOLEN PASSPORTS

The Consular Lost or Stolen Passport System contains information provided by applicants regarding their lost or stolen U.S. passports and is designed to prevent the misuse of lost or stolen U.S. passports. Anyone using a passport book reported as lost or stolen may be detained upon entry into the United States. Should you locate a U.S. passport previously reported as lost or stolen, immediately report the book as found and submit it for cancellation. It has been invalidated. You may not use that passport for travel.

Protect yourself against identity theft - Report your lost or stolen passport!
For more information or to report your lost or stolen passport by phone, call: NPIC or visit our website: *travel.state.gov*.

PLEASE DETACH AND RETAIN THIS INSTRUCTION SHEET FOR YOUR RECORDS.

U.S. Department of State

APPLICATION FOR A U.S. PASSPORT BY MAIL

TYPE OR PRINT IN CAPITAL LETTERS USING BLUE OR BLACK INK IN WHITE AREAS ONLY.

NAME	FIRST	MIDDLE

LAST

MAIL PASSPORT TO :

STREET / RFD # or P.O. BOX	APT. #

CITY	STATE	ZIP CODE

IN CARE OF *(IF APPLICABLE)*

Issue Date _____

R D O DP

End. # _____ Exp. _____

SEX	PLACE OF BIRTH	DATE OF BIRTH			SOCIAL SECURITY NUMBER *(SEE FEDERAL TAX LAW NOTICE ON REVERSE SIDE)*
☐ Male ☐ Female	City & State **OR** City & Country	Month	Day	Year	

HEIGHT	HAIR COLOR	EYE COLOR	HOME TELEPHONE	BUSINESS TELEPHONE
Feet	Inches				

NOTE: Most recent passport MUST be enclosed!

U.S. PASSPORT NUMBER	ISSUE DATE			PLACE OF ISSUANCE	OCCUPATION *(Not Mandatory)*
	Month	Day	Year		

DEPARTURE DATE	TRAVEL PLANS *(Not Mandatory)* COUNTRIES TO BE VISITED	LENGTH OF STAY *(Not Mandatory)*

PERMANENT ADDRESS (Do not list P.O. Box)

STREET / R.F.D. #	CITY	STATE	ZIP CODE

EMERGENCY CONTACT. If you wish, you may supply the name, address, and telephone number of a person not traveling with you to be contacted in case of emergency.

NAME

STREET

CITY	STATE	ZIP CODE

TELEPHONE	RELATIONSHIP

SUBMIT TWO RECENT COLOR PHOTOS WITH A LIGHT, PLAIN BACKGROUND

OATH AND SIGNATURE

I have not, since acquiring United States citizenship, performed any of the acts listed under "Acts or Conditions" on the reverse of this application form (unless an explanatory statement is attached.)

I solemnly swear (or affirm) that the statements made on this application are true, the photograph attached is a true likeness of me, and that I have not been issued a passport subsequent to the one submitted herein.

NOTE: APPLICANT MUST SIGN & DATE

SIGNATURE	DATE

DO NOT WRITE BELOW THIS SPACE **- FOR PASSPORT SERVICES USE ONLY -** DO NOT WRITE BELOW THIS SPACE

Application Approval	EVIDENCE OF NAME CHANGE	Fees
	☐ Marriage Cert. ☐ Court Order	
	Date _____	
	Place _____	
	From _____	
	To _____	

OMB No. 1405-0020   Expires: 03/31/2005   Estimated Burden   15 Minutes   (See Page 4)

DS-82

In accordance with 5 CFR 1320 5(b), persons are not required to respond to the collection of this information unless this form displays a currently valid OMB control number.

Page 3 of 4

U.S. Department of State

APPLICATION FOR U.S. PASSPORT BY MAIL

FEDERAL TAX LAW

26 U.S.C. 6039E (Internal Revenue Code) requires a passport applicant to provide his or her name and social security number. If you have not been issued a social security number, enter zeros in the appropriate boxes. The U.S. Department of State must provide this information to the Internal Revenue Service routinely. Any applicant who fails to provide the required information is subject to a $500 penalty enforced by the IRS. All questions on this matter should be referred to the nearest IRS office.

ACTS OR CONDITIONS

(If any of the below-mentioned acts or conditions has been performed by or apply to the applicant, the portion which applies should be lined out, and a supplementary explanatory statement under oath (or affirmation) by the applicant should be attached and made a part of this application.) I have not, since acquiring United States citizenship, been naturalized as a citizen of a foreign state; taken an oath or made an affirmation or other formal declaration of allegiance to a foreign state; entered or served in the armed forces of a foreign state; accepted or performed the duties of any office, post, or employment under the government of a foreign state or political subdivision thereof; made a formal renunciation of nationality either in the United States, or before a diplomatic or consular officer of the United States in a foreign state; or been convicted by a court or court martial of competent jurisdiction of committing any act of treason against, or attempting by force to overthrow, or bearing arms against, the United States, or conspiring to overthrow, put down, or to destroy by force, the Government of the United States.

WARNING: False statements made knowingly and willfully in passport applications or in affidavits or other supporting documents submitted therewith are punishable by fine and/or imprisonment under provisions of 18 U.S.C. 1001 and/or 18 U.S.C. 1542. Alteration or mutilation of a passport issued pursuant to this application is punishable by fine and/or imprisonment under the provisions of 18 U.S.C. 1543. The use of a passport in violation of the restrictions contained therein or of the passport regulations is punishable by fine and/or imprisonment under 18 U.S.C. 1544. All statements and documents submitted are subject to verification.

PRIVACY ACT AND PAPERWORK REDUCTION ACT STATEMENTS

AUTHORITIES: The information solicited on this form is requested pursuant to provisions in Titles 8, 18, and 22 of the United States Code, whether or not codified, including specifically 22 U.S.C. 211a, 212, 213, and all regulations issued pursuant to Executive Order 11295 (August 5, 1966), including Part 51, Title 22, Code of Federal Regulations (CFR). Also, as noted, 26 U.S.C. 6039E.

PURPOSE: The primary purpose for soliciting the information is to establish citizenship, identity, and entitlement to issuance of a U.S. passport. The information may also be used in connection with issuing other travel documents or evidence of citizenship, and in furtherance of the Secretary's responsibility for the protection of U.S. nationals abroad.

ROUTINE USES: The information solicited on this form may be made available as a routine use to other government agencies, to assist the U.S. Department of State in adjudicating passport applications, and for law enforcement and administration purposes. It may also be disclosed pursuant to court order. The information may be made available to foreign government agencies to fulfill passport control and immigration duties or to investigate or prosecute violations of law. The information may also be made available to private U.S. citizen 'wardens' designated by U.S. embassies and consulates.

Failure to provide the information requested on this form may result in the denial of a United States passport, related document, or service to the individual seeking such passport, document or service.

Public reporting burden for this collection of information is estimated to average 15 minutes per response, including time required for searching existing data sources, gathering the necessary data, providing the information required, and reviewing the final collection. You do not have to provide the information unless this collection displays a currently valid OMB number. Send comments on the accuracy of this estimate of the burden and recommendations for reducing it to: U.S. Department of State (A/RPS/DIR) Washington, DC 20520.

SOCIAL SECURITY ADMINISTRATION
Application for a Social Security Card

Applying for a Social Security Card is easy **AND** it is free!

USE THIS APPLICATION TO APPLY FOR:
- An **original** Social Security card
- A **duplicate** Social Security card (same name and number)
- A **corrected** Social Security card (name change and same number)
- A **change of information** on your record other than your name (no card needed)

IMPORTANT: You MUST provide the required evidence or we cannot process the application. Follow the instructions below to provide the information and evidence we need.

STEP 1 Read pages 1 through 3 which explain how to complete the application and what evidence we need.

STEP 2 Complete and sign the application using BLUE or BLACK ink. Do not use pencil or other colors of ink. Please print legibly.

STEP 3 Submit the completed and signed application with all required evidence to any Social Security office.

HOW TO COMPLETE THIS APPLICATION

Most items on the form are self-explanatory. Those that need explanation are discussed below. The numbers match the numbered items on the form. If you are completing this form for someone else, please complete the items as they apply to that person.

2. Show the address where you can receive your card 10 to 14 days from now.

3. If you check "Legal Alien **Not** Allowed to Work," you need to provide a document from the government agency requiring your Social Security number that explains why you need a number and that you meet all of the requirements for the benefit or service except for the number. A State or local agency requirement must conform with Federal law.

    If you check "Other," you need to provide proof you are entitled to a federally-funded benefit for which a Social Security number is required as a condition for you to receive payment.

5. Providing race/ethnic information is voluntary. However, if you do give us this information, it helps us prepare statistical reports on how Social Security programs affect people. We do not reveal the identities of individuals.

6. Show the month, day and full (4 digit) year of birth, for example, "1998" for year of birth.

8.B. Show the mother's Social Security number only if you are applying for an original Social Security card for a child under age 18.   You may leave this item blank if the mother does not have a number or you do not know the mother's number. We will still be able to assign a number to the child.

9.B. Show the father's Social Security number only if you are applying for an original Social Security card for a child under age 18.   You may leave this item blank if the father does not have a number or you do not know the father's number. We will still be able to assign a number to the child.

---

13. If the date of birth you show in item 6 is different from the date of birth you used on a prior application for a Social Security card, show the date of birth you used on the prior application and submit evidence of age to support the date of birth in item 6.

16. You **must** sign the application yourself if you are age 18 or older and are physically and mentally capable. If you are under age 18, you may also sign the application if you are physically and mentally capable. If you cannot sign your name, you should sign with an "X" mark and have two people sign as witnesses in the space beside the mark. If you are physically or mentally incapable of signing the application, generally a parent, close relative, or legal guardian may sign the application. Call us if you need clarification about who can sign.

ABOUT YOUR DOCUMENTS

- We need **ORIGINAL** documents or **copies certified by the custodian of the record**. We will return your documents after we have seen them.

- **We cannot accept photocopies or notarized copies of documents.**

- If your documents do not meet this requirement, we cannot process your application.

DOCUMENTS WE NEED

To apply for an **ORIGINAL CARD** (you have NEVER been assigned a Social Security number before), we need at least 2 documents as proof of:

- **Age,**
- **Identity, and**
- **U.S. citizenship or lawful alien status.**

To apply for a **DUPLICATE CARD** (same number, same name), we need proof of **identity**.

To apply for a **CORRECTED CARD** (same number, different name), we need proof of **identity**. We need one or more documents which identify you by the OLD NAME on our records and your NEW NAME. Examples include: a marriage certificate, divorce decree, or a court order that changes your name. Or we can accept two identity documents - one in your old name and one in your new name. (See IDENTITY, for examples of identity documents.)

IMPORTANT: If you are applying for a duplicate or corrected card and were **born outside the U.S.**, we also need proof of U.S. citizenship or lawful alien status. (See U.S. CITIZENSHIP or ALIEN STATUS for examples of documents you can submit.)

AGE: We prefer to see your birth certificate. However, we can accept another document that shows your age. Some of the other documents we can accept are:

- Hospital record of your birth (created at the time of your birth)
- Religious record showing your age made before you were 3 months old
- Passport
- Adoption record (the adoption record must indicate that the birth data was taken from the original birth certificate)

Call us for advice if you cannot obtain one of these documents.

IDENTITY: We must see a document in the name you want shown on the card. The identity document must be of recent issuance so that we can determine your continued existence. We prefer to see a document with a photograph. However, we can generally accept a non-photo identity document if it has enough information to identify you (e.g., your name, as well as age, date of birth or parents' names). **WE CANNOT ACCEPT A BIRTH CERTIFICATE, HOSPITAL SOUVENIR BIRTH CERTIFICATE, SOCIAL SECURITY CARD OR CARD STUB, OR SOCIAL SECURITY RECORD** as evidence of identity. Some documents we can accept are:

- Driver's license
- Employee ID card
- Passport

- Marriage or divorce record
- Adoption record (only if not being used to establish age)
- Health insurance card (not a Medicare card)

- Military record
- Life insurance policy
- School ID card

As evidence of identity for infants and young children, we can accept :

- Doctor, clinic, hospital record
- Daycare center, school record
- Religious record (e.g., baptismal record)

IMPORTANT: If you are **applying for a card on behalf of someone else**, you must provide evidence that establishes your authority to sign the application on behalf of the person to whom the card will be issued. In addition, we must see proof of identity for both you and the person to whom the card will be issued.

U. S. CITIZENSHIP: We can accept most documents that show you were born in the U.S. If you are a U.S. citizen born outside the U.S., show us a U.S. consular report of birth, a U.S. passport, a Certificate of Citizenship, or a Certificate of Naturalization.

ALIEN STATUS: We need to see an unexpired document issued to you by the Department of Homeland Security (DHS) showing your immigration status, such as Form I-551, I-94, I-688B, or I-766. We CANNOT accept a receipt showing you applied for the document. If you are not authorized to work in the U.S., we can issue you a Social Security card if you are lawfully here and need the number for a valid nonwork reason. (See HOW TO COMPLETE THIS APPLICATION, Item 3.) Your card will be marked to show you cannot work. If you do work, we will notify DHS.

To **CHANGE INFORMATION** on your record other than your name, we need proof of:

- **Identity,** and
- **Another document which supports the change** (for example, a birth certificate to change your date and/or place of birth or parents' names).

HOW TO SUBMIT THIS APPLICATION

In most cases, you can mail this application with your evidence documents to any Social Security office. We will return your documents to you. If you do not want to mail your original documents, take them with this application to the nearest Social Security office.

EXCEPTION: If you are age 12 or older and have never been assigned a number before, you **must apply in person.**

If you have any questions about this form, or about the documents we need, please contact any Social Security office. A telephone call will help you make sure you have everything you need to apply for a card or change information on your record. You can find your nearest office in your local phone directory or on our website at www.socialsecurity.gov.

SOCIAL SECURITY ADMINISTRATION
Application for a Social Security Card

Form Approved
OMB No. 0960-0066

1
NAME ——————————> TO BE SHOWN ON CARD	First	Full Middle Name	Last
FULL NAME AT BIRTH IF OTHER THAN ABOVE	First	Full Middle Name	Last
OTHER NAMES USED			

2 MAILING ADDRESS ——————> Do Not Abbreviate

Street Address, Apt. No., PO Box, Rural Route No.

City | State | Zip Code

3 CITIZENSHIP ——————> (Check One)

☐ U.S. Citizen ☐ Legal Alien Allowed To Work ☐ Legal Alien **Not** Allowed To Work (See Instructions On Page 1) ☐ Other (See Instructions On Page 1)

4 SEX ——————————————>

☐ Male ☐ Female

5 RACE/ETHNIC DESCRIPTION ——————> (Check One Only - Voluntary)

☐ Asian, Asian-American or Pacific Islander ☐ Hispanic ☐ Black (Not Hispanic) ☐ North American Indian or Alaskan Native ☐ White (Not Hispanic)

6 DATE OF BIRTH _____ Month, Day, Year

7 PLACE OF BIRTH _____ (Do Not Abbreviate) City   State or Foreign Country   FCI

Office Use Only

8
A. MOTHER'S MAIDEN NAME ——————>	First	Full Middle Name	Last Name At Her Birth

B. MOTHER'S SOCIAL SECURITY NUMBER ——————> ☐☐☐ – ☐☐ – ☐☐☐☐

9
A. FATHER'S NAME ——>	First	Full Middle Name	Last

B. FATHER'S SOCIAL SECURITY NUMBER ——————> ☐☐☐ – ☐☐ – ☐☐☐☐

10 Has the applicant or anyone acting on his/her behalf ever filed for or received a Social Security number card before?

☐ Yes (If "yes", answer questions 11-13.) ☐ No (If "no", go on to question 14.) ☐ Don't Know (If "don't know", go on to question 14.)

11 Enter the Social Security number previously assigned to the person listed in item 1. ——————> ☐☐☐ – ☐☐ – ☐☐☐☐

12 Enter the name shown on the most recent Social Security card issued for the person listed in item 1. ——————>

First   Middle Name   Last

13 Enter any different date of birth if used on an earlier application for a card. ——————>

_____ Month, Day, Year

14 TODAY'S DATE _____ Month, Day, Year

15 DAYTIME PHONE NUMBER (___) Area Code   Number

I declare under penalty of perjury that I have examined all the information on this form, and on any accompanying statements or forms, and it is true and correct to the best of my knowledge.

16 YOUR SIGNATURE ▶

17 YOUR RELATIONSHIP TO THE PERSON IN ITEM 1 IS:

☐ Self ☐ Natural Or Adoptive Parent ☐ Legal Guardian ☐ Other (Specify) _____

DO NOT WRITE BELOW THIS LINE (FOR SSA USE ONLY)

NPN			DOC	NTI	CAN		ITV
PBC	EVI	EVA	EVC	PRA	NWR	DNR	UNIT

EVIDENCE SUBMITTED

SIGNATURE AND TITLE OF EMPLOYEE(S) REVIEWING EVIDENCE AND/OR CONDUCTING INTERVIEW

_____ DATE

DCL _____ DATE

Form SS-5 (10-2003) EF (12-2004) Destroy Prior Editions

Chapter 3:
Forms for Estate Planning

This chapter explains the basics of wills and estate planning. It also gives the forms that may be used for both. An *estate* is everything that a person owns. It includes property, bank accounts, jewelry, stocks, etc. An estate is also everything that someone owes, such as loans, taxes, etc. A *will* is a way to gather your estate and distribute it after death. The will goes through a process called *probate* in which a court determines that a will is valid and decides how the estate should be distributed according to that will.

If you already have done some estate planning and merely want to make changes or if you have a simple estate, the information in this chapter may be enough information for you. However, if you have a large estate or want to make complicated arrangements such as disinheriting someone or avoiding taxes, you should consult a specialized book or an attorney.

Forms in Chapter:
- **Asset and Beneficiary List**
- **Will—Spouse and Children**
- **Will—Spouse and No Children**
- **Will—Children and No Spouse**
- **Will—No Spouse and No Children**
- **Will—Codicil**
- **Living Trust**
- **Living Trust—Schedule of Assets**
- **Declaration of Joint Property**
- **Declaration of Separate Property**
- **Living Trust—Amendment**
- **Living Trust—Termination**

- **General Power of Attorney**
- **Specific Power of Attorney**
- **Revocation of Power of Attorney**
- **Health Care Power of Attorney**
- **Living Will**
- **Uniform Donor Card**
- **Notice of Death to Social Security Administration**

When making out your will, trust, and other estate planning papers, it is helpful to have a list of all of your assets so you can get a big picture of what you own and who will get what. This list can also be used by your beneficiaries to be sure to locate all of your property. An ASSET AND BENEFICIARY LIST can be helpful in gathering this information. (see form 23, p.105.)

Will

A *will* is a document you can use to control who gets your property, who will be guardian of your children and their property, and who will manage your estate upon your death. Upon a person's death, a will is presented to a probate court. The court then appoints a person (*executor, personal representative,* or *administrator*) to manage the estate.

If you do not have a will, then the *intestacy laws* of your state decide who gets your property. In most states, this is your spouse and children, but in some states the intestacy law might not divide your property the way you want. For example, some states give half your property to your spouse and half to your children, whereas you might want it all to go to your spouse until he or she passes away.

Four different WILL forms, which cover simple situations, are included. If your situation is more complicated, check one of the resources listed in the back of the book.

The WILLS in this book cover the following situations.
- *Simple Will—Spouse and Minor Children—One Guardian.* Use this will if you have minor children and want all your property to go to your spouse. However, if your spouse dies before you, then your property would go to your minor children. It provides for one person to be guardian over your children and their estates. (see form 24, p.109.)
- *Simple Will—Spouse and No Children.* Use this will if you want your property to go to your spouse. If your spouse predeceases you, your property would go to others or to the descendants of the others. (see form 25, p.111.)

◆ *Simple Will—No Spouse—Minor Children—One Guardian.* Use this will if you do not have a spouse and want all your property to go to your children, at least one of whom is a minor. It provides for one person to be guardian over your children and their estates. (see form 26, p.113.)

◆ *Simple Will—No Spouse and No Children.* Use this will if you have no spouse or children and want your property to go to the survivor of the people you name. (see form 27, p.115.)

In some states, a will can be valid if it is completely handwritten. This is called a *holographic will*. However, in most states, a will must be witnessed by two persons (three in Vermont). In some states, the witnesses can be interested parties (people who will inherit). Generally, this is not a good idea, especially if there is someone who might contest the will. When signing a will, the witnesses do not have to read or know exactly what is in the will. The person making a will must tell the witnesses that it is a will and that it is being signed voluntarily.

The disadvantage of using a will to pass your property to people is that it requires a probate proceeding in court. This takes time and costs money. In many states, the law allows attorneys to charge a percentage of the assets in an estate, no matter how little work there is. Sometimes this fee can be negotiated down, but a better alternative is to avoid probate altogether as explained in the next section.

Self-Proving Statement

A will does not need to be notarized to be valid. However, if a notarized *self-proving statement* is attached to a will, this will usually allow it to be accepted by a probate court much quicker.

Codicil

A *codicil* is a document that changes something in a will. Since a codicil should be signed with the same formality and number of witnesses as a will, it is often just as easy to prepare a new will than to prepare a codicil. However, for simple changes, a form for a **CODICIL** is included. (see form 28, p.117.)

Avoiding Probate

Everyone who knows what probate is wants to avoid it. As stated earlier, probate is the determination that a will is valid and that the estate should be settled by the will's terms. It is often a long, arduous procedure. Luckily, the laws are changing to allow many different ways to avoid probate. This section explains the easiest ones. (For more detailed information, see one of the references at the end of this book.)

Joint Property

The easiest way to avoid probate is to own all property in *joint tenancy with right of survivorship*. When property is owned this way, it automatically passes to the survivor when the other owner dies. Three disadvantages of this are:

◆ either owner can secretly take the property at any time;

◆ either party's creditors can take it; and,

◆ if both parties die at the same time, there still has to be a probate.

To set up property in joint ownership, it must be titled with the names of both parties and the words:

as joint tenants with full rights of survivorship.

Merely putting two names on an account without this language does not mean the survivor gets it. This language can be on deeds of real estate, stock certificates, brokerage accounts, and bank accounts.

NOTE: *Some states allow married couples to jointly hold certain property (usually deeded property) as "tenants by the entirety." This allows for an extra level of protection from creditors in states that allow it.*

Most married couples who jointly own all their property and want all of it to go to their spouse do not need a will when the first one of them dies. The main reason they *should* have one is in the event of an accident that kills both of them.

One solution to this problem is for a couple to put their property in joint ownership with their children. Possible dangers of this is that the children can take all of the property at any time, and the creditors of a child might be able to seize it. (The next subsections *Totten Trust* and *Formal Trust* describe solutions for this.)

You should review how your bank accounts, stocks, mutual funds, motor vehicles, recreation vehicles, and other property are titled. If you want them to go to your relatives or through your will, they should be in your name alone. If you want them to go to your joint owner, you should be sure they are properly set up as a joint account with right of survivorship.

Totten Trust

A *Totten trust* can solve some of the problems of joint ownership. This is a method of setting up the title to property so that it automatically passes at death without the beneficiary having any rights to it until the first owner's life is over. It was named after the court case in which a court held that it was legal to do.

A Totten trust is established when the property is set up *in trust for* (I/T/F), with a named beneficiary. Some institutions may use the letters POD for *pay on death* or TOD for *transfer on death*. Either way the result is the same. No one, except you, can get the money until your death. Upon death, it immediately goes directly to the person you name, without a will or probate proceeding.

Totten trusts have been valid for a long time for bank accounts. During the last decade, more than half the states have passed laws allowing them to be used for securities such as stocks, bonds, and mutual funds. They are not yet used for real estate, though in some states the law seems to allow it. Check with a lawyer before attempting to use it for real estate.

If your financial advisor will not or cannot set up your mutual fund or brokerage account to pay on death, check with some others located in another state. Yours may be located in a state where the law has not passed.

Formal Trust

Another way to avoid needing a will (and to avoid probate) is to set up a formal trust. A *trust* is an agreement in which someone holds property that really belongs to someone else. It is then used for the latter person's benefit. For example, a person might transfer all their stocks to a bank to hold in trust. The trust would provide that during that person's life, he or she gets all the dividends from the stock. Then, after his or her death, the income goes to the children.

If the trust is *revocable*, the person setting up the trust (the *settlor*) can change the trust or even dissolve it. If it is *irrevocable*, it cannot be changed. The benefit of a revocable trust is that no one else can get to it, meaning if you or your children later have a large liability (medical bills or liability for an accident), the creditors cannot touch the money in the trust (if it is set up correctly).

A **LIVING TRUST**, often called a *Revocable Living Trust* or an *inter-vivos trust*, is usually a trust that a person or couple sets up in which they become their own trustees. The main benefit of this is that their property avoids probate. (see form 29, p.119.)

There are many other benefits of trusts. The laws differ from state to state as to the legal requirements, for example, whether a person can be his or her own trustee. (A thorough discussion is beyond the scope of this book; however, if you think a living trust could benefit you, consult one of the references at the end of this book.)

Personal Property

One of the biggest problems with setting up a living trust is that people forget to put their property into it! After the trust agreement is signed, all of the person's property must be transferred to the trust. Usually, all of the assets are listed on a **SCHEDULE OF ASSETS** that goes with the trust. A form for this is included. (see form 30, p.121.) But for some types of property, such as real estate and motor vehicles, the title must be reregistered. This means getting a new deed or title certificate. Also, bank and brokerage accounts must be retitled, rather than just listed on the **SCHEDULE OF ASSETS**.

Personal property ownership is not registered or documented by a title certificate. As a result, ownership of such items can be questionable. For example, what if you own a valuable coin collection, and after your death your spouse claims ownership as joint property, while your child claims inheritance as personal property under your will?

To avoid problems like this, you can specifically list personal items you wish to give people in your will. You can sign a declaration with your spouse or partner as to how your personal property is titled. A **DECLARATION OF JOINT PROPERTY** can help do this. (see form 31, p.123.) Below is an example of such a form.

Sample: **Declaration of Joint Property**

DECLARATION OF JOINT PROPERTY

The undersigned, in consideration of the mutual agreement herein contained, agrees that all property owned by them and located in their place of residence shall be owned in joint tenancy with full rights of survivorship, except the following items which shall remain separate property for all purposes:

Except John Smith's coin collection which will be willed to his son.

Except Mildred Smith's family photo album which will be willed to her sister's children.

In addition to the property located at the residence, the following property shall also be owned in joint tenancy with full rights of survivorship:

John Smith's canoe which is usually kept by the river.

In witness whereof, the parties affix their signatures and seals this ___29th___ day of ___January___, 20_06_ .

In some cases, you might be more concerned that the title to your property is separate. For example, in California and many other western states, all property acquired during marriage is considered *community property* and each spouse has 50% interest in it. If you and your spouse want to keep your property separate (for example, to leave it to your separate children), you could execute a **DECLARATION OF SEPARATE PROPERTY**. (see form 32, p.125.)

Amendments and Termination

If a living trust needs to be changed (such as when one beneficiary dies), this is done with an **AMENDMENT**. (see form 33, p.127.) A **TERMINATION** form to end the trust is also included. (see form 34, p.129.)

Power of Attorney

A *power of attorney* is a document that gives someone the right to take legal action in your name. For example, you might give someone a power of attorney to sign a deed selling your house if you are going to be out of the country. Or, you could give someone power of attorney to handle all of your legal affairs in case you were medically disabled.

A person holding a power of attorney to act for someone is called an *attorney in fact*. (This has no relationship to an *attorney at law*.) The person giving someone a power of attorney is called the *grantor*. While an attorney in fact should only take action that the grantor wishes, he or she has the *power* to do anything that the power of attorney grants. For example, an attorney in fact can withdraw money from an account and spend it for personal gain. (Of course, this would be criminal.)

For this reason, a power of attorney should only be given to a trusted person. It should be limited to necessary acts. For example, if you need someone to sign a real estate deed, it is not necessary to give them a **GENERAL POWER OF ATTORNEY** allowing them to do anything regarding all of your property. (see form 35, p.131.) Instead, you would give them a **SPECIFIC POWER OF ATTORNEY** for the specific act of signing the deed. (see form 36, p.133.) A sample of a **SPECIFIC POWER OF ATTORNEY** is shown on the following page.

Sample: **Specific Power of Attorney**

POWER OF ATTORNEY—SPECIFIC

_____Jon Dough_____ (the "Grantor") hereby grants to _____Jane Rowe_____ (the "Agent") a limited power of attorney. As the Grantor's attorney in fact, the Agent shall have full power and authority to undertake and perform the following on behalf of the Grantor:

By accepting this grant, the Agent agrees to act in a fiduciary capacity consistent with the reasonable best interests of the Grantor. This power of attorney may be revoked by the Grantor at any time; however, any person dealing with the Agent as attorney in fact may rely on this appointment until receipt of actual notice of termination.

IN WITNESS WHEREOF, the undersigned grantor has executed this power of attorney under seal as of the date stated above.

There may be times when you have given someone a power of attorney and then later decide to cancel it. This is done with a form called a **REVOCATION OF POWER OF ATTORNEY**. (see form 37, p.135.) You should deliver it to the person with the power of attorney as well as anyone whom you think has or will see the original power of attorney.

Health Care Power of Attorney

When you enter a hospital, you never know if you will be able to make all the judgment calls necessary throughout your treatment. To solve this, in most states you can sign a **HEALTH CARE POWER OF ATTORNEY**, which allows someone else to make decisions for you.

The form included in this book is a generic one. If your hospital has its own form, you should use that one. If there is no other form available, you can use this one and check with your hospital to see if they will honor it. (see form 38, p.137.)

Living Will

A *living will* is a document that allows you to state that if you become so ill that you will never recover, you do not wish unusual medical techniques to be used to prolong your life. Today, medical science can keep a body alive long after it is able to fully function on its own. Doctors often feel they should do everything possible to keep a body alive (or else risk the possibility of getting sued). In some cases, people have been in comas or in pain for years with no hope for recovery.

For this reason, laws allow people to sign a **LIVING WILL** stating that they wish to die naturally. (see form 39, p.139.)

Anatomical Gifts (Organ Donation)

Lives can now be saved by using organs of people who have died. For example, a person who has died of head injuries in a motorcycle crash can donate a heart, two kidneys, a liver, and several organs to people who would otherwise die without them. Permission can be given by the family of a deceased, but often family members are squeamish about giving away the organs of a loved one. For this reason, the law allows us to sign a card giving permission for organ donation. In some states, this is included on the back of the drivers' license. If not, you can use an **UNIFORM DONOR CARD**. (see form 40, p.143.)

Social Security

Entitlement to Social Security benefits ends at death. The payments are made in arrears. For example, the May 1st payment is for the month of April, so if a person dies May 2nd you do not need to return most of the May payment, you are just not entitled to the June 1st payment.

If any payments are made by the Social Security Administration (SSA) after death, they must be returned. To avoid any problems you should promptly notify the SSA of the death of a recipient. Sometimes the funeral home will take care of this for you.

If the payments are made directly into the decedent's bank account, you should notify the bank to return any amounts received after the date of death.

The form **NOTICE OF DEATH TO SOCIAL SECURITY ADMINISTRATION** should be sent to the local office. You can get their address by calling their local office listed in the beginning of the phone book under "federal government." (see form 41, p.145.)

ASSET AND BENEFICIARY LIST

PROPERTY INVENTORY

Assets

Bank Accounts (checking, savings, certificates of deposit)

_____

_____

_____

_____

_____

_____

_____

Real Estate

_____

_____

_____

_____

_____

_____

_____

Vehicles (cars, trucks, boats, planes, RVs, etc.)

_____

_____

_____

_____

_____

_____

_____

Personal Property (collections, jewelry, tools, artwork, household items, etc.)

_____

_____

_____

_____

_____

_____

_____

_____

_____

_____

106

Stocks/Bonds/Mutual Funds

_____
_____
_____
_____
_____
_____
_____
_____
_____
_____
_____
_____
_____

Retirement Accounts (IRAs, 401(k)s, pension plans, etc.)

_____
_____
_____
_____
_____
_____
_____

Receivables (mortgages held, notes, accounts receivable, personal loans)

_____
_____
_____
_____
_____

Life Insurance

_____
_____
_____
_____
_____
_____
_____

Other Property (trusts, partnerships, businesses, profit sharing, copyrights, etc.)

_____
_____
_____
_____
_____
_____
_____

LIABILITIES

Real Estate Loans

_____
_____
_____
_____
_____
_____
_____

Vehicle Loans

_____
_____
_____
_____
_____
_____
_____

Other Secured Loans

_____
_____
_____
_____
_____
_____
_____

Unsecured Loans and Debts (taxes, child support, judgments, etc.)

_____
_____
_____
_____
_____

BENEFICIARY LIST

_____

_____

_____

_____

_____

_____

_____

(Name)   (Address)   (phone)

LAST WILL AND TESTAMENT

I, _____, a resident of _____
County, _____ do hereby make, publish, and declare this to be my Last Will and Testament,
hereby revoking any and all Wills and Codicils heretofore made by me.

FIRST: I direct that all my just debts and funeral expenses be paid out of my estate as soon after my death as is
practicable.

SECOND: I give, devise, and bequeath the following specific gifts:

_____

_____

_____

_____

_____

_____

THIRD: I give, devise, and bequeath all my estate, real, personal, and mixed, of whatever kind and wherever situated,
of which I may die seized or possessed, or in which I may have any interest or over which I may have any power of
appointment or testamentary disposition, to my spouse, _____. If my
said spouse does not survive me, I give and bequeath the said property to my children, _____
_____
_____ ,

plus any afterborn or adopted children, in equal shares or their lineal descendants, per stirpes.

FOURTH: In the event that any beneficiary fails to survive me by thirty days, then this will shall take effect as if that
person had predeceased me.

FIFTH: Should my spouse not survive me, I hereby nominate, constitute, and appoint
_____ as guardian over the person and estate of any of my children
who have not reached the age of majority at the time of my death. In the event that said guardian is unable or
unwilling to serve, then I nominate, constitute, and appoint _____ as
guardian. Said guardian shall serve without bond or surety.

SIXTH: I hereby nominate, constitute, and appoint _____ as Executor or Personal
Representative of this, my Last Will and Testament. In the event that such named person is unable or unwilling to
serve at any time or for any reason, then I nominate, constitute, and appoint _____
as Executor or Personal Representative in the place and stead of the person first named herein. It is my will and I
direct that my Executor or Personal Representative shall not be required to furnish a bond for the faithful
performance of his or her duties in any jurisdiction, any provision of law to the contrary notwithstanding, and I
give my Executor or Personal Representative full power to administer my estate, including the power to settle
claims; pay debts; and, sell, lease, or exchange real and personal property without court order.

IN WITNESS WHEREOF I declare this to be my Last Will and Testament, and execute it willingly as my free and voluntary act for the purposes expressed herein. I am of legal age and sound mind and make this under no constraint or undue influence, this _____ day of _____, 20____ at _____ State of _____.

· · · · ·

The foregoing instrument was on said date subscribed at the end thereof by _____, the above named Testator who signed, published, and declared this instrument to be his/her Last Will and Testament in the presence of us and each of us, who thereupon at his/her request, in his/her presence, and in the presence of each other, have hereunto subscribed our names as witnesses thereto. We are of sound mind and proper age to witness a will and understand this to be his/her will, and to the best of our knowledge, the testator is of legal age to make a will, of sound mind, and under no constraint or undue influence.

_____ residing at _____

_____ residing at _____

_____ residing at _____

LAST WILL AND TESTAMENT

I, _____, a resident of _____ County, _____ do hereby make, publish, and declare this to be my Last Will and Testament, hereby revoking any and all Wills and Codicils heretofore made by me.

FIRST: I direct that all my just debts and funeral expenses be paid out of my estate as soon after my death as is practicable.

SECOND: I give, devise, and bequeath the following specific gifts:

_____

_____

_____

_____

_____

_____

_____

_____

THIRD: I give, devise, and bequeath all my estate, real, personal, and mixed, of whatever kind and wherever situated, of which I may die seized or possessed, or in which I may have any interest or over which I may have any power of appointment or testamentary disposition, to my spouse, _____. If my said spouse does not survive me, I give and bequeath the said property to _____

_____

_____,

or to their lineal descendants, per stirpes.

FOURTH: In the event that any beneficiary fails to survive me by thirty days, then this will shall take effect as if that person had predeceased me.

FIFTH: I hereby nominate, constitute, and appoint _____ as Executor or Personal Representative of this, my Last Will and Testament. In the event that such named person is unable or unwilling to serve at any time or for any reason, then I nominate, constitute, and appoint _____ as Executor or Personal Representative in the place and stead of the person first named herein. It is my will and I direct that my Executor or Personal Representative shall not be required to furnish a bond for the faithful performance of his or her duties in any jurisdiction, any provision of law to the contrary notwithstanding, and I give my Executor or Personal Representative full power to administer my estate, including the power to settle claims; pay debts; and, sell, lease, or exchange real and personal property without court order.

IN WITNESS WHEREOF I declare this to be my Last Will and Testament, and execute it willingly as my free and voluntary act for the purposes expressed herein. I am of legal age and sound mind and make this under no constraint or undue influence, this _____ day of _____, 20___ at _____ State of _____.

. . . . .

The foregoing instrument was on said date subscribed at the end thereof by _____ , the above named Testator who signed, published, and declared this instrument to be his/her Last Will and Testament in the presence of us and each of us, who thereupon at his/her request, in his/her presence, and in the presence of each other, have hereunto subscribed our names as witnesses thereto. We are of sound mind and proper age to witness a will and understand this to be his/her will, and to the best of our knowledge, the testator is of legal age to make a will, of sound mind, and under no constraint or undue influence.

_____ residing at _____

_____ residing at _____

_____ residing at _____

LAST WILL AND TESTAMENT

I, _____, a resident of _____
County, _____ do hereby make, publish, and declare this to be my Last Will and Testament,
hereby revoking any and all Wills and Codicils heretofore made by me.

FIRST: I direct that all my just debts and funeral expenses be paid out of my estate as soon after my death as is
practicable.

SECOND: I give, devise, and bequeath the following specific gifts:

_____

_____

_____

_____

_____

_____

_____

_____

THIRD: I give, devise, and bequeath all my estate, real, personal, and mixed, of whatever kind and wherever situated, of which I may die seized or possessed, or in which I may have any interest or over which I may have any power of
appointment or testamentary disposition, to my children, _____

_____

_____, plus any afterborn or adopted children, in equal shares or to their lineal
descendants per stirpes.

FOURTH: In the event that any beneficiary fails to survive me by thirty days, then this will shall take effect as if that
person had predeceased me.

FIFTH: In the event any of my children have not attained the age of 18 years at the time of my death, I hereby
nominate, constitute, and appoint _____ as guardian over the person and
estate of any of my children who have not reached the age of majority at the time of my death. In the event
that said guardian is unable or unwilling to serve, then I nominate, constitute, and appoint
_____ as guardian. Said guardian shall serve without bond or surety.

SIXTH: I hereby nominate, constitute, and appoint _____ as Executor or
Personal Representative of this, my Last Will and Testament. In the event that such named person is unable or
unwilling to serve at any time or for any reason, then I nominate, constitute, and appoint
_____ as Executor or Personal Representative in the place and stead of the
person first named herein. It is my will and I direct that my Executor or Personal Representative shall not be required
to furnish a bond for the faithful performance of his or her duties in any jurisdiction, any provision of law to the contrary notwithstanding, and I give my Executor or Personal Representative full power to administer my estate, including
the power to settle claims; pay debts; and, sell, lease or exchange real and personal property without court order.

IN WITNESS WHEREOF I declare this to be my Last Will and Testament, and execute it willingly as my free and voluntary act for the purposes expressed herein. I am of legal age and sound mind and make this under no constraint or undue influence, this _____ day of _____, 20___ at _____ State of _____.

· · · · ·

The foregoing instrument was on said date subscribed at the end thereof by _____, the above named Testator who signed, published, and declared this instrument to be his/her Last Will and Testament in the presence of us and each of us, who thereupon at his/her request, in his/her presence, and in the presence of each other, have hereunto subscribed our names as witnesses thereto. We are of sound mind and proper age to witness a will and understand this to be his/her will, and to the best of our knowledge, the testator is of legal age to make a will, of sound mind, and under no constraint or undue influence.

_____ residing at _____

_____ residing at _____

_____ residing at _____

LAST WILL AND TESTAMENT

I, _____, a resident of _____
County, _____ do hereby make, publish, and declare this to be my Last Will and Testament,
hereby revoking any and all Wills and Codicils heretofore made by me.

FIRST: I direct that all my just debts and funeral expenses be paid out of my estate as soon after my death as is
practicable.

SECOND: I give, devise, and bequeath the following specific gifts:

_____

_____

_____

_____

_____

_____

_____

THIRD: I give, devise, and bequeath all my estate, real, personal, and mixed, of whatever kind and wherever situated, of which I may die seized or possessed, or in which I may have any interest or over which I may have any power
of appointment or testamentary disposition, to the following:

_____

_____

_____,

in equal share, or to the survivor of them.

FOURTH: In the event that any beneficiary fails to survive me by thirty days, then this will shall take effect as if that
person had predeceased me.

FIFTH: I hereby nominate, constitute, and appoint _____ as Executor
or Personal Representative of this, my Last Will and Testament. In the event that such named person is unable or
unwilling to serve at any time or for any reason, then I nominate, constitute, and appoint
_____ as Executor or Personal Representative in the place and stead of
the person first named herein. It is my will and I direct that my Executor or Personal Representative shall not be
required to furnish a bond for the faithful performance of his or her duties in any jurisdiction, any provision of law
to the contrary notwithstanding, and I give my Executor or Personal Representative full power to administer my
estate, including the power to settle claims; pay debts; and, sell, lease, or exchange real and personal property without court order.

IN WITNESS WHEREOF I declare this to be my Last Will and Testament, and execute it willingly as my free and
voluntary act for the purposes expressed herein. I am of legal age and sound mind and make this under no constraint or undue influence, this _____ day of _____, 20____ at _____ State of
_____.

· · · · ·

The foregoing instrument was on said date subscribed at the end thereof by _____, the above named Testator who signed, published, and declared this instrument to be his/her Last Will and Testament in the presence of us and each of us, who thereupon at his/her request, in his/her presence, and in the presence of each other, have hereunto subscribed our names as witnesses thereto. We are of sound mind and proper age to witness a will and understand this to be his/her will, and to the best of our knowledge testator is of legal age to make a will, of sound mind, and under no constraint or undue influence.

_____ residing at _____

_____ residing at _____

_____ residing at _____

FIRST CODICIL TO THE WILL OF

_____

I, _____, a resident of _____ County, _____ declare this to be the first codicil to my Last Will and Testament, dated _____, 20____.

FIRST: I hereby revoke the clause of my Will that reads as follows: _____
_____
_____
_____
_____.

SECOND: I hereby add the following clause to my Will:_____
_____
_____
_____.

THIRD: In all other respects, I hereby confirm and republish my Last Will and Testament dated _____, _____.

IN WITNESS WHEREOF, I have signed, published, and declared the foregoing instrument as and for a codicil to my Last Will and Testament, this _____ day of _____, 20____.

· · · · ·

The foregoing instrument was on the _____ day of _____, 20____, signed at the end thereof, and at the same time published and declared by _____, as and for a codicil to his/her Last Will and Testament, dated _____, 20_____, in the presence of each of us, who, this attestation clause having been read to us, did at the request of the said testator/testatrix, in his/her presence, and in the presence of each other signed our names as witnesses thereto.

_____ residing at _____

_____ residing at _____

_____ residing at _____

This page intentionally left blank.

LIVING TRUST

THE

_____

REVOCABLE LIVING TRUST

I, _____, of _____
_____, hereby make and declare this Living
Trust, as Grantor and Trustee, on _____, 20____.

This Trust shall be known as the _____ Revocable Living Trust.
I, _____, will be trustee of this trust. Upon my death or if I am unable to
manage this trust and my financial affairs, I appoint _____,
my _____, of _____
_____ as successor trustee, to serve without bond. In addition to any powers,
authority, and discretion granted by law, I grant such Trustee and Successor Trustee any and all powers to perform
any acts, in his or her sole discretion and without court approval, for the management and distribution of this trust.

TRANSFER OF PROPERTY. I hereby transfer to this trust the property listed on the attached Schedule of Assets
which is made a part of this trust. I shall have the right at any time to add property to the trust or delete property
from the trust.

DISPOSITION OF INCOME AND PRINCIPAL. During my lifetime, the Trustee shall pay so much or all of the net
income and principal of the trust as I from time to time may request to me. Upon my death, the successor trustee shall
pay all claims, expenses and taxes and shall distribute the trust estate to the following beneficiary or beneficiaries who
shall survive me:

_____
_____
_____
_____

The share of a beneficiary who is under _____ years of age shall not be paid to such beneficiary but shall be held in
trust by the Trustee. The Trustee shall pay so much or all of the net income and principal of such trust to the beneficiary as he thinks necessary for his or her support, welfare, and education. The Trustee shall pay the beneficiary the
remaining principal, if any, when he or she attains the age of _____ years.

In case a beneficiary for whom a share is held in trust dies before receiving the remaining principal, it shall be paid to
his or her living child or children, or if none, to my then living descendants.

This trust shall terminate twenty-one (21) years after the death of the last beneficiary named in the trust.

REVOCATION AND AMENDMENT. I may, by signed instrument delivered to the Trustee, revoke or amend this Trust Agreement in whole or in part.

GOVERNING LAW. This Trust will be governed under the laws of the State of _____.

In Witness Whereof, I as Grantor and Trustee, have executed this Agreement on the date above written.

_____ _____
Witness   Grantor

_____ _____
Witness   Trustee

STATE OF   )
COUNTY OF   )

The foregoing instrument was acknowledged before me this _____ day of _____, 20___, by _____, as Grantor and Trustee, who is personally known to me or who has produced _____ as identification.

_____
Notary Public

My Commission Expires:

LIVING TRUST—SCHEDULE OF ASSETS

This Schedule of Assets of Living Trust is attached and made part of the _____
Revocable Living Trust, dated _____, 20____.

The following assets are made part of this Living Trust:

This page intentionally left blank.

DECLARATION OF JOINT PROPERTY

The undersigned, in consideration of the mutual agreement herein contained, agree that all property owned by them and located in their place of residence shall be owned in joint tenancy with full rights of survivorship, except the following items, which shall remain separate property for all purposes:

In addition to the property located at the residence, the following property shall also be owned in joint tenancy with full rights of survivorship:

In witness whereof, the parties affix their signatures and seals this _____ day of _____, 20_____.

_____ (seal)

_____ (seal)

This page intentionally left blank.

DECLARATION OF SEPARATE PROPERTY

The undersigned, in consideration of the mutual agreement herein contained, agree that all property owned by them and located in their place of residence shall be owned as separate property of the person by whom it was purchased, except the following items, which are owned as joint property with full rights of survivorship.

In addition to the property located at the residence, the following property shall also be owned as separate property:

In witness whereof, the parties affix their signatures and seals this _____ day of _____, 20_____.

_____ (seal)

_____ (seal)

This page intentionally left blank.

LIVING TRUST—AMENDMENT

AMENDMENT TO THE

_____

REVOCABLE LIVING TRUST

This Amendment to the _____ Revocable Living Trust, dated _____, 20 _____, is made by _____, Grantor, on _____, 20_____.

The Grantor hereby amends the Trust as follows:

State of _____

County of _____

On _____, 20_____, before me personally appeared _____, who is personally known to me or who provided _____ as identification, and signed the above document in my presence.

_____

Notary Public

My Commission expires:

This page intentionally left blank.

LIVING TRUST—TERMINATION

I, _____, of _____

_____, hereby revoke the _____

Living Trust, dated _____, 20____.

Dated: _____, 20_____

_____

Grantor

State of _____

County of _____

On _____, 20_____, before me personally appeared _____,

who is personally known to me or who provided _____ as

identification, and signed the above document in my presence.

_____

Notary Public

My Commission expires:

This page intentionally left blank.

GENERAL POWER OF ATTORNEY

_____ (the Grantor) hereby grants to _____ (the Agent) a general power of attorney. As the Grantor's attorney in fact, the Agent shall have full power and authority to undertake any and all acts, which may be lawfully undertaken on behalf of the grantor, including but not limited to: the right to buy, sell, lease, mortgage, assign, rent, or otherwise dispose of any real or personal property belonging to the Grantor; to execute, accept, undertake, and perform contracts in the name of the Grantor; to deposit, endorse, or withdraw funds to or from any bank depository of the Grantor; to initiate, defend, or settle legal actions on behalf of the Grantor; and to retain any accountant, attorney or other advisor deemed by the Agent to be necessary to protect the interests of the Grantor in relation to such powers.

By accepting this grant, the Agent agrees to act in a fiduciary capacity consistent with the reasonable best interests of the Grantor. This power of attorney may be revoked by the Grantor at any time; however, any person dealing with the Agent as attorney in fact may rely on this appointment until receipt of actual notice of termination.

IN WITNESS WHEREOF, the undersigned grantor has executed this power of attorney under seal as of the date stated above.

_____(Seal)

Grantor

STATE OF
COUNTY OF

I certify that _____ , who ❑ is personally known to me to be the person whose name is subscribed to the foregoing instrument ❑ produced _____ as identification, personally appeared before me on _____ , 20_____, and acknowledged the execution of the foregoing instrument.

_____

Notary Public, State of

Notary's commission expires:

I hereby accept the foregoing appointment as attorney in fact on _____ , 20_____.

_____

Attorney in Fact

This page intentionally left blank.

SPECIFIC POWER OF ATTORNEY

_____ (the Grantor) hereby grants to _____ (the Agent) a limited power of attorney. As the Grantor's attorney in fact, the Agent shall have full power and authority to undertake and perform the following on behalf of the Grantor:

By accepting this grant, the Agent agrees to act in a fiduciary capacity consistent with the reasonable best interests of the Grantor. This power of attorney may be revoked by the Grantor at any time; however, any person dealing with the Agent as attorney in fact may rely on this appointment until receipt of actual notice of termination.

IN WITNESS WHEREOF, the undersigned grantor has executed this power of attorney under seal as of the date stated above.

_____(Seal)

Grantor

STATE OF
COUNTY OF

I certify that _____ , who ❑ is personally known to me to be the person whose name is subscribed to the foregoing instrument ❑ produced _____ as identification, personally appeared before me on _____, 20_____, and acknowledged the execution of the foregoing instrument.

_____

Notary Public, State of

Notary's commission expires:

I hereby accept the foregoing appointment as attorney in fact on _____, 20_____.

_____

Attorney in Fact

This page intentionally left blank.

REVOCATION OF POWER OF ATTORNEY

I, _____ (the Grantor) granted a Power of Attorney to _____ (the Agent) dated _____, do hereby revoke said Power of Attorney as of _____, 20____.

STATE OF
COUNTY OF

I certify that _____ , who ☐ is personally known to me to be the person whose name is subscribed to the foregoing instrument ☐ produced _____ as identification, personally appeared before me on _____, 20_____, and acknowledged the execution of the foregoing instrument.

_____
Notary Public, State of

Notary's commission expires:

This page intentionally left blank.

HEALTH CARE POWER OF ATTORNEY

I, _____, as principal, designate
_____ as my agent for all matters relating to my
health care, including, without limitation, full power to give or refuse consent to all medical, surgical, hospital, and
related health care. This power of attorney is effective on my inability to make or communicate health care decisions.
All of my agent's actions under this power during any period when I am unable to make or communicate health care
decisions or when there is uncertainty whether I am dead or alive have the same effect on my heirs, devisees, and personal representatives as if I were alive, competent, and acting for myself.

If my agent is unwilling or unable to serve or continue to serve, I hereby appoint _____
as my agent.

❏ I have ❏ I have not completed and attached a living will for purposes of providing specific direction to my agent
in situations that may occur during any period when I am unable to make or communicate health care decisions or
after my death. My agent is directed to implement those choices I have initialed in the living will.

This health care directive continues in effect for all who may rely on it except those to whom I have given notice of its
revocation.

_____   _____
Witness   Signature of Principal

_____   _____
Address   Date

                                         _____
                                         Time

_____   _____
Witness   Address of Agent

_____   _____
Address   Telephone of Agent

This page intentionally left blank.

LIVING WILL

I, _____, being of sound mind, willfully and voluntarily make known my desires regarding my medical care and treatment under the circumstances as indicated below:

_____   1.   If I should have an incurable or irreversible condition that will cause my death within a relatively short time, and if I am unable to make decisions regarding my medical treatment, I direct my attending physician to withhold or withdraw procedures that merely prolong the dying process and are not necessary to my comfort or to alleviate pain. This authorization includes, but is not limited to, the withholding or the withdrawal of the following types of medical treatment (subject to any special instructions in paragraph 5 below):

_____   a. Artificial feeding and hydration.

_____   b. Cardiopulmonary resuscitation (this includes, but is not limited to, the use of drugs, electric shock, and artificial breathing).

_____   c. Kidney dialysis.

_____   d. Surgery or other invasive procedures.

_____   e. Drugs and antibiotics.

_____   f. Transfusions of blood or blood products.

_____   g. Other: _____

_____

_____   2.   If I should be in an irreversible coma or persistent vegetative state that my attending physician reasonably believes to be irreversible or incurable, I direct my attending physician to withhold or withdraw medical procedures and treatment other than such medical procedures and treatment necessary to my comfort or to alleviate pain. This authorization includes, but is not limited to, the withholding or withdrawal of the following types of medical treatment (subject to any special instructions in paragraph 5 below):

_____   a. Artificial feeding and hydration.

_____   b. Cardiopulmonary resuscitation (this includes, but is not limited to, the use of drugs, electric shock, and artificial breathing).

_____   c. Kidney dialysis.

_____   d. Surgery or other invasive procedures.

_____   e. Drugs and antibiotics.

_____   f. Transfusions of blood or blood products.

_____   g. Other: _____

_____

_____ 3. If I have a medical condition where I am unable to communicate my desires as to treatment and my physician determines that the burdens of treatment outweigh the expected benefits, I direct my attending physician to withhold or withdraw medical procedures and treatment, other than such medical procedures and treatment necessary to my comfort or to alleviate pain. This authorization includes, but is not limited to, the withholding or withdrawal of the following types of medical treatment (subject to any special instructions in paragraph 5 below):

_____   a.   Artificial feeding and hydration.

_____   b.   Cardiopulmonary resuscitation (this includes, but is not limited to, the use of drugs, electric shock, and artificial breathing).

_____   c.   Kidney dialysis.

_____   d.   Surgery or other invasive procedures.

_____   e.   Drugs and antibiotics.

_____   f.   Transfusions of blood or blood products.

_____   g.   Other: _____

_____

_____ 4. I want my life prolonged to the greatest extent possible (subject to any special instructions in paragraph 5 below).

_____ 5. Special instructions (if any) _____

_____

_____

_____

Signed this _____ day of _____, 20_____.

_____

Signature

Address:_____

_____

The declarant is personally known to me and voluntarily signed this document in my presence.

Witness: _____   Witness: _____

Name: _____   Name: _____

Address: _____   Address: _____

_____   _____

State of _____)

County of _____)

On this _____ day of _____, 20____, before me, personally appeared _____,
principal, and _____ and _____, witnesses, who are
personally known to me or who provided _____
as identification, and signed the foregoing instrument in my presence.

_____

Notary Public

This page intentionally left blank.

UNIFORM DONOR CARD

UNIFORM DONOR CARD

The undersigned hereby makes this anatomical gift, if medically acceptable, to take effect on death. The words and marks below indicate my desires:

I give:

(a) _____ any needed organs or parts;

(b) _____ only the following organs or parts

_____

for the purpose of transplantation, therapy, medical research, or education;

(c) _____ my body for anatomical study if needed.

Limitations or special wishes, if any:

_____

Signed by the donor and the following witnesses in the presence of each other:

_____   _____
Signature of Donor   Date of birth

_____   _____
Date signed   City & State

_____   _____
Witness   Witness

_____   _____
Address   Address

UNIFORM DONOR CARD

The undersigned hereby makes this anatomical gift, if medically acceptable, to take effect on death. The words and marks below indicate my desires:

I give:

(a) _____ any needed organs or parts;

(b) _____ only the following organs or parts

_____

for the purpose of transplantation, therapy, medical research, or education;

(c) _____ my body for anatomical study if needed.

Limitations or special wishes, if any:

_____

Signed by the donor and the following witnesses in the presence of each other:

_____   _____
Signature of Donor   Date of birth

_____   _____
Date signed   City & State

_____   _____
Witness   Witness

_____   _____
Address   Address

UNIFORM DONOR CARD

The undersigned hereby makes this anatomical gift, if medically acceptable, to take effect on death. The words and marks below indicate my desires:

I give:

(a) _____ any needed organs or parts;

(b) _____ only the following organs or parts

_____

for the purpose of transplantation, therapy, medical research, or education;

(c) _____ my body for anatomical study if needed.

Limitations or special wishes, if any:

_____

Signed by the donor and the following witnesses in the presence of each other:

_____   _____
Signature of Donor   Date of birth

_____   _____
Date signed   City & State

_____   _____
Witness   Witness

_____   _____
Address   Address

UNIFORM DONOR CARD

The undersigned hereby makes this anatomical gift, if medically acceptable, to take effect on death. The words and marks below indicate my desires:

I give:

(a) _____ any needed organs or parts;

(b) _____ only the following organs or parts

_____

for the purpose of transplantation, therapy, medical research, or education;

(c) _____ my body for anatomical study if needed.

Limitations or special wishes, if any:

_____

Signed by the donor and the following witnesses in the presence of each other:

_____   _____
Signature of Donor   Date of birth

_____   _____
Date signed   City & State

_____   _____
Witness   Witness

_____   _____
Address   Address

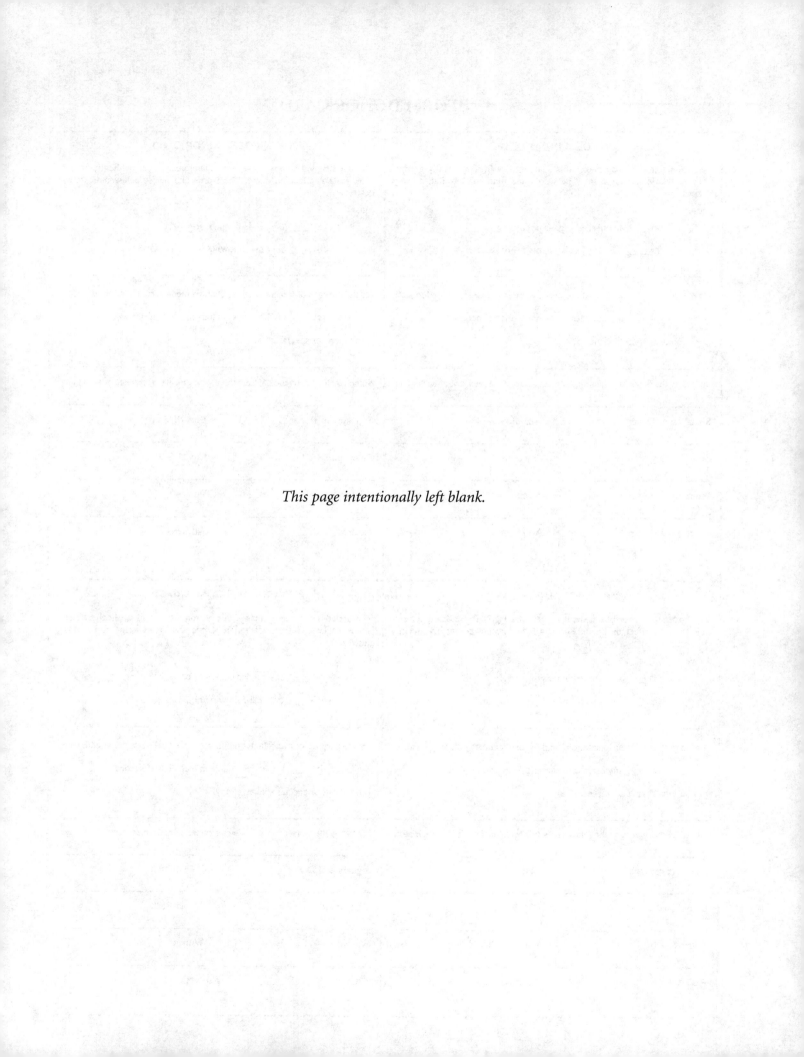

This page intentionally left blank.

NOTICE OF DEATH TO SOCIAL SECURITY ADMINISTRATION

To: Social Security Administration

_____

_____

This letter is to inform you that _____, whose Social Security number

is _____-_____-_____, and resided at _____,

died on _____, 20_____.

Any payments made after death are being returned with this letter or will be returned as received. Please stop all future payments.

Sincerely,

_____

_____

_____

Chapter 4:
Financial Legal Forms

Some of the most commonly used forms are those regarding financial matters. The forms in this chapter will help you if you are selling or buying an item outside of a merchant setting, lending or borrowing money, or ensuring your personal credit is properly maintained.

Forms in Chapter:
- Receipt
- Promissory Note—Lump Payment
- Promissory Note—Amortized with Guarantee
- Promissory Note—Payable on Demand
- Authorization to Check Credit
- Guarantee
- Request for Credit Report
- Request for Correction of Credit Report
- Denial of Debt
- Request to Stop Harassment on Debt
- Satisfaction and Release of Judgment
- Notice of Lost Credit Card
- Request to Cancel Credit Card
- ID Theft Affidavit
- Request for Forbearance on Loan
- Request for Consolidation of Loans
- Notice of Death of Debtor

Receipt

A *receipt* is a written confirmation that you have received something, usually cash. Whenever you pay cash for anything, it is important to get a receipt, otherwise the recipient can deny that the cash was ever received.

However, receipts have another use. They can prove and give the terms of a *contract*. If you buy something, a car for example, and do not have a written contract, the receipt for the transaction can be used to prove the terms of the sale. If you put the make, model, mileage, and other description on the receipt, and the car does not comply, you have a better legal case than if you did not write it on the receipt.

Courts have ruled that a document such as a receipt can help a person win a case even if they have no written contract—whether or not the law says they must have one. As explained in Chapter 1, the *statute of frauds* require that certain contracts be in writing. Many court cases have held that if a receipt (or other documentation such as letters between the parties) contains enough details of the intended transaction, then those documents can constitute the contract.

Whenever you complete a transaction with someone and do not have a written contract spelling out the terms, you should be sure that you have a **RECEIPT** with as much detail as possible. (see form 42, p.157.) If you are the seller, you might want to add something like "sold in as-is condition with no warranties" to protect yourself.

Sample: **Receipt**

RECEIPT

The undersigned hereby acknowledges receipt of the sum of __one thousand__
($__1,000__) in for form of

☒ cash

❑ a check numbered _____, dated _____, 20_____

as payment for: __1956 Chevrolet Belair, Blue and white, ID #6J503021, 89,651 miles__
__and all spare parts in trunk__
_____
_____
_____

Balance due: __five hundred__   ($__500.00__)

Date __May 10__, 20 __06__

Promissory Note

A **PROMISSORY NOTE** is a promise to pay (or repay) money. It is the legal term for an "IOU." The variety of terms of how a note can be repaid are unlimited. A lump sum can be due on a certain day. (see form 43, p.159.) Smaller payments can be due each week or month. (see form 44, p.161.) Or, the note can be payable *on demand*, meaning whenever the lender needs the money. (see form 45, p.163.)

NOTE: *Do not sign duplicate copies of a promissory note! Each signed note is an enforceable promise to pay the money referred to in the note. So if you sign three copies of the same note, you have promised to pay the same amount of money three times. Even machine copies of a note should be made before the note is signed (and the copy should not be signed) so there will not be any mistakes.*

Amortization

When a note is paid in regular payments (such as monthly), the amount is usually calculated to allow the entire loan to be paid off by a certain date. For example, if you borrow $1,000 at 12% interest and want to pay it off within a year, you need to make payments of $93.33 each month for twelve months. Prior to the Great Depression, people usually only paid the interest on the loan each month and then had to come up with the entire principal amount at the end of the loan. That is why most people defaulted. Now many loans are amortized to pay off a little of the principal each payment.

How do you know the amount of payment for any sum? In the past, there were little books called *amortization tables* or *mortgage payment tables*. Now, the Internet has several sites that provide free amortization calculators—such as **http://ray.met.fsu.edu/~bret/amortize.html**. Some electronic calculators also calculate amortizations of loans. Using these tables or calculators, you can be sure that the principal and correct interest is paid.

Interest

There is nearly an infinite number of ways to calculate interest on a loan. When not using an amortization calculation, the most common way is *simple interest*—or the percentage per year times the balance. To get more interest from the same percentage rate, you can calculate it by the month. For example, 12% of $1,000 is $120 for one year. But, if it is calculated by the month, it is $126.84. (Not much of a difference on a small loan, but for large amounts it adds up.)

One thing to be careful of when setting the interest rate is your state's *usury* law. This is the law that sets a limit on the amount of interest that can be charged on loans. The purpose is to eliminate loan sharking, but the laws usually apply to all loans. The penalties can be severe. If you charge too much interest, you may lose the right to collect interest or have to pay double interest to the borrower. You could even be charged with the crime of criminal usury.

NOTE: *Most people are surprised to learn how low their state's usury rate is (often under 10%). This is because credit card companies, banks, pawn shops, payday loan operations, etc. are governed by a different set of laws regarding the interest they can charge.*

Negotiability

Sometimes a person holding a promissory note needs the money before the loan is due. One way to get it is to sell the note. A note can be sold if it is *negotiable*. A note is negotiable if:

- ◆ the promise to pay the money is not subject to any conditions;
- ◆ it is written and signed;
- ◆ it is payable to a named person (a person to whom the note has been *negotiated* (sold), or to the *bearer* or *holder* of the note); and,
- ◆ it is to be paid either on a specified date or on the demand of the person the debt is to be paid to.

These requirements account for some of the odd language that notes and other negotiable instruments use—such as checks. For example, the words "pay to the order of" mean that the person who owes the money has to pay it to the person named or to whomever that person orders it to be paid. That is, to whomever it has been negotiated. There are other kinds of contracts that create an obligation to repay money, but promissory notes are the most reliable and readily enforceable.

Before agreeing to accept a promissory note from someone, it is common to check out their *credit history* to be sure that they pay their bills. To obtain a person's credit report, you need to have them sign an **AUTHORIZATION TO CHECK CREDIT**. (see form 46, p.165.)

Guarantee

When a person does not have either good credit history or any assets, lenders often look for another person to guarantee (*co-sign*) the loan. For young people, this is often a parent. For others, it may be a successful friend or other relative.

If you sell something to someone whose credit looks questionable, consider asking if they have someone who could guarantee the amount owed. This is done either by having the guarantor sign the note or by requiring a separate **GUARANTEE** form. (see form 47, p.167.)

If you are using a **AMORTIZED NOTE** (form 44), it has a paragraph for a guarantee by another party. This note can be used without a guarantee.

NOTE: *The guarantee clause can be added to any of the other notes.*

Sample: **Guarantee**

GUARANTEE

Date: _____ May 7 _____, 20 __06__

The undersigned, to induce the acceptance of the above Promissory Note hereby unconditionally guarantees the payment of this note according to its terms. The undersigned waives presentment, demand for payment, protest and notice of nonpayment, dishonor or protest. This guarantee shall inure to the benefit of all subsequent holders of this note.

Gary Guaranteer _____ _Carl Cosigner_ _____

Security

Except for small loan amounts, a loan represented by a promissory note is often *secured*, meaning the person owing the money pledges some property to guarantee payment of the loan. If it is not paid on time, the lender can take the property and sell it to recover the amount owed.

The forms for securing a loan with real estate are explained in Chapter 6 and those for personal property are explained in Chapter 5.

Forms for Credit Matters

A good credit profile is important in that it allows you to borrow the money necessary to buy a home, car, business, and other large items. It allows the purchase of large assets with payments spread over a long period. Imagine having to save up the cash to buy a house, rather than borrowing the money and paying each month.

Credit Report

Whether or not you are given credit will be determined by your *credit report*. It is important to you that it contain accurate information. Often the wrong information gets into these reports.

It used to cost money to get a copy of your credit report unless you were denied credit. In 2005, a new law, the *Fair and Accurate Credit Transactions Act*, was passed that allows you to get a free copy once a year.

The three main credit reporting companies, Equifax, Experian, and TransUnion, have a toll-free number (877-322-8228) you can call to order your report. To make your request by mail, you can use the REQUEST FOR CREDIT REPORT (see form 48, p.169) and send it to:

Annual Credit Report Request Service
P.O. Box 105283
Atlanta, GA, 30348-5283

You can also make your request online at **www.annualcreditreport.com**.

If you find an error on your report, explain to the agency what the error is and ask them to remove it from your report. A REQUEST FOR CORRECTION OF CREDIT REPORT can help accomplish this. (see form 49, p.171.) A sample of how to fill in this form follows.

Sample: **Request for Correction of Credit Report**

REQUEST FOR CORRECTION OF CREDIT REPORT

To: Acme Credit Bureau
      125 Side Street
      Anytown, USA 12345

From: Jon Dough
Address: 9 Leisure Lane
         Midville, USA 12345
Social Security No: 123-45-6789

Your report on my credit history contains the following error(s):

1. You show that I owe $45,000 to Midville Bank. This loan was paid in full when I sold my house on May 6, 1999.

2. You show a Visa card with MajorBanc. I never had a credit card with MajorBanc, so this account must belong to another Jon Dough.

Kindly correct these errors and provide me with a corrected copy of my report.

Dealing with Debts

Most state's laws provide that if you do not deny owing a debt you can be held legally responsible for it. The legal theory is called *account stated*. If a merchant sends you a statement and it is wrong (for example, it includes billing for something you never ordered or received), you need to contest it to avoid being liable for it.

This is not likely to happen if you have never done business with someone. If you have done regular business with them and you accept statements without complaint, you could become liable for the amounts in dispute. Use a a **DENIAL OF DEBT** to challenge these charges. (see form 50, p.173.)

Under the federal law *Fair Debt Collection Practices Act*, collection agencies are not allowed to harass you over a debt once you request that they stop. A **REQUEST TO STOP HARASSMENT ON DEBT** provides a written request for this to stop. (see form 51, p.175.)

Judgments

If someone gets a judgment against you and you pay it off, they are required to notify the court that the judgment was satisfied and where it was originally filed. This is their legal responsibility. However, if they do not know what to do and you want to speed the process along, you can provide them with a **SATISFACTION AND RELEASE OF JUDGMENT** form. (see form 52, p.177.) Be sure to first check with the clerk where the judgment is filed to see if there are any special requirements. (They may even have their own form.)

Credit Cards

If you lose your credit cards, you should immediately inform the issuers, or you may be liable for any amounts charged on them. Usually, they have a toll-free number that can be used for this purpose. Make the call immediately. But, after calling you should also confirm this in writing using a **NOTICE OF LOST CREDIT CARD**. (see form 53, p.179.)

Sometimes, just having credit cards, even if you do not use them, will keep you from getting new credit. The creditors feel that if you took your other cards to their limits you would be overextended. Therefore, it is sometimes necessary to close old accounts before qualifying for new ones. If you wish to close a credit card account, you should send a written **REQUEST TO CANCEL CREDIT CARD** to the issuer. (see form 54, p.181.) Some companies request that you cut your card in half and return it to them. However, they will usually accept your word that you destroyed the card.

Identity Theft

Identity theft is a concern for many people and occurs with great frequency. If you find that you have become a victim of identity theft, act immediately. If someone has opened an account using your personal information, you can use the **ID THEFT AFFIDAVIT** to assist in correcting the problem and clearing your name and credit report. (see form 55, p.183.)

In addition to using the **ID THEFT AFFIDAVIT**, report the fraud to the following organizations.

◆ All three national consumer reporting agencies:

Equifax
P.O. Box 740241
Atlanta, GA 30374
800-525-6285
www.equifax.com

Experian
P.O. Box 2002
Allen, TX 75013
888-397-3742
www.experian.com

Trans Union
Fraud Victim Assistance Division
P.O. Box 6790
Fullerton, CA 92834
800-680-7289
www.transunion.com

◆ The fraud department at each organization that issued credit, provided services, or sold goods to someone using your personal information.

◆ Your local police department. You may need to provide copies of a police report with the affidavit.

◆ The Federal Trade Commission (FTC), which maintains the Identity Theft Data Clearinghouse—a centralized database kept by the federal government. Contact the FTC at **www.consumer.gov/idtheft** or 877-ID-THEFT (877-438-4338). This information is shared within law enforcement nationwide, which is extremely important as the ID thief could be acting hundreds of miles from where you live.

Loans

If you get to a point in which you find it hard to meet your bills, you may be able to get a creditor to give you an extension of time to pay. Interest will still accrue on your loan, but you may be able to skip a payment or two and extend the life of the loan while you get caught up on your finances. Call your lender to discuss this.

For student loans, however, there are federal guidelines as to under what circumstances you may be granted a *forbearance*. A forbearance is a tactic used to put off payments, while still accruing interest, without defaulting. A default in a loan is a mark against your credit stating nonpayment when payment was due. You can get more information about this by contacting:

U.S. Department of Education
400 Maryland Avenue, SW
Washington, DC 20202
800-USA-LEARN
www.studentaid.ed.gov

You can make a **FORBEARANCE GENERAL REQUEST** of a student loan. (see form 56, p.189.)

If you have several loans at high interest rates (like credit cards), you may be able to get one new loan at a lower rate in which to pay off the others. This way, your monthly payment would be lower. Most lenders have a formal application for this, but you can start the ball rolling with a **REQUEST FOR CONSOLIDATION OF LOANS.** (see form 57, p.191.)

When a person dies, it is no longer required that their family pay their bills. If they owned property, the creditors can make claims against the estate. If not, then the creditors are out of luck. To inform a creditor that a person is deceased, you can use a **NOTICE OF DEATH OF DEBTOR.** (see form 58, p.193.)

Social Security

When a person who receives Social Security dies, his or her payments stop as of the last one received prior to death. If he or she has a surviving spouse, then the spouse's payment may be increased due to the death. To inform the Social Security Administration of a death, phone them at 800-772-1213. For more information you can access the Social Security Administration website at:

www.ssa.gov

RECEIPT

The undersigned hereby acknowledges receipt of the sum of _____ ($_____)
in the form of:

❏ cash

❏ a check numbered _____, dated _____, 20_____

as payment for: _____
_____
_____
_____.

Balance due: _____ ($_____)

Date _____20_____

_____

This page intentionally left blank.

PROMISSORY NOTE—LUMP PAYMENT

$_____   Date: _____, 20_____

_____ hereby promises to pay to the order of
_____ the sum of $_____,
with interest thereon from the date of this note to the date of payment at the rate of _____ per annum.

This note is due and payable in full on _____, 20___, if not paid sooner. The principal and interest shall be payable when due at _____, or at a place of which the undersigned may be notified in writing by the holder of this note.

This note is not assumable without the written consent of the lender. This note may be paid in whole or in part at any time prior without penalty. The borrower waives demand, presentment, protest, and notice. This note shall be fully payable upon demand of any holder in the event the undersigned shall default on the terms of this note or any agreement securing the payment of this note. In the event of default, the undersigned agrees to pay all costs of collection including reasonable attorney's fees.

IN WITNESS WHEREOF, the undersigned has executed this note under seal as of the date stated above (if the undersigned is a corporation, this note has been executed under seal and by authority of its board of directors).

_____

This page intentionally left blank.

PROMISSORY NOTE—AMORTIZED WITH GUARANTEE

$_____   Date: _____, 20_____

_____ hereby promises to pay to the order of
_____ the sum of $_____,
with interest thereon from the date of this note to the date of payment at the rate of _____ per annum.

This note is payable $_____ per _____, including principal and interest, until paid in
full. The principal and interest shall be payable when due at _____,
or at a place of which the undersigned may be notified in writing by the holder of this note.

This note is not assumable without the written consent of the lender. This note may be paid in whole or in part at any
time prior without penalty. The borrower waives demand, presentment, protest, and notice. This note shall be fully
payable upon demand of any holder in the event the undersigned shall default on the terms of this note or any agreement securing the payment of this note. In the event of default, the undersigned agrees to pay all costs of collection,
including reasonable attorney's fees.

IN WITNESS WHEREOF, the undersigned has executed this note under seal as of the date stated above (if the undersigned is a corporation, this note has been executed under seal and by authority of its board of directors).

_____

Guarantee

The undersigned, to induce the acceptance of the above Promissory Note, hereby unconditionally guarantees the
payment of this note according to its terms. The undersigned waives presentment, demand for payment, protest,
and notice of nonpayment, dishonor, or protest. This guarantee shall inure to the benefit of all subsequent holders of
this note.

_____

This page intentionally left blank.

PROMISSORY NOTE—PAYABLE ON DEMAND

$_____   Date: _____, 20_____

_____ hereby promises to pay to the order of
_____ the sum of $_____,
with interest thereon from the date of this note to the date of payment at the rate of _____ per annum.

This note is payable upon demand of the holder. The principal and interest shall be payable when due at
_____, or at a place of which the undersigned
may be notified in writing by the holder of this note.

This note is not assumable without the written consent of the lender. This note may be paid in whole or in part at any time prior without penalty. The borrower waives demand, presentment, protest, and notice. This note shall be fully payable upon demand of any holder in the event the undersigned shall default on the terms of this note or any agreement securing the payment of this note. In the event of default, the undersigned agrees to pay all costs of collection including reasonable attorneys fees.

IN WITNESS WHEREOF, the undersigned has executed this note under seal as of the date stated above (if the undersigned is a corporation, this note has been executed under seal and by authority of its board of directors).

_____

AUTHORIZATION TO CHECK CREDIT

To:

I hereby authorize you to release my credit report to:

_____

_____

_____

_____

Signature

This page intentionally left blank.

GUARANTEE

Date: _____, 20_____

The undersigned, to induce the acceptance of the above Promissory Note, hereby unconditionally guarantees the payment of this note according to its terms. The undersigned waives presentment, demand for payment, protest, and notice of nonpayment, dishonor, or protest. This guarantee shall inure to the benefit of all subsequent holders of this note.

_____

This page intentionally left blank.

REQUEST FOR CREDIT REPORT

Annual Credit Report Request Service
P.O. Box 105281
Atlanta, GA 30348-5281

As provided by the Fair and Accurate Credit Transactions Act, please send me a copy of my credit report from:

❏ Equifax

❏ Experian

❏ TransUnion

Name:_____   Soc. Sec. No.:_____

Address:_____

Thank you,

_____

This page intentionally left blank.

REQUEST FOR CORRECTION OF CREDIT REPORT

To:

From: _____

Address: _____

_____

Social Security No: _____

Your report on my credit history contains the following error(s):

Kindly correct these errors and provide me with a corrected copy of my report.

_____

This page intentionally left blank.

DENIAL OF DEBT

To:

Re: _____

Amount $_____

The records of your company regarding the above debt are in error for the following reasons:

Kindly correct your records accordingly.

_____

This page intentionally left blank.

REQUEST TO STOP HARASSMENT ON DEBT

To:

Re: _____

Amount $_____

Please do not continue to contact me regarding the above debt.

_____

This page intentionally left blank.

SATISFACTION AND RELEASE OF JUDGMENT

The Plaintiff, _____, hereby acknowledges that the judgment in this action, rendered on _____, has been fully satisfied by Defendant, _____, and hereby releases and discharges said Defendant from any and all further liability for said judgment.

Dated: _____, 20_____

_____

-OR-

This document is signed by _____, [insert: "individually" or "as agent of Plaintiff corporation"] on _____, 20_____ to acknowledge full payment of the judgment signed by the Judge on _____, 20_____. Plaintiff agrees that Defendant(s) do(es) not owe the Plaintiff any more monies on the judgment.

_____

This page intentionally left blank.

NOTICE OF LOST CREDIT CARD

To:

Re: Credit Card #_____

The referenced credit card was lost or stolen on or about _____, 20___. Any charges incurred after that date were not made by me. Please cancel this card and issue me a new one.

Thank you,

_____

Address:

_____

_____

_____

This page intentionally left blank.

REQUEST TO CANCEL CREDIT CARD

To:

Re: Credit Card #_____

Please cancel the above-referenced credit card account and report to the credit bureaus that the account has been closed. The card(s) issued for the account:

❏ are enclosed

❏ have been destroyed.

Thank you,

_____

Address:

_____

_____

_____

This page intentionally left blank.

Instructions for
Completing the ID Theft Affidavit

To make certain that you do not become responsible for the debts incurred by the identity thief, you must provide proof that you didn't create the debt to each of the companies where accounts where opened or used in your name.

A working group composed of credit grantors, consumer advocates and the Federal Trade Commission (FTC) developed this ID Theft Affidavit to help you report information to many companies using just one standard form. Use of this affidavit is optional for companies. While many companies accept this affidavit, others require that you submit more or different forms. Before you send the affidavit, contact each company to find out if they accept it.

You can use this affidavit where a **new account** was opened in your name. The information will enable the companies to investigate the fraud and decide the outcome of your claim. (If someone made unauthorized charges to an **existing account**, call the company to find out what to do.)

This affidavit has two parts:

■ **ID Theft Affidavit** is where you report general information about yourself and the theft.

■ **Fraudulent Account Statement** is where you describe the fraudulent account(s) opened in your name. Use a separate Fraudulent Account Statement for each company you need to write to.

When you send the affidavit to the companies, attach copies (**NOT** originals) of any supporting documents (for example, drivers license, police report) you have. Before submitting your affidavit, review the disputed account(s) with family members or friends who may have information about

the account(s) or access to them.

Complete this affidavit as soon as possible. Many creditors ask that you send it within two weeks of receiving it. Delaying could slow the investigation.

Be as accurate and complete as possible. You *may* choose not to provide some of the information requested. However, incorrect or incomplete information will slow the process of investigating your claim and absolving the debt. Please print clearly.

When you have finished completing the affidavit, mail a copy to each creditor, bank or company that provided the thief with the unauthorized credit, goods or services you describe. Attach to each affidavit a copy of the Fraudulent Account Statement with information only on accounts opened at the institution receiving the packet, as well as any other supporting documentation you are able to provide.

Send the appropriate documents to each company by certified mail, return receipt requested, so you can prove that it was received. The companies will review your claim and send you a written response telling you the outcome of their investigation. **Keep a copy of everything you submit for your records**.

If you cannot complete the affidavit, a legal guardian or someone with power of attorney may complete it for you. Except as noted, the information you provide will be used only by the company to process your affidavit, investigate the events you report and help stop further fraud. If this affidavit is requested in a lawsuit, the company might have to provide it to the requesting party.

Completing this affidavit does not guarantee that the identity thief will be prosecuted or that the debt will be cleared.

Name _____ Phone number _____ Page 1

ID Theft Affidavit

Victim Information

(1)   My full legal name is _____
                         (First)   (Middle)   (Last)   (Jr., Sr., III)

(2)   (If different from above) When the events described in this affidavit took place, I was known as

      _____
      (First)   (Middle)   (Last)   (Jr., Sr., III)

(3)   My date of birth is _____
                         (day/month/year)

(4)   My Social Security number is_____

(5)   My driver's license or identification card state and number are_____

(6)   My current address is _____

      City _____ State _____ Zip Code _____

(7)   I have lived at this address since _____
                                       (month/year)

(8)   (If different from above) When the events described in this affidavit took place, my address was

      _____

      City _____ State _____ Zip Code _____

(9)   I lived at the address in Item 8 from _____ until _____
                                          (month/year)   (month/year)

(10) My daytime telephone number is (____)_____

      My evening telephone number is (____)_____

Name _____ Phone number _____ *Page 2*

How the Fraud Occurred

Check all that apply for items 11 - 17:

(11) ❑ I did not authorize anyone to use my name or personal information to seek the money, credit, loans, goods or services described in this report.

(12) ❑ I did not receive any benefit, money, goods or services as a result of the events described in this report.

(13) ❑ My identification documents (for example, credit cards; birth certificate; driver's license; Social Security card; etc.) were ❑ stolen ❑ lost on or about _____.
   (day/month/year)

(14) ❑ To the best of my knowledge and belief, the following person(s) used my information (for example, my name, address, date of birth, existing account numbers, Social Security number, mother's maiden name, etc.) or identification documents to get money, credit, loans, goods or services without my knowledge or authorization:

_____	_____
Name (if known)	Name (if known)
_____	_____
Address (if known)	Address (if known)
_____	_____
Phone number(s) (if known)	Phone number(s) (if known)
_____	_____
Additional information (if known)	Additional information (if known)

(15) ❑ I do NOT know who used my information or identification documents to get money, credit, loans, goods or services without my knowledge or authorization.

(16) ❑ Additional comments: (For example, description of the fraud, which documents or information were used or how the identity thief gained access to your information.)

_____

_____

_____

_____

(Attach additional pages as necessary.)

Name _____ *Phone number* _____ *Page 3*

Victim's Law Enforcement Actions

(17) (check one) I ❑ am ❑ am not willing to assist in the prosecution of the person(s) who committed this fraud.

(18) (check one) I ❑ am ❑ am not authorizing the release of this information to law enforcement for the purpose of assisting them in the investigation and prosecution of the person(s) who committed this fraud.

(19) (check all that apply) I ❑ have ❑ have not reported the events described in this affidavit to the police or other law enforcement agency. The police ❑ did ❑ did not write a report. *In the event you have contacted the police or other law enforcement agency, please complete the following:*

(Agency #1)   (Officer/Agency personnel taking report)

(Date of report)   (Report number, if any)

(Phone number)   (email address, if any)

(Agency #2)   (Officer/Agency personnel taking report)

(Date of report)   (Report number, if any)

(Phone number)   (email address, if any)

Documentation Checklist

Please indicate the supporting documentation you are able to provide to the companies you plan to notify. Attach copies (NOT originals) to the affidavit before sending it to the companies.

(20) ❑ A copy of a valid government-issued photo-identification card (for example, your driver's license, state-issued ID card or your passport). If you are under 16 and don't have a photo-ID, you may submit a copy of your birth certificate or a copy of your official school records showing your enrollment and place of residence.

(21) ❑ Proof of residency during the time the disputed bill occurred, the loan was made or the other event took place (for example, a rental/lease agreement in your name, a copy of a utility bill or a copy of an insurance bill).

(22) ❑ A copy of the report you filed with the police or sheriff's department. If you are unable to obtain a report or report number from the police, please indicate that in Item 19. Some companies only need the report number, not a copy of the report. You may want to check with each company.

Signature

I declare under penalty of perjury that the information I have provided in this affidavit is true and correct to the best of my knowledge.

_____   _____
(signature)   (date signed)

Knowingly submitting false information on this form could subject you to criminal prosecution for perjury.

_____
(Notary)

[Check with each company. Creditors sometimes require notarization. If they do not, please have one witness (non-relative) sign below that you completed and signed this affidavit.]

Witness:

_____   _____
(signature)   (printed name)

_____   _____
(date)   (telephone number)

Fraudulent Account Statement

> ### Completing this Statement
>
> - Make as many copies of this page as you need. **Complete a separate page for each company you're notifying and only send it to that company.** Include a copy of your signed affidavit.
> - List only the account(s) you're disputing with the company receiving this form. **See the example below.**
> - If a collection agency sent you a statement, letter or notice about the fraudulent account, attach a copy of that document (**NOT** the original).

I declare (check all that apply):

❑ As a result of the event(s) described in the ID Theft Affidavit, the following account(s) was/were opened at your company in my name without my knowledge, permission or authorization using my personal information or identifying documents:

Creditor Name/Address *(the company that opened the account or provided the goods or services)*	Account Number	Type of unauthorized credit/goods/services provided by creditor *(if known)*	Date issued or opened *(if known)*	Amount/Value provided *(the amount charged or the cost of the goods/services)*
Example Example National Bank 22 Main Street Columbus, Ohio 22722	01234567-89	auto loan	01/05/2002	$25,500.00

❑ During the time of the accounts described above, I had the following account open with your company:

Billing name _____

Billing address_____

Account number _____

Direct Loans
William D. Ford Federal Direct Loan Program

GENERAL FORBEARANCE REQUEST
William D. Ford Federal Direct Loan Program

WARNING: Any person who knowingly makes a false statement or misrepresentation on this form or on any accompanying documents will be subject to penalties which may include fines, imprisonment, or both, under the U.S. Criminal Code and 20 U.S.C. 1097.

OMB No. 1845-0031
Form Approved
Exp. Date 06/30/2006

GFB
General

SECTION 1: BORROWER / ENDORSER IDENTIFICATION   *PLEASE PRINT LEGIBLY IN BLUE OR BLACK INK*

Last Name	First Name	Middle Initial	Social Security Number

Street Address

Area Code/Telephone Number (Home)
(   )

Area Code/Telephone Number (Other)
(   )

City	State	Zip Code

E-mail Address (optional)

SECTION 2: FORBEARANCE REQUEST

Before completing this form, carefully read the entire form, including the instructions and other information in Sections 3, 4, 5, and 6. You may complete and submit your forbearance request electronically at the Direct Loan Servicing Center's web site: *www.dl.ed.gov*.

■ I am willing but unable to make my current Direct Loan payments due to a temporary financial hardship. I am requesting this forbearance because: _____

_____

_____

■ **If this forbearance request is approved, I want to** (check one):
☐ temporarily stop making payments; or
☐ make smaller payments of $_____ per month.

■ If this forbearance request is approved, I am requesting that the U.S. Department of Education (ED) grant a forbearance on my loan(s) beginning (MM-DD-YYYY) |____| |____|-|____| |____|-|____| |____| |____| |____| and ending (MM-DD-YYYY) |____| |____|-|____| |____|-|____| |____| |____| |____| for a period not to exceed 12 months. At the end of the forbearance, I may apply to renew the forbearance if I am still experiencing a financial hardship.

SECTION 3: BORROWER / ENDORSER UNDERSTANDINGS AND CERTIFICATIONS

■ **I understand** that the following terms and conditions apply to this forbearance request:

(1) I will continue to receive billing statements for my current payment amount which I must pay until I am notified by the Direct Loan Servicing Center that my forbearance request has been granted.

(2) ED may grant me a forbearance on my loans for up to 60 days, if necessary, for the collection and processing of documentation related to my forbearance request. ED will not capitalize interest that accrues during this forbearance.

(3) ED will not grant this forbearance request unless this form is completed and any required documentation is provided.

(4) During the forbearance period, I am not required to make payments of loan principal and interest, but interest will be charged on all of my loans.

(5) If I requested a temporary suspension of payments, I will receive a quarterly interest statement, and I may pay the interest at any time. If I do not pay the interest that accrues on my loan(s), it will be capitalized at the end of the forbearance period.

(6) If I requested a reduced payment forbearance, I will receive a monthly bill for the requested payment amount until the forbearance ends, and any unpaid interest that has accrued during the period will be capitalized at the end of the forbearance period.

■ **I certify** that:

(1) The information I have provided on this form is true and correct.

(2) I will provide additional documentation to the Direct Loan Servicing Center, as required, to support my continued forbearance status.

(3) I will notify the Direct Loan Servicing Center immediately when the condition that qualified me for the forbearance ends.

(4) I have read, understand, and meet the eligibility requirements of the forbearance for which I have applied.

(5) Upon termination of this forbearance, I will repay my loan(s) according to the terms of my promissory note and repayment schedule.

BORROWER'S OR ENDORSER'S SIGNATURE: _____   **DATE:** _____

190

SECTION 4: INSTRUCTIONS FOR COMPLETING THE GENERAL FORBEARANCE REQUEST FORM

- Type or print using dark ink. Report dates as month-day-year. For example, show "January 31, 2003" as "01-31-2003". **REMEMBER TO SIGN AND DATE THE FORM.**

Send the completed form and any required documentation to:	If you need help completing this form, call: **1-800-848-0979**
U.S. Department of Education Direct Loan Servicing Center P.O. Box 5609 Greenville, TX 75403-5609	If you use a telecommunications device for the deaf (TDD), call: **1-800-848-0983** Direct Loan Servicing Center web site: **www.dl.ed.gov**

SECTION 5: DEFINITIONS

- If unpaid interest is **capitalized**, this means that it is added to the principal balance of your loan(s). This will increase the principal amount and the total cost of your loan(s).

- An **endorser** is someone who promises to repay a PLUS loan or the PLUS portion of a consolidation loan if the parent borrower does not repay it.

- A **forbearance** allows you to temporarily postpone making payments on your loan(s), or lets you temporarily make smaller payments than previously scheduled. Interest is charged during a forbearance on all types of Direct Loans.

- The **William D. Ford Federal Direct Loan (Direct Loan) Program** includes Federal Direct Stafford/Ford (Direct Subsidized) Loans, Federal Direct Unsubsidized Stafford/Ford (Direct Unsubsidized) Loans, Federal Direct PLUS (Direct PLUS) Loans, and Federal Direct Consolidation (Direct Consolidation) Loans. These loans are known collectively as "Direct Loans".

SECTION 6: IMPORTANT NOTICES

Privacy Act Notice. The Privacy Act of 1974 (5 U.S.C. 552a) requires that the following notice be provided to you:

The authority for collecting the requested information from and about you is §451 et seq. of the Higher Education Act of 1965, as amended (20 U.S.C. 1087a et seq.) and the authority for collecting and using your Social Security Number (SSN) is §484(a)(4) of the HEA (20 U.S.C. 1091(a)(4)). Participating in the William D. Ford Federal Direct Loan (Direct Loan) Program and giving us your SSN are voluntary, but you must provide the requested information, including your SSN, to participate.

The principal purposes for collecting the information on this form, including your SSN, are to verify your identity, to determine your eligibility to receive a loan or a benefit on a loan (such as a deferment, forbearance, discharge, or forgiveness) under the Direct Loan Program, to permit the servicing of your loan(s), and, if it becomes necessary, to locate you and to collect on your loan(s) if your loan(s) become delinquent or in default. We also use your SSN as an account identifier and to permit you to access your account information electronically.

The information in your file may be disclosed to third parties as authorized under routine uses in the appropriate systems of records. The routine uses of this information include its disclosure to federal, state, or local agencies, to other federal agencies under computer matching programs, to agencies that we authorize to assist us in administering our loan programs, to private parties such as relatives, present and former employers, business and personal associates, to credit bureau organizations, to financial and educational institutions, to guaranty agencies, and to contractors in order to verify your identity, to determine your eligibility to receive a loan or a benefit on a loan, to permit the servicing or collection of your loan(s), to counsel you in repayment efforts, to enforce the terms of the loan(s), to investigate possible fraud and to verify compliance with federal student financial aid program regulations, or to locate you if you become delinquent in your loan payments or if you default, to provide default rate calculations, to provide financial aid history information, to assist program administrators with tracking refunds and cancellations, or to provide a standardized method for educational institutions efficiently to submit student enrollment status.

In the event of litigation, we may send records to the Department of Justice, a court, adjudicative body, counsel, party, or witness if the disclosure is relevant and necessary to the litigation. If this information, either alone or with other information, indicates a potential violation of law, we may send it to the appropriate authority for action. We may send information to members of Congress if you ask them to help you with federal student aid questions. In circumstances involving employment complaints, grievances, or disciplinary actions, we may disclose relevant records to adjudicate or investigate the issues. If provided for by a collective bargaining agreement, we may disclose records to a labor organization recognized under 5 U.S.C. Chapter 71. Disclosures may also be made to qualified researchers under Privacy Act safeguards.

Paperwork Reduction Notice. According to the Paperwork Reduction Act of 1995, no persons are required to respond to a collection of information unless it displays a currently valid OMB control number. The valid OMB control number for this information collection is 1845-0031. The time required to complete this information collection is estimated to average 0.2 hours (12 minutes) per response, including the time to review instructions, search existing data resources, gather and maintain the data needed, and complete and review the information collection. **If you have comments concerning the accuracy of the time estimate(s) or suggestions for improving this form, please write to:** U.S. Department of Education, Washington, DC 20202-4651. *Do not send the completed form to this address.*

If you have questions about the status of *your individual submission of this form*, contact the Direct Loan Servicing Center (see Section 4).

REQUEST FOR CONSOLIDATION OF LOANS

To:

I wish to consolidate the following loans with a new loan from your institution:

Please let me know if this will be possible, and if so, send information on the terms available and any application forms which need to be completed.

Thank you,

_____

Address:

_____

_____

_____

This page intentionally left blank.

NOTICE OF DEATH OF DEBTOR

To:

Re: Name: _____

    Social Security Number: _____

    Date of Death: _____

    Account Number: _____

The above-referenced debtor is deceased.

❏ No probate proceedings are planned.

❏ Probate proceedings have been filed in the following court:

_____

File No. _____

                                    Very truly yours,

                                    _____

                                    Address:

                                    _____

                                    _____

                                    _____

Chapter 5:
Personal Property Forms

This chapter explains legal forms you could use for transactions relating to personal property. Examples are buying a car from a private party, loaning a valuable tool to a neighbor, or selling a collection of baseball cards. While such transactions are usually done without legal forms, these simple pieces of paper, signed in a few seconds, can save you months of aggravation and thousands of dollars in legal fees if the transaction goes wrong.

For example, what if you buy a car you believe has 35,000 miles on it, but later discover it has 135,000, and all you have is a cancelled check? Or, you let your neighbor borrow a farm implement, and then he dies, and his heirs claim it was his. Or, you sell your valuable baseball card collection to a neighbor, two months later he wants to rescind the deal, but the cards are no longer in the condition they were in when you sold them. The forms in this chapter will help you avoid most legal problems that could come up in these types of situations.

__Forms in Chapter:__
• **Request for Quotation**
• **Bill of Sale—with Warranty**
• **Bill of Sale**
• **Chattel Mortgage**
• **UCC-1 Financing Statement**
• **UCC-3 Financing Statement Amendment**
• **Receipt for Personal Property**

Placing an Order

When you purchase something from a catalog or off the rack, you usually know exactly what you are getting. When you need something made to your specifications, such as a driveway or a cabinet, you may get something completely different from what you expected because you and the seller were assuming different specifications. Do not assume anything. To be sure you will get what you want, you should put in writing all of the specifications you are expecting.

The best form for this is a **REQUEST FOR QUOTATION.** (see form 59, p.201.) While many companies have their own specification form, this form will help you remember and organize all of the specifications you are looking for.

Sample: **Request for Quotation**

REQUEST FOR QUOTATION

To: Acme Supply
      321 Fleet St.
      Mytown, USA

We are considering the purchase of the following:

12 cubic yards of clean top soil
25 pounds of Bahai grass seed
12 pressure-treated 4 x 4 inch posts 8 feet long

All to be delivered to 100 Easy Street, Mytown, USA on or before May 12, 2006

If you are able to provide this as specified, kindly provide us with a quotation of total price and completion or delivery date.

Buying and Selling

While a sale of real estate usually involves a contract, a simple cash purchase will usually just involve a *bill of sale*. A bill of sale is like the deed used for real estate, but it is used for personal property. For some types of property, such as motor vehicles and boats, you can transfer title by signing over the state registration (the title). However, it is always a good idea to have a bill of sale as well, because this can include the important terms of the transaction. The price can be used for tax reasons, and the description and/or mileage can be used as evidence that the property was misrepresented (if it was).

A bill of sale can be with warranty or without warranty. The most basic *warranty* is that the seller actually owns the property being sold. Since stolen property nearly always must be returned to its original owner, even if an innocent person buys it, a seller's warranty of ownership will help you collect from the seller in the event you lose the item because it was originally stolen.

A bill of sale can also include warranties as to condition, age, or other aspects of the property. As a *buyer* of property, you want as many warranties as possible. As a *seller*, you want to give as few warranties as possible, because then there will be less things you can be accountable for. A BILL OF SALE—WITH WARRANTY is included. (see form 60, p.203.)

For both parties, it is best to describe the property as accurately as possible. If the item has a serial number, that should be included. If not, the make, model, style, color, and other identifying aspects should be included.

A bill of sale needs only to be signed by the person selling the property. Below is a sample of a BILL OF SALE with no warranty. (see form 61, p.205.)

Sample: **Bill of Sale**

BILL OF SALE

For $_____50.00_____, the receipt of which is hereby acknowledged, the undersigned hereby sells and transfers to _____Jon Dough_____ all of the undersigned's rights in the following property:

> Toro 21" lawn mower model Go%, serial no. CV123456 with grass catcher and instruction book

Executed under seal on _____August 9_____, 20_06_.

Installment Sales

When a person cannot afford to pay cash for an item, he or she can still purchase it by borrowing the money or by buying it on an *installment purchase agreement*. If you are buying something from a private party, he or she will probably want cash. If you can convince them to take payments, you might be able to get a better deal than borrowing from a bank or your credit cards.

If you are selling something, you would rather get cash. In some cases you might get a higher price if you agree to sell on an installment agreement. Keep in mind that this is risky. The buyer might disappear with the property and never pay you. Or, if the buyer fails to pay and gives the property back, it might be in such bad condition you cannot resell it at the balance due. Then again, if the buyer puts a big enough down payment, you might be able to sell the property again and make a double profit. You will need to weigh the benefits of selling on an installment agreement against the risks.

When selling on an installment agreement, the most important thing to do is to place a *lien* on the property so that it cannot be resold without you being paid off. Like a *mortgage* (a lien on real estate), a **Chattel Mortgage** is a lien on personal property. (see form 62, p.207.) In addition to a chattel mortgage, you should file a *financing statement* in the public records. This protects you by giving notice to the world of your interest in the property. A financing statement is usually called a *UCC-1* because it is covered by the *Uniform Commercial Code (UCC)*.

Forms

While the Uniform Commercial Code is supposed to be uniform, each state has made its own changes to it. One unfortunate situation is that most states prefer that you use their own form. They may not supply the form. They may instruct you to purchase it from a private company. Some of those states charge a few dollars extra if the form you use does not exactly match theirs. Because the official forms can be hard to obtain, generic **UCC-1** and **UCC-3** forms are included. You may find it preferable to pay a couple dollars extra than to take the effort and delay to track down the right one.

The **UCC-1** form is usually filed with both the secretary of state and a county recording office. (see form 63, p.209.) After the debt has been paid, the **UCC-1** is released by filing a **UCC-3** form. (see form 64, p.213.) If you need more room to add names of additional debtors, secured parties, collateral, or additional information, you can use the **UCC Financing Statement Addendum** and **UCC Financing Statement Amendment Addendum** included with each form respectively.

In addition to the chattel mortgage, you should have a *promissory note* that the buyer signs promising to pay the balance due. (See Chapter 4 for more information on promissory notes. These notes can be used to purchase goods as well as for loans.) You can also have a formal *sales agreement*, but for a simple transaction, it is not necessary.

For motor vehicles, some boats, and other property that has a registration with a government agency, there is an easier system. Usually the agency that registers the titles has a form that you can use to register a financial interest in the vehicle or property. Check with your state or county registration office as to what forms are available to place a lien on property that will be sold.

Loaning Property

If you loan something valuable to someone, want to be sure of getting it back, and are not liable for its use, you should use a written **RECEIPT FOR PERSONAL PROPERTY**. (see form 65, p.217.)

For example, if your neighbor will be borrowing one of your farm implements and storing it on his property, or if someone will be borrowing something valuable on a long-term basis, you should get something in writing. Insuring that you get it back can protect you from potential liability. When using the receipt for personal property, be sure to describe the property carefully, so that it cannot be mistaken for other property.

Again, you do not need to be pulling out legal forms whenever someone borrows something, but keep in mind that if you loan someone a dangerous tool, like a chain saw, and they are injured, you could be liable. This would be especially likely if they injured someone else, or if you had somehow modified the tool making it more dangerous. Other than not loaning dangerous tools, one thing you can do is tell the borrower that you will only loan it on the condition that you will not be held responsible for any injuries. While a verbal agreement like this is harder to prove than a written one, it could still work in court if it came to that. If a disinterested third party heard the agreement, that would be even better.

REQUEST FOR QUOTATION

To:

I am considering the purchase of the following:

If you are able to provide this as specified, kindly provide me with a quotation of total price and completion or delivery date.

_____

This page intentionally left blank.

BILL OF SALE—WITH WARRANTY

For valuable consideration, the receipt and sufficiency of which is hereby acknowledged, the undersigned hereby sells and transfers to _____ the following:

The undersigned warrants and represents that it has good title to and full authority to sell and transfer the same, and that the property is sold and transferred free and clear of all liens, claims, and encumbrances, except:

The undersigned warrants that, subject to the exceptions stated above, it will indemnify the buyer, and defend title to the property, against the adverse claims of all persons.

Executed under seal on _____, 20_____.

_____

_____
[print name]

This page intentionally left blank.

BILL OF SALE

For $_____, the receipt of which is hereby acknowledged, the undersigned hereby sells and transfers to _____ all of the undersigned's rights in the following property:

Executed under seal on _____, 20_____.

_____

_____
[print name]

This page intentionally left blank.

CHATTEL MORTGAGE

Date: _____

FOR VALUE RECEIVED, receipt of which is hereby acknowledged, the undersigned debtor hereby grants a security interest in the following property _____
_____
to _____ as secured party.

This security agreement is to secure indebtedness in the amount of _____
_____ ($_____), evidenced by a promissory note of even date.

The undersigned warrants that he/she is the owner of all interest in said property, and that such interest is subject to no other liens, charges, encumbrances or claims.

This agreement shall be secured with a UCC financing statement. A copy of this security agreement and the UCC financing statement shall be lodged with the trustee of said land trust. The undersigned consents that no further pledge of the beneficial interest shall be made, or conveyance or encumbrance of the real property of the trust, without the consent of the secured party.

Upon default, the secured party shall have all the rights and remedies provided a secured party under the _____ [State] Uniform Commercial Code, including the right to sell the beneficial interest at a public or private sale, with or without advertising. The undersigned agrees that the requirements of the UCC shall be met if notice is mailed to the undersigned at the address below, not less than five days prior to the sale or other disposition.

Default shall be: any failure to pay principal or interest under the promissory note as it comes due; breach of any warranty made by the debtor; attachment, seizure, foreclosure, forfeiture, or levy on the beneficial interest of the trust or the real property held by the trust; institution of any action in bankruptcy by or against debtor; or, any reasonable insecurity of the secured party.

The undersigned acknowledges receipt of a completed copy of this security agreement.

Secured party: Debtor:

_____   _____

_____   _____

Address: Address:

_____   _____

_____   _____

This page intentionally left blank.

Instructions for UCC Financing Statement (Form UCC1)

Please type or laser-print this form. Be sure it is completely legible. Read all instructions, especially Instruction 1; correct Debtor name is crucial. Follow Instructions completely.

Fill in form very carefully; mistakes may have important legal consequences. If you have questions, consult your attorney. Filing office cannot give legal advice.

Do not insert anything in the open space in the upper portion of this form; it is reserved for filing office use.

When properly completed, send Filing Office Copy, with required fee, to filing office. If you want an acknowledgment, complete item B and, if filing in a filing office that returns an acknowledgment copy furnished by filer, you may also send Acknowledgment Copy; otherwise detach. If you want to make a search request, complete item 7 (after reading Instruction 7 below) and send Search Report Copy, otherwise detach. Always detach Debtor and Secured Party Copies.

If you need to use attachments, you are encouraged to use either Addendum (Form UCC1Ad) or Additional Party (Form UCC1AP).

A. To assist filing offices that might wish to communicate with filer, filer may provide information in item A. This item is optional.

B. Complete item B if you want an acknowledgment sent to you. If filing in a filing office that returns an acknowledgment copy furnished by filer, present simultaneously with this form a carbon or other copy of this form for use as an acknowledgment copy.

1. **Debtor name**: Enter only one Debtor name in item 1, an organization's name (1a) or an individual's name (1b). Enter Debtor's exact full legal name. Don't abbreviate.

1a. Organization Debtor. "Organization" means an entity having a legal identity separate from its owner. A partnership is an organization; a sole proprietorship is not an organization, even if it does business under a trade name. If Debtor is a partnership, enter exact full legal name of partnership; you need not enter names of partners as additional Debtors. If Debtor is a registered organization (e.g., corporation, limited partnership, limited liability company), it is advisable to examine Debtor's current filed charter documents to determine Debtor's correct name, organization type, and jurisdiction of organization.

1b. Individual Debtor. "Individual" means a natural person; this includes a sole proprietorship, whether or not operating under a trade name. Don't use prefixes (Mr., Mrs., Ms.). Use suffix box only for titles of lineage (Jr., Sr., III) and not for other suffixes or titles (e.g., M.D.). Use married woman's personal name (Mary Smith, not Mrs. John Smith). Enter individual Debtor's family name (surname) in Last Name box, first given name in First Name box, and all additional given names in Middle Name box.

For both organization and individual Debtors: Don't use Debtor's trade name, DBA, AKA, FKA, Division name, etc. in place of or combined with Debtor's legal name; you may add such other names as additional Debtors if you wish (but this is neither required nor recommended).

1c. An address is always required for the Debtor named in 1a or 1b.

1d. Reserved for Financing Statements to be filed in North Dakota or South Dakota only. If this Financing Statement is to be filed in North Dakota or South Dakota, the Debtor's taxpayer identification number (tax ID#) — social security number or employer identification number must be placed in this box.

1e,f,g. "Additional information re organization Debtor" is always required. Type of organization and jurisdiction of organization as well as Debtor's exact legal name can be determined from Debtor's current filed charter document. Organizational ID #, if any, is assigned by the agency where the charter document was filed; this is different from tax ID #; this should be entered preceded by the 2-character U.S. Postal identification of state of organization if one of the United States (e.g., CA12345, for a California corporation whose organizational ID # is 12345); if agency does not assign organizational ID #, check box in item 1g indicating "none."

Note: If Debtor is a trust or a trustee acting with respect to property held in trust, enter Debtor's name in item 1 and attach Addendum (Form UCC1Ad) and check appropriate box in item 17. If Debtor is a decedent's estate, enter name of deceased individual in item 1b and attach Addendum (Form UCC1Ad) and check appropriate box in item 17. If Debtor is a transmitting utility or this Financing Statement is filed in connection with a Manufactured-Home Transaction or a Public-Finance Transaction as defined in applicable Commercial Code, attach Addendum (Form UCC1Ad) and check appropriate box in item 18.

2. If an additional Debtor is included, complete item 2, determined and formatted per Instruction 1. To include further additional Debtors, attach either Addendum (Form UCC1Ad) or Additional Party (Form UCC1AP) and follow Instruction 1 for determining and formatting additional names.

3. Enter information for Secured Party or Total Assignee, determined and formatted per Instruction 1. To include further additional Secured Parties, attach either Addendum (Form UCC1Ad) or Additional Party (Form UCC1AP) and follow Instruction 1 for determining and formatting additional names. If there has been a total assignment of the Secured Party's interest prior to filing this form, you may either (1) enter Assignor S/P's name and address in item 3 and file an Amendment (Form UCC3) [see item 5 of that form]; or (2) enter Total Assignee's name and address in item 3 and, if you wish, also attaching Addendum (Form UCC1Ad) giving Assignor S/P's name and address in item 12.

4. Use item 4 to indicate the collateral covered by this Financing Statement. If space in item 4 is insufficient, put the entire collateral description or continuation of the collateral description on either Addendum (Form UCC1Ad) or other attached additional page(s).

5. If filer desires (at filer's option) to use titles of lessee and lessor, or consignee and consignor, or seller and buyer (in the case of accounts or chattel paper), or bailee and bailor instead of Debtor and Secured Party, check the appropriate box in item 5. If this is an agricultural lien (as defined in applicable Commercial Code) filing or is otherwise not a UCC security interest filing (e.g., a tax lien, judgment lien, etc.), check the appropriate box in item 5, complete items 1-7 as applicable and attach any other items required under other law.

6. If this Financing Statement is filed as a fixture filing or if the collateral consists of timber to be cut or as-extracted collateral, complete items 1-5, check the box in item 6, and complete the required information (items 13, 14 and/or 15) on Addendum (Form UCC1Ad).

7. This item is optional. Check appropriate box in item 7 to request Search Report(s) on all or some of the Debtors named in this Financing Statement. The Report will list all Financing Statements on file against the designated Debtor on the date of the Report, including this Financing Statement. There is an additional fee for each Report. If you have checked a box in item 7, file Search Report Copy together with Filing Officer Copy (and Acknowledgment Copy). Note: Not all states do searches and not all states will honor a search request made via this form; some states require a separate request form.

8. This item is optional and is for filer's use only. For filer's convenience of reference, filer may enter in item 8 any identifying information (e.g., Secured Party's loan number, law firm file number, Debtor's name or other identification, state in which form is being filed, etc.) that filer may find useful.

Instructions for UCC Financing Statement Addendum (Form UCC1Ad)

9.   Insert name of first Debtor shown on Financing Statement to which this Addendum relates, exactly as shown in item 1 of Financing Statement.

10.   Miscellaneous: Under certain circumstances, additional information not provided on Financing Statement may be required. Also, some states have non-uniform requirements. Use this space to provide such additional information or to comply with such requirements; otherwise, leave blank.

11.   If this Addendum adds an additional Debtor, complete item 11 in accordance with Instruction 1 of Financing Statement. To include further additional Debtors, attach either an additional Addendum (Form UCC1Ad) or Additional Party (Form UCC1AP) and follow Instruction 1 of Financing Statement for determining and formatting additional names.

12.   If this Addendum adds an additional Secured Party, complete item 12 in accordance with Instruction 3 of Financing Statement. To include further additional Secured Parties, attach either an additional Addendum (Form UCC1Ad) or Additional Party (Form UCC1AP) and follow Instruction 1 of Financing Statement for determining and formatting additional names. In the case of a total assignment of the Secured Party's interest before the filing of this Financing Statement, if filer has given the name and address of the Total Assignee in item 3 of Financing Statement, filer may give the Assignor S/P's name and address in item 12.

13-15.   If collateral is timber to be cut or as-extracted collateral, or if this Financing Statement is filed as a fixture filing, check appropriate box in item 13; provide description of real estate in item 14; and, if Debtor is not a record owner of the described real estate, also provide, in item 15, the name and address of a record owner. Also provide collateral description in item 4 of Financing Statement. Also check box 6 on Financing Statement. Description of real estate must be sufficient under the applicable law of the jurisdiction where the real estate is located.

16.   Use this space to provide continued description of collateral, if you cannot complete description in item 4 of Financing Statement.

17.   If Debtor is a trust or a trustee acting with respect to property held in trust or is a decedent's estate, check the appropriate box.

18.   If Debtor is a transmitting utility or if the Financing Statement relates to a Manufactured-Home Transaction or a Public-Finance Transaction as defined in the applicable Commercial Code, check the appropriate box.

UCC FINANCING STATEMENT
FOLLOW INSTRUCTIONS (front and back) CAREFULLY

A. NAME & PHONE OF CONTACT AT FILER [optional]

B. SEND ACKNOWLEDGMENT TO: (Name and Address)

THE ABOVE SPACE IS FOR FILING OFFICE USE ONLY

1. DEBTOR'S EXACT FULL LEGAL NAME - insert only one debtor name (1a or 1b) - do not abbreviate or combine names

1a. ORGANIZATION'S NAME

OR 1b. INDIVIDUAL'S LAST NAME | FIRST NAME | MIDDLE NAME | SUFFIX

1c. MAILING ADDRESS | CITY | STATE | POSTAL CODE | COUNTRY

1d. SEE INSTRUCTIONS | ADD'L INFO RE ORGANIZATION DEBTOR | 1e. TYPE OF ORGANIZATION | 1f. JURISDICTION OF ORGANIZATION | 1g. ORGANIZATIONAL ID #, if any | NONE

2. ADDITIONAL DEBTOR'S EXACT FULL LEGAL NAME - insert only one debtor name (2a or 2b) - do not abbreviate or combine names

2a. ORGANIZATION'S NAME

OR 2b. INDIVIDUAL'S LAST NAME | FIRST NAME | MIDDLE NAME | SUFFIX

2c. MAILING ADDRESS | CITY | STATE | POSTAL CODE | COUNTRY

2d. SEE INSTRUCTIONS | ADD'L INFO RE ORGANIZATION DEBTOR | 2e. TYPE OF ORGANIZATION | 2f. JURISDICTION OF ORGANIZATION | 2g. ORGANIZATIONAL ID #, if any | NONE

3. SECURED PARTY'S NAME (or NAME of TOTAL ASSIGNEE of ASSIGNOR S/P) - insert only one secured party name (3a or 3b)

3a. ORGANIZATION'S NAME

OR 3b. INDIVIDUAL'S LAST NAME | FIRST NAME | MIDDLE NAME | SUFFIX

3c. MAILING ADDRESS | CITY | STATE | POSTAL CODE | COUNTRY

4. This FINANCING STATEMENT covers the following collateral:

5. ALTERNATIVE DESIGNATION [if applicable]: LESSEE/LESSOR CONSIGNEE/CONSIGNOR BAILEE/BAILOR SELLER/BUYER AG. LIEN NON-UCC FILING
6. This FINANCING STATEMENT is to be filed [for record] (or recorded) in the REAL ESTATE RECORDS. Attach Addendum [if applicable] 7. Check to REQUEST SEARCH REPORT(S) on Debtor(s) [ADDITIONAL FEE] [optional] All Debtors Debtor 1 Debtor 2
8. OPTIONAL FILER REFERENCE DATA

FILING OFFICE COPY — UCC FINANCING STATEMENT (FORM UCC1) (REV. 05/22/02)

212

UCC FINANCING STATEMENT **ADDENDUM**

FOLLOW INSTRUCTIONS (front and back) CAREFULLY

9. NAME OF FIRST DEBTOR (1a or 1b) ON RELATED FINANCING STATEMENT

	9a. ORGANIZATION'S NAME

OR

9b. INDIVIDUAL'S LAST NAME	FIRST NAME	MIDDLE NAME, SUFFIX

10. MISCELLANEOUS:

THE ABOVE SPACE IS FOR FILING OFFICE USE ONLY

11. ADDITIONAL DEBTOR'S EXACT FULL LEGAL NAME - insert only <u>one</u> name (11a or 11b) - do not abbreviate or combine names

	11a. ORGANIZATION'S NAME			

OR

11b. INDIVIDUAL'S LAST NAME	FIRST NAME	MIDDLE NAME	SUFFIX

11c. MAILING ADDRESS	CITY	STATE	POSTAL CODE	COUNTRY

11d. <u>SEE INSTRUCTIONS</u>	ADD'L INFO RE ORGANIZATION DEBTOR	11e. TYPE OF ORGANIZATION	11f. JURISDICTION OF ORGANIZATION	11g. ORGANIZATIONAL ID #, if any
				☐ NONE

12. ☐ ADDITIONAL SECURED PARTY'S <u>or</u> ☐ ASSIGNOR S/P'S NAME - insert only <u>one</u> name (12a or 12b)

	12a. ORGANIZATION'S NAME			

OR

12b. INDIVIDUAL'S LAST NAME	FIRST NAME	MIDDLE NAME	SUFFIX

12c. MAILING ADDRESS	CITY	STATE	POSTAL CODE	COUNTRY

13. This FINANCING STATEMENT covers ☐ timber to be cut or ☐ as-extracted collateral, or is filed as a ☐ fixture filing.

14. Description of real estate:

16. Additional collateral description:

15. Name and address of a RECORD OWNER of above-described real estate (if Debtor does not have a record interest):

17. Check <u>only</u> if applicable and check <u>only</u> one box.

Debtor is a ☐ Trust or ☐ Trustee acting with respect to property held in trust or ☐ Decedent's Estate

18. Check <u>only</u> if applicable and check <u>only</u> one box.

☐ Debtor is a TRANSMITTING UTILITY

☐ Filed in connection with a Manufactured-Home Transaction — effective 30 years

☐ Filed in connection with a Public-Finance Transaction — effective 30 years

FILING OFFICE COPY — UCC FINANCING STATEMENT ADDENDUM (FORM UCC1Ad) (REV. 05/22/02)

Instructions for UCC Financing Statement Amendment (Form UCC3)

Please type or laser-print this form. Be sure it is completely legible. Read all Instructions, especially Instruction 1a; correct file number of initial financing statement is crucial. Follow Instructions completely.

Fill in form very carefully; mistakes may have important legal consequences. If you have questions, consult your attorney. Filing office cannot give legal advice.

Do not insert anything in the open space in the upper portion of this form; it is reserved for filing office use.

An Amendment may relate to only one financing statement. Do not enter more than one file number in item 1a.

When properly completed, send Filing Office Copy, with required fee, to filing office. If you want an acknowledgment, complete item B and, if filing in a filing office that returns an acknowledgment copy furnished by filer, you may also send Acknowledgment Copy, otherwise detach. Always detach Debtor and Secured Party Copies.

If you need to use attachments, you are encouraged to use either Amendment Addendum (Form UCC3Ad) or Amendment Additional Party (Form UCC3AP). Always complete items 1a and 9.

A. To assist filing offices that might wish to communicate with filer, filer may provide information in item A. This item is optional.

B. Complete item B if you want an acknowledgment sent to you. If filing in a filing office that returns an acknowledgment copy furnished by filer, present simultaneously with this form a carbon or other copy of this form for use as an acknowledgment copy.

1a. **File number:** Enter file number of initial financing statement to which this Amendment relates. Enter only one file number. In some states, the file number is not unique; in those states, also enter in item 1a, after the file number, the date that the initial financing statement was filed.

1b. Only if this Amendment is to be filed or recorded in the real estate records, check box 1b and also, in item 13 of Amendment Addendum, enter Debtor's name, in proper format exactly identical to the format of item 1 of financing statement, and name of record owner if Debtor does not have a record interest.

Note: Show purpose of this Amendment by checking box 2, 3, 4, 5 (in item 5 you must check two boxes) or 8; also complete items 6, 7 and/or 8 as appropriate. Filer may use this Amendment form to simultaneously accomplish both data changes (items 4, 5, and/or 8) and a Continuation (item 3), although in some states filer may have to pay a separate fee for each purpose.

2. To terminate the effectiveness of the identified financing statement with respect to security interest(s) of authorizing Secured Party, check box 2. See Instruction 9 below.

3. To continue the effectiveness of the identified financing statement with respect to security interest(s) of authorizing Secured Party, check box 3. See Instruction 9 below.

4. To assign (i) all of assignor's interest under the identified financing statement, or (ii) a partial interest in the security interest covered by the identified financing statement, or (iii) assignor's full interest in some (but not all) of the collateral covered by the identified financing statement: Check box in item 4 and enter name of assignee in item 7a if assignee is an organization, or in item 7b, formatted as indicated, if assignee is an individual. Complete 7a or 7b, but not both. Also enter assignee's address in item 7c. Also enter name of assignor in item 9. If partial Assignment affects only some (but not all) of the collateral covered by the identified financing statement, filer may check appropriate box in item 8 and indicate affected collateral in item 8.

5,6,7.To change the name of a party: Check box in item 5 to indicate whether this Amendment amends information relating to a Debtor or a Secured Party; also check box in item 5 to indicate that this is a name change; also enter name of affected party (current record name) in item 6a or 6b as appropriate; and enter new name (7a or 7b). If the new name refers to a Debtor complete (7c); also complete 7e-7g if 7a was completed.

5,6,7.To change the address of a party: Check box in item 5 to indicate whether this Amendment amends information relating to a Debtor or a Secured Party; also check box in item 5 to indicate that this is an address change; also enter name of affected party (current record name) in item 6a or 6b as appropriate; and enter new address (7c) in item 7.

5,6,7.To change the name and address of a party: Check box in item 5 to indicate whether this Amendment amends information relating to a Debtor or a Secured Party; also check box in item 5 to indicate that this is a name/address change; also enter name of affected party (current record name) in items 6a or 6b as appropriate; and enter the new name (7a or 7b). If the new name refers to a Debtor complete item 7c; also complete 7e-7g if 7a was completed.

5,6. To delete a party: Check box in item 5 to indicate whether deleting a Debtor or a Secured Party; also check box in item 5 to indicate that this is a deletion of a party; and also enter name (6a or 6b) of deleted party in item 6.

5,7. To add a party: Check box in item 5 to indicate whether adding a Debtor or Secured Party; also check box in item 5 to indicate that this is an addition of a party and enter the new name (7a or 7b). If the new name refers to a Debtor complete item 7c; also complete 7e-7g if 7a was completed. To include further additional Debtors or Secured Parties, attach Amendment Additional Party (Form UCC3AP), using correct name format.

Note: The preferred method for filing against a new Debtor (an individual or organization not previously of record as a Debtor under this file number) is to file a new Financing Statement (UCC1) and not an Amendment (UCC3).

7d. Reserved for Financing Statement Amendments to be filed in North Dakota or South Dakota only. If this Financing Statement Amendment is to be filed in North Dakota or South Dakota, the Debtor's taxpayer identification number (tax ID#) — social security number or employer identification number must be placed in this box.

8. Collateral change. To change the collateral covered by the identified financing statement, describe the change in item 8. This may be accomplished either by describing the collateral to be added or deleted, or by setting forth in full the collateral description as it is to be effective after the filing of this Amendment, indicating clearly the method chosen (check the appropriate box). If the space in item 8 is insufficient, use item 13 of Amendment Addendum (Form UCC3Ad). A partial release of collateral is a deletion. If, due to a full release of all collateral, filer no longer claims a security interest under the identified financing statement, check box 2 (Termination) and not box 8 (Collateral Change). If a partial assignment consists of the assignment of some (but not all) of the collateral covered by the identified financing statement, filer may indicate the assigned collateral in item 8, check the appropriate box in item 8, and also comply with instruction 4 above.

9. Always enter name of party of record authorizing this Amendment; in most cases, this will be a Secured Party of record. If more than one authorizing Secured Party, give additional name(s), properly formatted, in item 13 of Amendment Addendum (Form UCC3Ad). If the indicated financing statement refers to the parties as lessee and lessor, or consignee and consignor, or seller and buyer, instead of Debtor and Secured Party, references in this Amendment shall be deemed likewise so to refer to the parties. If this is an assignment, enter assignor's name. If this is an Amendment authorized by a Debtor that adds collateral or adds a Debtor, or if this is a Termination authorized by a Debtor, check the box in item 9 and enter the name, properly formatted, of the Debtor authorizing this Amendment, and, if this Amendment or Termination is to be filed or recorded in the real estate records, also enter, in item 13 of Amendment Addendum, name of Secured Party of record.

10. This item is optional and is for filer's use only. For filer's convenience of reference, filer may enter in item 10 any identifying information (e.g., Secured Party's loan number, law firm file number, Debtor's name or other identification, state in which form is being filed, etc.) that filer may find useful.

Instructions for National UCC Financing Statement AMENDMENT Addendum (Form UCC3Ad)

11.   Enter information exactly as given in item 1a on Amendment form.

12.   Enter information exactly as given in item 9 on Amendment form.

13.   If space on Amendment form is insufficient or you must provide additional information, enter additional information in item 13.

UCC FINANCING STATEMENT **AMENDMENT**

FOLLOW INSTRUCTIONS (front and back) CAREFULLY

A. NAME & PHONE OF CONTACT AT FILER [optional]

B. SEND ACKNOWLEDGMENT TO: (Name and Address)

THE ABOVE SPACE IS FOR FILING OFFICE USE ONLY

1a. INITIAL FINANCING STATEMENT FILE #	1b. ☐ This FINANCING STATEMENT AMENDMENT is to be filed [for record] (or recorded) in the REAL ESTATE RECORDS.

2. ☐ **TERMINATION:** Effectiveness of the Financing Statement identified above is terminated with respect to security interest(s) of the Secured Party authorizing this Termination Statement.

3. ☐ **CONTINUATION:** Effectiveness of the Financing Statement identified above with respect to security interest(s) of the Secured Party authorizing this Continuation Statement is continued for the additional period provided by applicable law.

4. ☐ **ASSIGNMENT** (full or partial): Give name of assignee in item 7a or 7b and address of assignee in item 7c; and also give name of assignor in item 9.

5. **AMENDMENT (PARTY INFORMATION):** This Amendment affects ☐ Debtor _or_ ☐ Secured Party of record. Check only _one_ of these two boxes.

Also check _one_ of the following three boxes _and_ provide appropriate information in items 6 and/or 7.

☐ CHANGE name and/or address: Please refer to the detailed instructions in regards to changing the name/address of a party.   ☐ DELETE name: Give record name to be deleted in item 6a or 6b.   ☐ ADD name: Complete item 7a or 7b, and also item 7c; also complete items 7e-7g (if applicable).

6. CURRENT RECORD INFORMATION:

	6a. ORGANIZATION'S NAME			
OR	6b. INDIVIDUAL'S LAST NAME	FIRST NAME	MIDDLE NAME	SUFFIX

7. CHANGED (NEW) OR ADDED INFORMATION:

	7a. ORGANIZATION'S NAME			
OR	7b. INDIVIDUAL'S LAST NAME	FIRST NAME	MIDDLE NAME	SUFFIX

7c. MAILING ADDRESS	CITY	STATE	POSTAL CODE	COUNTRY

7d. SEE INSTRUCTIONS	ADD'L INFO RE ORGANIZATION DEBTOR	7e. TYPE OF ORGANIZATION	7f. JURISDICTION OF ORGANIZATION	7g. ORGANIZATIONAL ID #, if any ☐ NONE

8. **AMENDMENT (COLLATERAL CHANGE):** check only _one_ box.

Describe collateral ☐ deleted or ☐ added, or give entire ☐ restated collateral description, or describe collateral ☐ assigned.

9. **NAME** OF **SECURED PARTY** OF RECORD AUTHORIZING THIS AMENDMENT (name of assignor, if this is an Assignment). If this is an Amendment authorized by a Debtor which adds collateral or adds the authorizing Debtor, or if this is a Termination authorized by a Debtor, check here ☐ and enter name of **DEBTOR** authorizing this Amendment.

	9a. ORGANIZATION'S NAME			
OR	9b. INDIVIDUAL'S LAST NAME	FIRST NAME	MIDDLE NAME	SUFFIX

10. OPTIONAL FILER REFERENCE DATA

FILING OFFICE COPY — UCC FINANCING STATEMENT AMENDMENT (FORM UCC3) (REV. 05/22/02)

216

UCC FINANCING STATEMENT AMENDMENT ADDENDUM

FOLLOW INSTRUCTIONS (front and back) CAREFULLY

11. INITIAL FINANCING STATEMENT FILE # (same as item 1a on Amendment form)

12. NAME OF PARTY AUTHORIZING THIS AMENDMENT (same as item 9 on Amendment form)

	12a. ORGANIZATION'S NAME		
OR	12b. INDIVIDUAL'S LAST NAME	FIRST NAME	MIDDLE NAME,SUFFIX

13. Use this space for additional information

THE ABOVE SPACE IS FOR FILING OFFICE USE ONLY

RECEIPT FOR PERSONAL PROPERTY

The undersigned hereby certifies and acknowledges that on _____, 20____, he/she received from _____ the following personal property:

The purpose for which such items were received was _____.

These items shall be returned _____

In consideration for use of the property, the undersigned agrees to be fully responsible for its use and to hold the owner harmless from any claims resulting from the undersigned's use of the property. The undersigned understands that the owner has made no representations or warranties as to the condition of the property or its fitness for any use.

_____

Chapter 6:
Real Estate Forms

The purchase or sale of real estate is a major financial transaction. If you have not done it before, you should be represented by an attorney or broker. Keep in mind that a real estate agent or broker works on commission.

While traditionally a real estate broker has been paid by and responsible to the seller, a *buyer's broker* is a real estate broker who represents the buyer. This can offer more protection to a new buyer. One who comes recommended by other happy buyers will probably be good to work with.

Some people think that if they are getting a loan, the bank will make sure that the real estate papers are right. You must keep in mind that the bank is looking out for its own interest, and that is not always the same as yours.

There are many types of problems that only an experienced investor or attorney would notice. For example, beachfront property might have a strip of land owned by someone else blocking access to the beach; a utility easement might run through the middle of the house; the house you looked at might not actually be on the lot you are buying; deed restrictions might prevent you from building what you want on the property; or, the deed might not include all the property you expected. All of these are actual examples of what happens at some real estate closings. Some of them are things that a broker or bank would not notice or care about. Until you are able to notice problems like this in the closing papers, you should have a real estate attorney review the papers when you are buying property.

If you find property you really want, you should tell an attorney that you want it. If there are problems with it, tell the attorney you would prefer to solve them than to walk away.

Buying and Selling Real Estate

The seller in a real estate transaction has less concerns than the buyer. If the buyer fails to pay, then the seller wants to be protected so that the property is returned in good condition.

Another concern for the seller is not to have any responsibilities after the sale. This means a seller usually does not want to guarantee anything to help avoid getting sued if the buyer is not happy about something with the property. The ancient principle *caveat emptor*—buyer beware—has been changed in most states in recent years to "seller beware." Today sellers are often expected to disclose to the buyer problems with the property, even if not asked. Real estate agents often demand disclosures from sellers before listing a property to protect themselves from lawsuits by buyers. Legally, real estate agents are not liable if a seller lies on the disclosure. Only the seller is liable.

Real Estate Contract

Most buyers of real estate do not realize the importance of the initial contract. They sign a contract with no legal advice and then hire an attorney for the closing. But if the contract is not prepared right, there is little the attorney can do. One way to protect yourself is to add a clause to the contract such as:

subject to approval of buyer's attorney.

Unless you understand every clause of a real estate contract, you should not sign it without some guidance. Once you have done a few transactions, you may be comfortable enough to handle most of the legal issues yourself. A sample **REAL ESTATE SALES CONTRACT** is included. (see form 66, p.235.) Keep in mind that real estate transactions are covered by state law, and your state might have some local requirements. The best way to learn the local requirements is to get a sample contract from an attorney or real estate broker. Keep in mind that both of these may include clauses that are not required by law. Usually, an office supply store is not a good place to get a contract because most of them stock only bare bones national forms that do not include any state requirements. A sample of how to fill in a real estate contract is included below.

Sample: **Real Estate Sales Contract**

REAL ESTATE SALES CONTRACT

Date: June 6, 2005

PARTIES: Jon Dough as "Buyer"
of _____ Phone: (123) 456-7890 and
Mary Smith as "Seller"
of _____ Phone: (987) 654-3210 hereby
agree that the Buyer shall buy and the Seller shall sell real property described below under the following terms and conditions:

Street Address: 6 Hilltop Lane, Mytown, USA

continued

Legal Description:

Lot 1, Shady Oaks Subdivision according to the plat recorded in Plat Book 6, Page 12, Public Records of Harrison County

1. PURCHASE PRICE: The full purchase price shall be $ __$100,000__ payable as follows:

a) Deposit held in escrow by __Acme Title Co.__ $ __$2,000.00__

b) New mortgage* to be obtained by Buyer __within 30 days__ _____
$ __$80,000.00__

c) Subject to [ ] , or assumption of [ ] mortgage* to _____ with interest rate of _____%, payable $_____ per month, having an approximate balance of $_____

d) Mortgage* and Note to be held by seller at _____% interest payable _____ for _____ years in the amount of $_____

e) Other _____
_____ $_____

f) Balance to close (U.S. cash, certified or cashier's check) subject to adjustments and prorations, plus closing costs $ __$18,000.00__

Total.. $ __$100,000__

*or deed of trust

1. FINANCING: Contingent upon Buyer obtaining a firm commitment for a mortgage loan for a minimum of $ __$80,000.00__ at a maximum interest rate of _____% for a term of at least __8__ years. Buyer agrees to make application for and use reasonable diligence to obtain said loan.

~~2. EXISTING MORTGAGES: Seller represents to Buyer that the existing mortgage on the property is held by _____ and bears interest at _____% per annum with monthly payments of $_____ principal and interest plus $_____ for escrow. Said loan is fully assumable under the following terms:~~
_____
_____

3. CLOSING DATE & PLACE: Closing shall be on __August 1__ , __2005__ at the office of the attorney or title agent selected by Seller.

4. ACCEPTANCE: If this contract is not executed by both parties on or before __June 7__ , __2005__ it shall be void and Buyer's deposit returned.

5. PERSONAL PROPERTY: This sale includes all personal property listed on Schedule A. The parties agree that the portion of the purchase price attributable to these items is $ __$2,000.00__ to provide access for inspection upon reasonable notice.

NOTE: *Federal law requires that a* **Lead Paint Disclosure** *form be completed by the buyer and seller of property built before 1978. (see form 75, p.255.)*

Real Estate Deed

A *deed* is a document that formally transfers title or ownership of property. There are several types of deeds in regular use. In most cases, you probably need a **Warranty Deed** in which the seller guarantees, among other things, that the seller has good title to the property, and that, after selling it, the buyer will have good title. (see form 67, p.239.) A warranty deed is special because of language such as the following:

> *To have and to hold such property together with all rights and appurtenances thereto belonging. The grantor is seized of the premises in fee simple and has the right to convey the same in fee simple clear of all encumbrances, and the grantor hereby covenants to warrant and forever defend title to the property against the lawful claims of all persons whomsoever except for the exceptions above stated.*

An alternative deed, and the type you would prefer to use if you are the seller, is the **Quitclaim Deed**. (see form 68, p.241.) It merely says that the seller sells to the buyer whatever the seller owns, if anything, with no guarantees. Quitclaim deeds have their uses, but you should not buy property relying on a quitclaim deed alone. It is unlikely that a knowledgeable person would accept one from you.

These days, most deeds are fill-in-the-blank forms. Each state has its own preferred form. The forms in this book should suffice in most states, but check with your recorder of deeds for any special local requirements.

Transfers of real property are usually acknowledged and made under seal. They are within the *Statute of Frauds* and must be in *writing*. (see Chapter 1.) Since real property cannot be literally handed over to the buyer, recording of deeds is critical. It is the way you prove your ownership, as well as the way you prevent someone else from purporting to sell the property that belongs to you.

As always, the signatures on options, contracts for purchase and sale, and deeds must be appropriate for the situation, depending upon whether the property owner is an individual, married couple, partnership, corporation, etc. (See the section on signatures in Chapter 1.)

Financing Real Estate

Since few people pay cash for real estate, the transfer usually includes a loan transaction. The buyer borrows money, usually from a bank or the seller, and signs papers pledging the real estate as a guarantee of payment of the loan.

Mortgage or Deed of Trust

This is usually done with a *mortgage*, although some states use a document called a *deed of trust*. A mortgage or deed of trust will describe the real estate, refer to the promissory note it secures, and have numerous provisions relating to what happens if the promissory note goes into default.

If your property is being mortgaged, the lender on the promissory note will probably prepare the mortgage documents. If you are going to take a mortgage to secure money someone owes to you, you will need to prepare the documents. Since the form for a mortgage and the requirements for its execution and recording vary from state to state, no useful form can be provided in a book like this. Mortgage forms or *Deed of Trust* forms can usually be obtained from an office supply store, or possibly from a real estate agent, bank, or mortgage company.

If you hold a mortgage, you may want to sell it to another party. To do so, you will need to execute an ASSIGNMENT OF MORTGAGE. (see form 69, p.243.) If you hold the mortgage until it is paid off, you will need to execute a SATISFACTION OF MORTGAGE. (see form 70, p.245.)

Real Estate Options

An *option* is a kind of contract within a contract. It is an agreement to keep an offer *open* for a period of time in exchange for some consideration—such as money. As always in a contract, the consideration part is important. It must be real and not just a formal recital. Otherwise, you might find that you do not have an option at all. Options may be recorded just as deeds. Recording will protect the party with the option from subsequent claims, but it may also trigger a *due on sale* clause in some mortgages. An OPTION AGREEMENT form is included. (see form 71, p.247.)

The *optionor* is the person granting the option to someone and the *optionee* is the person getting the option to buy the property. One common mistake with options is for the *optionee* to neglect to follow the terms of the option. If the seller is eager to sell the property, this might not matter. If the seller would rather keep the property and the option money, forgetting to follow the terms of the option (such as giving notice prior to the end) could cause the optionee to lose all rights. To help prevent this, use the EXERCISE OF OPTION form. (see form 72, p.249.)

Leasing and Renting Real Estate

A *lease* or *rental agreement* is the document that grants the right to temporary possession of real estate. Although it transfers an interest in real estate, as does a deed, a lease is very different. Deeds are usually quite short. Leases are usually quite long. Deeds look very much alike, while leases vary tremendously depending upon the type and function of the property being leased.

If you go into the rental business by investing in real estate, you should get a good lease form to use with your tenants and be sure that you understand every clause of it. In the beginning, you may wish to get the advice of an attorney. The best way to find one who is both knowledgeable about real estate and charges reasonable fees is to join a local landlords' association. Many of these clubs are mostly small-time landlords who can give you valuable advice about the business and legalities of renting real estate.

If you do not plan to get so deeply into rentals, and only occasionally need to do so, such as when you are transferred out of town and need to rent out your home, you should still consider getting legal advice. Your home is probably the most valuable piece of property you own. By renting your home to someone, you risk damage to it.

Rental Application

The first thing you should do when renting is screen the tenants carefully. Get permission to get a copy of their credit report and check their references. Do not just check with their current landlord—he or she may be eager to get rid of them. Ask one or two past landlords if they took care of the property. Use a **RENTAL APPLICATION** to gather information about prospective tenants. (see form 73, p.251.)

Property Inspections

One big issue between landlords and tenants is the condition of the property when the tenant leaves versus when the tenant moved in. By doing a room-by-room inspection before and after the tenancy, you can have a more accurate record of what damage was done by the tenant. An **INSPECTION REPORT** can be used for this purpose. (see form 74, p.253.) Taking photos is also important if you need to go to court.

Lead-Based Paint

Whenever you lease property built before 1978, you are required to give the tenant a **DISCLOSURE OF INFORMATION ON LEAD-BASED PAINT AND/OR LEAD-BASED PAINT HAZARDS.** (see form 75, p.255.) You are also required to give the tenant a copy of the ten page booklet, *Protect Your Family from Lead in Your Home.* This can be obtained by phone by calling 800-424-5323 or on the Internet at:

www.epa.gov/opptintr/lead/leadprot.htm

Lease Agreement

Forms are included in the appendix for leasing property. Two **House Leases** are included—one that can be used for renting a single family home for a **Set Term** (see form 76, p.257) and one on a **Month-to-Month** basis. (see form 77, p.261.) Two **Apartment Rental Agreements** are included—one that can be used to rent a room or apartment on a **Set Term** (see form 78, p.265) and one on a month-to-month basis. (see form 79, p.269.)

Your state might require clauses or *riders* relating to matters such as security deposits, lead-based paints, and radon testing not included in those forms. The failure to include one of these required clauses could render the lease unenforceable or create some kind of penalty for the land-lord. Check with a knowledgeable real estate agent or attorney. You can add them to the lease by using an addendum.

As a tenant, you will usually be offered a lease on a *take it or leave it* basis by a landlord. If the landlord is desperate to get a tenant, you may be able to negotiate more favorable terms. If you do so, these should always be in writing. Verbal agreements are usually not enforceable when you have a written agreement to the contrary.

Pets

If the tenant has pets or wants to get a pet in the future, a **Pet Agreement** can be used to identify what will or will not be allowed. (see form 80, p.273.) An additional deposit may also be request-ed by the landlord to cover damages caused by the pets.

Amendment to Lease

If there is no way to fit all of your changes onto the landlord's lease form, you can use an **Amendment to Lease Agreement**. (see form 81, p.275.)

Sample: **Amendment to Lease Agreement**

AMENDMENT TO LEASE AGREEMENT

For valuable consideration, the receipt and sufficiency of which is hereby acknowledged by each of the parties, this agreement amends a lease agreement (the "Lease") between ___Jon Dough_____ (the "Landlord") and ___Jane Rowe_____ (the "Tenant") dated _____, relating to property located at _____ __9 Shady Lane, Mytown, USA_____. This agreement is hereby incorporated into the Lease

continued...

---

1. Paragraph 5 of the Lease is hereby amended to read in its entirety as follows:

> 5. Assignment. The Tenant shall not assign this Agreement or sublet the Premises in whole or in part without the written consent of the Landlord.

2. Paragraph 20.3 of the Lease is hereby deleted in its entirety.

3. There is hereby added to the Lease a new paragraph number 9.4 which shall read in its entirety as follows:

> 9.4. Provide the Tenant with 10 designated and sign-posted parking spaces in the center parking lot.

Except as changed by this amendment, the Lease shall continue in effect according to its terms. The amendments herein shall be effective on the date this document is executed by both parties.

Executed on ___May 1, 2006_____.

___*Jon Dough*___ (Seal)   ___*Jane Rowe*___ (Seal)

_____ (Seal)   _____ (Seal)

Lease Assignments and Subleases

Chapter 1 discussed the assignment of contracts. From the tenant's point of view, assigning a lease means moving out and finding a new tenant. When a landlord assigns a lease, it is usually when the building is sold.

In a **Lease Assignment** by a tenant, the new tenant steps into the shoes of the old tenant and deals with the landlord directly. (see form 82, p.277.) If all goes well, the old tenant is out of the picture. Remember that, while a tenant can assign his or her right to use the property, he or she can only delegate the duty to pay rent. This means that, absent an agreement by the landlord, the old tenant always remains ultimately responsible for payment of the rent if the lease assignee fails to do so.

A sublease is quite different from an assignment. In a *sublease*, the old tenant stands between the landlord and the subtenant. In essence, the tenant becomes the landlord to the subtenant. The subtenant will pay rent to the old tenant, who will then pay rent to the landlord. The subtenant may pay more rent to the tenant than the tenant will pay to landlord, leaving the tenant a profit. A sublease is actually a special type of lease and is just as complex as a lease. The failure to include certain provisions required by a state or local law can invalidate a sublease; therefore, you should consult an attorney or a book specifically about leases before preparing or signing one. Because of the variety of state and local leasing laws, it is not practical to provide a sublease form in this book.

Almost every written lease agreement will require the landlord's permission and **CONSENT TO SUBLEASE** before the tenant can validly assign the lease or sublet the premises. (see form 83, p.279.) Examples of a **LEASE ASSIGNMENT** and a **CONSENT TO SUBLEASE** follow. The sample form makes the landlord the party giving consent to an assignment. (As stated earlier, an assignment may or may not release the original tenant from further liability to the landlord, so be sure to note the optional language for paragraph 4 in the example.)

Sample: **Lease Assignment**

LEASE ASSIGNMENT

This Lease Assignment is entered into by and among __Jane Rowe_____
(the "Assignor"), __Freddie Foe_____ (the "Assignee"), and
__Jon Dough_____ (the "Landlord"). For valuable consideration, it is agreed by the parties as follows:

1. The Landlord and the Assignor have entered into a lease agreement (the "Lease") dated __May 1, 2006_____ concerning the premises described as:

    1264 Main Street, #24, Decatur, Georgia.

2. The Assignor hereby assigns, transfers, and delivers to the Assignee all of Assignor's rights and delegates all of Assignor's duties under the Lease effective on __September 1, 2006_____ (the "Effective Date").

3. The Assignee hereby accepts such assignment of rights and delegation of duties and agrees to pay all rents promptly when due and perform all of Assignor's obligations under the Lease accruing on and after the Effective Date. The Assignee further agrees to indemnify and hold the Assignor harmless from any breach of Assignee's duties hereunder.

4. ❏   The Assignor agrees to transfer possession of the leased premises to the Assignee on the Effective Date. All rents and obligations of the Assignor under the Lease accruing before the Effective Date shall have been paid or discharged as of the Effective Date.

continued...

❑   The Landlord hereby assents to the assignment of the Lease hereunder and as of the Effective Date hereby releases and discharges the Assignor from all duties and obligations under the Lease accruing after the Effective Date.

❑   The Landlord hereby assents to the assignment of the Lease hereunder provided that the Landlord's assent hereunder shall not discharge the Assignor of his or her obligations under the Lease in the event of breach by the Assignee. The Landlord will give notice to the Assignor of any such breach by the Assignee, and, provided the Assignor pays all accrued rents and cures any other default of the Assignee, the Assignor may enforce the terms of the Lease and this Assignment against the Assignee, in the name of the Landlord, if necessary.

5. There shall be no further assignment of the Lease without the written consent of the Landlord.

6. This agreement shall be binding upon and inure to the benefit of the parties, their successors, assigns, and personal representatives.

This assignment was executed under seal on __May 1, 2006_____.

Sample: **Landlord's Consent to Sublease**

LANDLORD'S CONSENT TO SUBLEASE

FOR VALUABLE CONSIDERATION, the undersigned (the "Landlord") hereby consents to the sublease of all or part of the premises located at __9 Shady Lane, Mytown, USA____
__Jane Rowe_____, which is the subject of a lease agreement between Landlord and _____ (the "Tenant"), pursuant to an Agreement to Sublease dated __May 1, 2006_____, between the Tenant and __Freddie Foe_____ as Subtenant dated __May 1, 2006_____.

This consent was signed by the Landlord on __May 1, 2006_____.

Roommates

Getting a roommate can be a great way to afford a much better place to live. Usually a $1,000 place is more than twice as big as two $500 places, as you do not have to duplicate the kitchen and bath facilities.

When searching for a roommate, be sure to check him or her out as thoroughly as possible. If you can visit where he or she presently lives, you can see the living conditions. If you can talk with the current landlord or neighbors, you can find out if he or she is a good tenant.

One thing to keep in mind when renting a place with other roommates is that the lease you sign will probably make each of you liable for the full rent. That means that if your roommates stop paying the rent after the first month, you can be sued for the full amount of rent for the full term.

One way to protect yourself is to have an agreement with your roommates that they can be evicted for not paying rent and that you can sue them in a small claims court for it. Such an agreement will not stop the landlord from suing you, but it may give you leverage against your roommates. A **ROOMMATE AGREEMENT** is included. (see form 84, p.281.) A sample of how to fill it out follows.

Sample: **Roommate Agreement**

ROOMMATE AGREEMENT

The undersigned, intending to share a dwelling unit located at _____446 Main St._____
____Mayberry, USA____, in consideration of the mutual promises contained in this agreement, agree as follows:

1. They shall share the unit as follows: _____Mary Cunningham gets north bedroom,_____
_Joan Peterson gets south bedroom_____

_____

2. Rent shall be paid as follows: _$400 each_____

_____

3. Each party shall be responsible for his/her own long distance and toll charges on the telephone bill(s) regardless of whose name the bill is in.

4. The other utilities and fees shall be paid as follows: _water, electricity, gas, trash—_
_50% each. cable tv—25% by Mary, 75% by Joan_____

5. No party is obligated to pay another party's share of the rent or other bills, but in the event one party finds it necessary to pay a bill for another party to stop eviction or termination of service, the party paying shall have the right to reimbursement in full plus a $_20_ charge. In the event the nonpaying party fails to reimburse such amounts, the paying party shall be entitled to interest at the highest legal rate, attorneys' fees, and court costs if legal action is necessary.

continued...

---

6. The parties also agree:

Smoking ___only outside_____

Overnight guests ___only on weekends (Friday and Saturday)_____

7. The parties agree to respect each other's privacy, to keep the shared areas reasonably clean, not to make unreasonable noise during normal sleeping hours, not to leave food where it would invite infestation, and to be courteous and considerate of the other's needs. They agree that if their guests do not follow these rules, such guests shall not be permitted in the unit. They further agree not to do anything which violates the lease and could cause eviction.

One way to avoid the risk of being liable for your roommates' share(s) of the rent is to have a lease that only makes you responsible for your share. For example, it would state that you are to pay $400 per month, roommate A is to pay $400 per month, and roommate B is to pay $400 per month. Unless there is another clause in the lease that states that you are liable for the others' rent, this would protect you. Unfortunately, most landlords will not go for such an arrangement because they do not want just to evict one roommate.

Another way to protect yourself is to rent the place in your own name and then sublease rooms to roommates. That way, you could evict them and replace them if they violated the terms of the sublease with you. To do this, you would need your lease with the landlord to allow you to have subtenants. In this arrangement you would still be liable for the full rent, but you would have control over your roommates' stay.

Tenant Maintenance Problems

Occasionally a tenant of a home or apartment will have a maintenance problem that is not repaired promptly. Depending upon the type and severity of the problem, the tenant may be allowed to fix the problem and deduct the cost from rent, decrease the rent paid, or move out.

The tenant's rights are determined by state laws that are usually specific as to how and when the tenant can take these actions. It is important to follow state law precisely before taking any action. Therefore, you should obtain a copy of your state's landlord/tenant act. You can usually get it from your state legislator, a local housing official, or you can photocopy it at your local library.

In all cases a tenant should give written notice to the landlord of the problem at the earliest possible time. A **NOTICE TO LANDLORD TO MAKE REPAIRS** can be used for this purpose. (see form 85, p.283.) However, be sure to check your state statute to be sure you include everything necessary. In most cases, it must be sent by certified mail.

Expiring Leases

At the end of a lease term, it is a good idea for a landlord to contact the tenant to determine what his or her future plans are. If the tenant wishes to stay and the landlord agrees, a new lease can be signed. To learn the intention of tenants, a landlord can send an ANNUAL LETTER—CONTINUATION OF TENANCY to the tenant. (see form 86, p.285.) If a landlord does not wish to keep the tenant, then a LETTER TO VACATING TENANT can be used to notify the tenant that the landlord does not intend to renew the lease. (see form 87, p.287.) It also directs the tenant to vacate the premises at the expiration of the lease term and return the keys to the landlord.

In some states tenants are assumed to renew their leases unless they give notice to the landlord that they are moving out at the end of the lease. This notice must be given within a set time such as fifteen or thirty days or more. You should check your state's law to be sure you comply. The NOTICE OF INTENT TO VACATE AT END OF LEASE can be used for this purpose unless your state requires a special form. (see form 88, p.289.)

Security Deposits

Many landlords are not eager to return a tenant's security deposit, and some may hope the tenant forgets about it. To make sure your landlord remembers to have it ready for you when you move out, you should use the DEMAND FOR RETURN OF SECURITY DEPOSIT. (see form 89, p.291.)

Be sure to check your state's laws regarding security deposits. Some states allow the landlord to wait fifteen or thirty days before returning it (in order to examine and repair any damages to the unit). Some states require the landlord to pay the tenant's attorney fees if the deposit is illegally kept or if the landlord forgets to send the tenant the proper notice that it is being kept.

Waiver and Assumption of Risk

One risk of being a landlord is the potential for lawsuits. You could be the target of one of these lawsuits if someone is injured on your property. The first way to protect yourself is to have insurance. Many awards, however, are well in excess of insurance limits.

Another step you can take to protect yourself is to require anyone engaging in risky or dangerous behavior on your property to sign a WAIVER AND ASSUMPTION OF RISK. (see form 90, p.293.) This is a document in which a person agrees that in exchange for the right to use your property, they agree not to sue you if they are injured. However, such an agreement would probably not work if you did something negligent or if there was some hidden danger on your property. If the person was just injured or killed doing some normal activity on your property, you might be protected. Sometimes, you might use such a form if you have rural property and you allow people to hunt, fish, or swim on it. You might also use such a form if you let neighbors use your swimming pool, trampoline, or other dangerous property. If it is a child using it, you must get the signature of the parent or guardian.

It might seem difficult or tacky to make neighbors sign such a document, but if you present it in a nonthreatening manner, it might go over well. You could say something like "I would love to invite you over to swim in our lake, but I am told I would be liable if anything happened. If you would sign something stating that I am not responsible, I would be glad to have you over."

While these do not always hold up in court, they may dissuade some people from suing.

Declaration of Homestead

When a person uses property as his or her home, in many states he or she obtains special legal benefits. These may include lower taxes and immunity from having the property taken by creditors. Also, when a person makes a state his or her personal residence, he or she may obtain benefits, such as lower tuition at state schools.

Usually, these benefits can be obtained by filing a **DECLARATION OF HOMESTEAD** at the county courthouse. Some states and counties have their own form for this, but if one is not available, use the one included. (see form 91, p.295.)

REAL ESTATE SALES CONTRACT

Date:_____, 20_____

PARTIES: _____ as "Buyer" of
_____ Phone: _____
and _____ as "Seller" of
_____ Phone: _____
hereby agree that the Buyer shall buy and the Seller shall sell real property described below under the following terms and conditions:

Street Address:_____

Legal Description:

PURCHASE PRICE: The full purchase price shall be $_____ payable as follows:
   a) Deposit held in escrow by _____......................$_____
   b) New mortgage* to be obtained by Buyer _____ ....$_____
   c) Subject to [ ] , or assumption of [ ] mortgage* to
   _____ with interest rate of _____%, payable
   $_____ per month, having an approximate balance of ....$_____
   d) Mortgage* and Note to be held by seller at ___% interest payable
   _____ for _____ years in the amount of ....$_____
   e) Other _____ ....$_____
   f) Balance to close (U.S. cash, certified or cashier's check) subject to
      adjustments and prorations, plus closing costs ....$_____
Total ....$_____
             *or deed of trust

1. FINANCING: Contingent upon Buyer obtaining a firm commitment for a mortgage loan for a minimum of $_____ at a maximum interest rate of _____% for a term of at least ____ years. Buyer agrees to make application for and use reasonable diligence to obtain said loan.

2. EXISTING MORTGAGES: Seller represents to Buyer that the existing mortgage on the property is held by _____ and bears interest at _____% per annum with monthly payments of $_____ principal and interest plus $_____ for escrow. Said loan is fully assumable under the following terms:

_____.

3. CLOSING DATE & PLACE: Closing shall be on _____, 20_____ at the office of the attorney or title agent selected by Seller.

4. ACCEPTANCE: If this contract is not executed by both parties on or before _____, 20_____, it shall be void and Buyer's deposit returned.

5. PERSONAL PROPERTY: This sale includes all personal property listed on Schedule A. The parties agree that the portion of the purchase price attributable to these items is $_____.

6. TITLE EVIDENCE: Seller shall purchase and deliver to Buyer at or before closing a title insurance policy, or if it is the prevailing custom in the locality, an abstract of title.

7. TITLE DEFECTS: In the event title is found defective, Seller shall have 60 days within which to remove such defects. If Seller is unable to cure them within such time, Buyer may cancel this contract and have all earnest money refunded or may allow Seller additional time to cure. Seller agrees to use diligent effort to correct the defects including the bringing of necessary suits.

8. PRORATIONS: Real and personal property taxes shall be prorated based upon the most recent available information. If closing occurs at a date when the current year's millage is not fixed, and the current year's assessment is available, taxes will be prorated based upon such assessment and the prior year's millage. If current year's assessment is not available, then taxes will be prorated on the prior year's tax; provided, however, that if there are improvements on the property completed by January 1st of the year of closing, which were not in existence on January 1st of the prior year, then taxes shall be prorated based upon the prior year's millage and at an equitable assessment to be agreed upon between the parties, failing which, request will be made to the County Property Appraiser for an informal assessment. Any tax proration based upon an estimate may, at the request of either party, be subsequently readjusted upon receipt of the tax bill. Prepaid rents and other tenant deposits shall be prorated to the date of closing.

9. EXPENSES: The parties herein shall each pay half of the costs and fees for closing costs, documentary stamps and transfer and recording fees.

10. SPECIAL ASSESSMENTS: Certified, confirmed, and ratified special assessment liens as of date of closing (and not as of closing date) are to be paid by Seller. Pending liens as of date of closing shall be assumed by Buyer.

11. LIEN AFFIDAVIT: Seller shall, as to both the real and personal property being sold hereunder, furnish to Buyer at time of closing an affidavit attesting to the absence, unless otherwise provided for herein, of any financing statements, claims of lien or potential lienors known to Seller, and further attesting that there have been no improvements to the property for 90 days immediately preceding the date of closing. If the property has been improved within said time Seller shall deliver releases or waivers of all mechanic's liens, executed by general contractors, subcontractors, suppliers and materialmen, in addition to Seller's affidavit, setting forth the names of all such parties and further reciting that in fact all bills for work to the property which could serve as a basis for a mechanic's lien have been paid or will be paid at closing.

12. CONTINGENCIES: Contingent upon satisfactory inspection of the premises by a licensed contractor.

13. TERMITES: Within 30 days of closing, the premises shall be inspected by a certified pest control operator acceptable to Buyer, and the cost of said inspection shall be paid equally by Buyer and Seller. In the event infestation by wood destroying organisms is indicated, either party may cancel this contract or Seller may treat the premises at own expense if acceptable to Buyer.

14. PLUMBING AND ELECTRICAL: Major appliances, heating, cooling, electrical, and plumbing systems are to be in working order as of 6 days prior to closing. Buyer may inspect said items and shall report in writing to seller such items as found not to be in working condition. Unless Buyer reports failures by said date, he shall be deemed to have waived Seller's warranty as to failures not reported. Valid reported failures shall be corrected at Seller's cost. Seller agrees to provide access for inspection upon reasonable notice.

15. RESTRICTIONS & EASEMENTS: Property is subject to easements, covenants and restrictions of record provided they do not affect Buyer's intended use of the property.

16. CONDOMINIUMS–1: If this property is a condominium, sale is contingent upon Buyer or his attorney approving the Declaration of Condominium and all Amendments thereto and any rules and regulations promulgated thereunder within 15 days of receipt from Seller.

17. CONDOMINIUMS–2: If this property is a condominium, Seller shall convey all rights therein including common elements such as parking spaces and cabanas, if any. This contract is contingent upon the approval by the association or developer, if required, and the parties shall equally pay all costs of approval and transfer. Any assessments shall be prorated as of closing.

18. ZONING & ORDINANCES: Property is subject to governmental zoning and ordinances. VIOLATIONS: Seller represents that he or she has received no notice of violation on the property of any building, health or other governmental codes or ordinances.

19. INGRESS & EGRESS: Seller warrants that there is ingress and egress to the property which is insurable by a title insurance underwriter.

20. POSSESSION: Seller shall deliver exclusive possession of the premises to Buyer at closing subject only to leases assigned to Buyer.

21. RISK OF LOSS: If the improvements are damaged by fire or other casualty prior to closing and the cost of restoring same does not exceed 3% of the assessed valuation of the improvements so damaged, Buyer shall have the option of either taking the property as is together with either the 3% or any insurance proceeds available by virtue of such loss or damage, or of cancelling this contract and receiving return of deposits made hereunder.

22. DEFAULT: If the Buyer fails to perform under this contract within the time specified, the deposit(s) paid by the Buyer may be retained by the Seller as liquidated damages, consideration for the execution of this contract and full settlement of any claims, whereupon all parties shall be relieved of all obligations under this contract. If, for any

reason other than failure of Seller to render his title marketable after diligent effort, Seller fails, neglects, or refuses to perform under this contract, Buyer may proceed at law or in equity to enforce his rights under this contract.

23. ARBITRATION: In the event of any dispute under this contract, the parties agree to binding arbitration under the rules of the American Arbitration Association.

24. CONVEYANCE: Conveyance shall be by Warranty Deed subject only to matters excepted in this contract. Personal property shall, at the request of Buyer, be conveyed by an absolute Bill of Sale with warranty of title subject only to such liens as provided herein.

25. SEVERABILITY: In the event any clause in this contract is held to be unenforceable or against public policy, such holding shall not affect the validity of the remainder of the contract unless it materially alters the terms hereof.

26. OTHER AGREEMENTS: No prior or present agreements or representations shall be binding upon the parties unless incorporated into this contract. No modification or change in this contract shall be binding unless in writing and signed by the party to be bound thereby.

Having read the foregoing, the undersigned hereby ratify, approve and confirm the same as our agreement.

Witnesses: Sellers:

_____   _____

_____   _____

                                                        Buyers:

_____   _____

_____   _____

WARRANTY DEED

This Warranty Deed, executed on _____, 20_____, between _____, Grantor, of _____ and _____, Grantee, of _____.

The Grantor, for and in consideration of the sum of $ _____ and other good and valuable consideration paid by the Grantee, the receipt whereof is hereby acknowledged, does hereby grant, bargain, sell, convey, and warrant to the Grantee forever, all the following described real estate, located at _____ _____:

[Legal Description of Property]

To have and to hold the same in fee simple forever, together with all the buildings, improvements, and appurtenances thereto belonging.

And the Grantor hereby covenants with said Grantee that the Grantor is lawfully seized of said land in fee simple; that the Grantor has good right and lawful authority to sell and convey said land; that the Grantor hereby fully warrants the title to said land and will defend the same against the lawful claims of all persons whosoever; and, that said land is free of all encumbrances, except _____.

Signed, sealed, and delivered:

_____   _____
                                         Grantor

_____   _____
                                         Grantor

STATE OF _____)
COUNTY OF _____)

On _____, 20____, before me personally appeared _____, who is personally known to me or who provided _____ as identification, and signed the above document in my presence.

_____
Notary Public
My Commission expires:

This page intentionally left blank.

QUITCLAIM DEED

This Quitclaim Deed, executed on _____, 20____, between _____,

Grantor, of _____ and _____, Grantee, of

_____.

The Grantor, for and in consideration of the sum of $ _____ and other good and valuable consideration paid by the Grantee, the receipt whereof is hereby acknowledged, does hereby remise, release and quitclaim unto the Grantee forever, all the right, title, and interest the Grantor has in and to the following described real estate, located at:

_____:

[Legal Description of Property]

To have and to hold the same together with all buildings, improvements, and appurtenances thereto belonging.

Signed, sealed and delivered in presence of:

_____   _____

Witness   Grantor

_____

Witness

STATE OF _____)

COUNTY OF _____)

On _____, 20____, before me personally appeared _____, who is personally known to me or who provided _____ as identification, and signed the above document in my presence.

_____

Notary Public

My Commission expires:

This page intentionally left blank.

ASSIGNMENT OF MORTGAGE

For value received, _____, the holder(s) of that certain mortgage, dated _____, 20_____, executed by _____, and recorded at _____ _____, hereby assigns and transfers _____ all of the undersigned's right title and interest in said mortgage.

IN WITNESS WHEREOF, the undersigned has executed this assignment of mortgage on the _____ day of _____, 20_____.

Witnessed by:

_____   _____

_____   _____

STATE OF _____)

COUNTY OF _____)

The foregoing instrument was acknowledged before me this _____ day of _____, 20_____, by _____, who is personally known to me or who has produced _____ as identification.

_____
Signature

_____
(Typed Name of Acknowledger)

NOTARY PUBLIC

Commission Number:_____

My Commission Expires:

This page intentionally left blank.

SATISFACTION OF MORTGAGE

For value received, _____, the holder(s) of that certain
mortgage dated _____, 20_____, executed by _____,
and recorded at _____
_____,
hereby acknowledge(s) full payment, satisfaction and discharge of said mortgage.

IN WITNESS WHEREOF, the undersigned has executed this satisfaction of mortgage on the _____ day of
_____, 20_____.

Witnessed by:

_____   _____

_____   _____

STATE OF _____)
COUNTY OF _____)

I certify that _____, who ❏ is personally known to me to be the person
whose name is subscribed to the foregoing instrument ❏ produced _____
as identification, personally appeared before me on _____, 20_____, and acknowledged
the execution of the foregoing instrument.

_____

Notary Public, State of _____

My commission expires:

This page intentionally left blank.

OPTION AGREEMENT

This Option to Purchase is granted on _____, 20____, by _____,
Optionor, whose post office address is _____ to
_____, Optionee, whose post office address is _____
_____.

The Optionor is the owner of the following described real estate, situated at
_____:

1. PURPOSE OF AGREEMENT. The Optionor wishes to grant to the Optionee an Option to Purchase the Property. The Optionee wishes to buy from Optionor an Option to Purchase the Property.

2. GRANT OF OPTION. The Optionor, in consideration of the payment of the sum of _____ ($_____), the receipt of which is hereby acknowledged, grants to the Optionee the exclusive Option to Purchase the Property.

3. OPTION PERIOD. The option period will be from the date of this Agreement until, if not exercised, its expiration on _____, 20____.

4. EXERCISE OF OPTION. This Option may be exercised at any time during the option period and prior to its expiration. The Optionee must give written notice of exercise of the Option to the Optionor. If the Option is exercised, the consideration will be applied to the purchase price of the property.

5. FAILURE TO EXERCISE OPTION. If the option is not exercised, the Optionor will retain the consideration.

6. CONTRACT OF SALE/TERMS OF PURCHASE. Attached to this Option Agreement is a completed Contract of Sale. If the Optionee gives the Optionor written notice of exercise of the Option, the parties agree to enter into this Contract of Sale.

7. GOVERNING LAW. This agreement shall be governed by the laws of _____.

8. BINDING EFFECT. This Agreement shall be binding upon the parties and upon their successors.

9. ENTIRE AGREEMENT. This instrument, including any attachments, constitutes the entire Agreement of the parties. This Agreement may not be modified except in writing signed by both parties.

_____   _____
Signature of Optionor   Signature of Optionee

_____   _____
Printed Name of Optionor   Printed Name of Optionee

This page intentionally left blank.

EXERCISE OF OPTION

Date:

To:

Dear _____ :

I, as Optionee of the Option Agreement made by you, as Optionor, dated _____, 20_____ for the purchase of property located in _____, hereby exercise the Option to purchase.

Enclosed you will find two copies of the Contract of Sale signed by me. Please sign and return one copy of the Contract of Sale to me.

Sincerely,

_____
Signature

This page intentionally left blank.

RENTAL APPLICATION

Name _____ Date of Birth _____

Name _____ Date of Birth _____

Social Security Numbers _____

Driver's License Numbers _____

Children & Ages _____

Present Landlord _____ Phone _____

Address _____

How Long Have You Lived at Your Current Residence? _____

Previous Landlord _____ Phone _____

Address _____

Second Previous Landlord _____ Phone _____

Address _____

Nearest Relative _____ Phone _____

Address _____

Employer _____ Phone _____

Address _____

Second Applicant's Employer _____ Phone _____

Address _____

Pets _____

Other persons who will stay at premises for more than one week _____

_____

Bank Name_____ Acct. # _____

Bank Name_____ Acct. # _____

Have you ever been evicted? _____

Have you ever been in litigation with a landlord? _____

The undersigned hereby attest that the above information is true.

_____

_____

This page intentionally left blank.

INSPECTION REPORT

Date: _____

Unit: _____

AREA	CONDITION			
	Move-In		Move-Out	
	Good	Poor	Good	Poor
Yard/garden				
Driveway				
Patio/porch				
Exterior				
Entry light/bell				
Living room/dining room/halls				
Floors/carpets				
Walls/ceilings				
Doors/locks				
Fixtures/light				
Outlets/switches				
Other				
Bedrooms				
Floors/carpets				
Walls/ceilings				
Doors/locks				
Fixtures/light				
Outlets/switches				
Other				
Bathrooms				
Faucets				
Toilet				
Sink/tub				
Floors/carpets				
Walls/ceiling				
Doors/locks				
fixtures/lights				
Outlet/switches				
Other				
Kitchen				
Refrigerator				
Range				
Oven				
Dishwasher				
Sink/disposal				
Cabinets/counters				
Floors/carpets				
Walls/ceiling				
Doors/locks				
Fixtures/lights				
Outlets/switches				
Other				
Misc.				
Closets/pantry				
Garage				
Keys				
Other				

_____   _____

       Tenant   Landlord

This page intentionally left blank.

Disclosure of Information on Lead-Based Paint and/or Lead-Based Paint Hazards

Lead Warning Statement

Housing built before 1978 may contain lead-based paint. Lead from paint, paint chips, and dust can pose health hazards if not managed properly. Lead exposure is especially harmful to young children and pregnant women. Before renting pre-1978 housing, lessors must disclose the presence of known lead-based paint and/or lead-based paint hazards in the dwelling. Lessees must also receive a federally approved pamphlet on lead poisoning prevention.

Lessor's Disclosure

(a) Presence of lead-based paint and/or lead-based paint hazards (check (i) or (ii) below):

   (i) _____ Known lead-based paint and/or lead-based paint hazards are present in the housing (explain).

   _____

   _____

   (ii) _____ Lessor has no knowledge of lead-based paint and/or lead-based paint hazards in the housing.

(b) Records and reports available to the lessor (check (i) or (ii) below):

   (i) _____ Lessor has provided the lessee with all available records and reports pertaining to lead-based paint and/or lead-based paint hazards in the housing (list documents below).

   _____

   _____

   (ii) _____ Lessor has no reports or records pertaining to lead-based paint and/or lead-based paint hazards in the housing.

Lessee's Acknowledgment (initial)

(c) _____ Lessee has received copies of all information listed above.

(d) _____ Lessee has received the pamphlet *Protect Your Family from Lead in Your Home.*

Agent's Acknowledgment (initial)

(e) _____ Agent has informed the lessor of the lessor's obligations under 42 U.S.C. 4852(d) and is aware of his/her responsibility to ensure compliance.

Certification of Accuracy

The following parties have reviewed the information above and certify, to the best of their knowledge, that the information they have provided is true and accurate.

_____ _____ _____ _____
Lessor   Date   Lessor   Date

_____ _____ _____ _____
Lessee   Date   Lessee   Date

_____ _____ _____ _____
Agent   Date   Agent   Date

This page intentionally left blank.

HOUSE LEASE—SET TERM

LANDLORD: _____ TENANT: _____

_____ _____

PROPERTY:_____

IN CONSIDERATION of the mutual covenants and agreements herein contained, Landlord hereby leases to Tenant and Tenant hereby leases from Landlord the above-described property together with any personal property listed on "Schedule A" attached hereto, under the following terms and conditions:

1. TERM. This lease shall be for a term of _____ beginning _____, 20_____ and ending _____, 20_____.

2. RENT. The rent shall be $_____ per _____ and shall be due on or before the _____ day of each _____. In the event the full amount of rent is not received on the due date, a late charge of $_____ shall be due. In the event a check bounces or an eviction notice must be posted, Tenant agrees to pay a $15.00 charge.

3. PAYMENT. Payment must be received by Landlord on or before the due date at the following address: _____ or such place as designated by Landlord in writing. Tenant understands that this may require early mailing. In the event a check bounces, Landlord may require cash or certified funds.

4. DEFAULT. In the event Tenant defaults under any term of this lease, Landlord may recover possession as provided by law and seek monetary damages.

5. SECURITY. Tenant shall pay Landlord the sum of $_____ as the last month's rent under this lease, plus $_____ as security deposit. In the event Tenant terminates the lease prior to its expiration date, said amounts are non-refundable as a charge for Landlord's trouble in securing a new tenant, but Landlord reserves the right to seek additional damages if they exceed the above amounts.

6. UTILITIES. Tenant agrees to pay all utility charges on the property except: _____ _____.

7. MAINTENANCE. Tenant has examined the property, acknowledges it to be in good repair and in consideration of the reduced rent, Tenant agrees to be responsible for and to promptly complete all maintenance to the premises.

8. LOCKS. If Tenant adds or changes locks on the premises, Landlord shall be given copies of the keys. Landlord shall at all times have keys for access to the premises in case of emergencies.

9. ASSIGNMENT. Tenant may not assign this lease or sublet any part of the premises without Landlord's written consent, which consent shall be at Landlord's sole discretion.

10. USE. Tenant agrees to use the premises for residential purposes only and not for any illegal purpose or any purpose which will increase the rate of insurance. Tenant further agrees not to violate any zoning laws or subdivision restrictions or to engage in any activity which would injure the premises or constitute a nuisance to the neighbors or Landlord.

11. LAWN. Tenant shall be responsible for maintaining the lawn and shrubbery on the premises at Tenant's expense and for any damages caused by his neglect or abuse thereof.

12. LIABILITY. Tenant agrees to hold Landlord harmless from any and all claims for damages occurring on the premises, and to be solely responsible for insuring Tenant's own possessions on the premises.

13. ACCESS. Landlord reserves the right to enter the premises for the purposes of inspection, repair, or showing to prospective tenants or purchasers.

14. PETS. No pets shall be allowed on the premises except: _____ and there shall be a $_____ nonrefundable pet deposit. Landlord reserves the right to revoke consent if pet becomes a nuisance.

15. OCCUPANCY. The premises shall not be occupied by more than _____ persons.

16. TENANT'S APPLIANCES. Tenant agrees not to use any heaters, fixtures or appliances drawing excessive current without the written consent of the Landlord.

17. PARKING. Tenant agrees that no parking is allowed on the premises except: _____ _____. Campers, trailers, boats, recreational vehicles, or inoperable vehicles shall not be stored on the premises without the written consent of the Landlord.

18. FURNISHINGS. Any articles provided to Tenant and listed on attached schedule are to be returned in good condition at the termination of this lease.

19. ALTERATIONS AND IMPROVEMENTS. Tenant shall make no alterations or improvements to the premises (including paint) without the written consent of the Landlord and any such alterations or improvements shall become the property of the Landlord unless otherwise agreed in writing.

20. ENTIRE AGREEMENT. This lease constitutes the entire agreement between the parties and may not be modified except in writing signed by both parties.

21. HARASSMENT. Tenant shall not do any acts to intentionally harass the Landlord or other tenants.

22. ATTORNEY'S FEES. In the event it becomes necessary to enforce this Agreement through the services of an attorney, Tenant shall be required to pay Landlord's attorney's fees.

23. SEVERABILITY. In the event any section of this Agreement shall be held to be invalid, all remaining provisions shall remain in full force and effect.

24. RECORDING. This lease shall not be recorded in any public records.

25. WAIVER. Any failure by Landlord to exercise any rights under this agreement shall not constitute a waiver of Landlord's rights.

26. ABANDONMENT. In the event Tenant abandons the property prior to the expiration of this lease, Landlord may relet the premises and hold Tenant liable for any costs, lost rent or damage to the premises. Landlord may dispose of any property abandoned by Tenant.

27. SUBORDINATION. Tenant's interest in the premises shall be subordinate to any encumbrances now or hereafter placed on the premises, to any advances made under such encumbrances, and to any extensions or renewals thereof. Tenant agrees to sign any documents indicating such subordination which may be required by lenders.

28. SURRENDER OF PREMISES. At the expiration of the term of this lease, Tenant shall immediately surrender the premises in as good condition as at the start of this lease. The Tenant shall turn over to Landlord all keys to the premises, including keys made by Tenant or Tenant's agents.

29. HOLDOVER BY TENANT. If Tenant fails to deliver possession of the premises to Landlord at the expiration of this lease, the tenancy shall still be governed by this lease on a month-to-month basis. If such holdover is without the consent of the Landlord, Tenant shall be liable for double the monthly rent for each month or fraction thereof.

30. DAMAGE TO PREMISES. In the event the premises are damaged or destroyed by fire or other casualty or are declared uninhabitable by a governmental authority, Landlord may terminate this lease or may repair the premises.

31. PEST CONTROL. Tenant agrees to be responsible for pest control and extermination services on the premises, and to keep the premises clean and sanitary to avoid such problems. Tenant shall notify Landlord immediately of any evidence of termites. Landlord shall not be responsible to provide living arrangements for Tenant in the event the premises must be vacated for termite or other pest control treatment.

32. LIENS. The estate of Landlord shall not be subject to any liens for improvements contracted by Tenant.

33. WATERBEDS. In the event Tenant uses a flotation type bedding device on the premises, Tenant shall maintain an insurance policy of at least $_____ to cover damages from such device and shall list Landlord as a named insured on said policy.

34. MISCELLANEOUS PROVISIONS. _____

_____

_____

_____

_____

WITNESS the hands and seals of the parties hereto as of this _____ day of _____, 20_____.

LANDLORD: TENANT:

_____   _____

_____   _____

HOUSE LEASE—MONTH-TO-MONTH

LANDLORD: _____ TENANT: _____

_____ _____

PROPERTY:_____

IN CONSIDERATION of the mutual covenants and agreements herein contained, Landlord hereby leases to Tenant and Tenant hereby leases from Landlord the above-described property together with any personal property listed on "Schedule A" attached hereto, under the following terms and conditions:

1. TERM. This rental agreement shall be for a month-to-month tenancy which may be cancelled by either party upon giving notice to the other party at least 30 days prior to the end of the month.

2. RENT. The rent shall be $_____ per _____ and shall be due on or before the _____ day of each _____. In the event the full amount of rent is not received on the due date, a late charge of $_____ shall be due. In the event a check bounces or an eviction notice must be posted, Tenant agrees to pay a $15.00 charge.

3. PAYMENT. Payment must be received by Landlord on or before the due date at the following address: _____ or such place as designated by Landlord in writing. Tenant understands that this may require early mailing. In the event a check bounces, Landlord may require cash or certified funds.

4. DEFAULT. In the event Tenant defaults under any term of this lease, Landlord may recover possession as provided by law and seek monetary damages.

5. SECURITY. Tenant shall pay Landlord the sum of $_____ as the last month's rent under this lease, plus $_____ as security deposit. In the event Tenant terminates the lease prior to its expiration date, said amounts are nonrefundable as a charge for Landlord's trouble in securing a new tenant, but Landlord reserves the right to seek additional damages if they exceed the above amounts.

6. UTILITIES. Tenant agrees to pay all utility charges on the property except: _____ _____.

7. MAINTENANCE. Tenant has examined the property, acknowledges it to be in good repair and in consideration of the reduced rent, Tenant agrees to be responsible for and to promptly complete all maintenance to the premises.

8. LOCKS. If Tenant adds or changes locks on the premises, Landlord shall be given copies of the keys. Landlord shall at all times have keys for access to the premises in case of emergencies.

9. ASSIGNMENT. Tenant may not assign this lease or sublet any part of the premises without Landlord's written consent, which consent shall be at Landlord's sole discretion.

10. USE. Tenant agrees to use the premises for residential purposes only and not for any illegal purpose or any purpose which will increase the rate of insurance. Tenant further agrees not to violate any zoning laws or subdivision restrictions or to engage in any activity which would injure the premises or constitute a nuisance to the neighbors or Landlord.

11. LAWN. Tenant shall be responsible for maintaining the lawn and shrubbery on the premises at Tenant's expense and for any damages caused by his neglect or abuse thereof.

12. LIABILITY. Tenant agrees to hold Landlord harmless from any and all claims for damages occurring on the premises, and to be solely responsible for insuring Tenant's own possessions on the premises.

13. ACCESS. Landlord reserves the right to enter the premises for the purposes of inspection, repair, or showing to prospective tenants or purchasers.

14. PETS. No pets shall be allowed on the premises except: _____ and there shall be a $_____ nonrefundable pet deposit. Landlord reserves the right to revoke consent if pet becomes a nuisance.

15. OCCUPANCY. The premises shall not be occupied by more than _____ persons.

16. TENANT'S APPLIANCES. Tenant agrees not to use any heaters, fixtures or appliances drawing excessive current without the written consent of the Landlord.

17. PARKING. Tenant agrees that no parking is allowed on the premises except: _____ _____. Campers, trailers, boats, recreational vehicles or inoperable vehicles shall not be stored on the premises without the written consent of the Landlord.

18. FURNISHINGS. Any articles provided to Tenant and listed on attached schedule are to be returned in good condition at the termination of this lease.

19. ALTERATIONS AND IMPROVEMENTS. Tenant shall make no alterations or improvements to the premises (including paint) without the written consent of the Landlord and any such alterations or improvements shall become the property of the Landlord unless otherwise agreed in writing.

20. ENTIRE AGREEMENT. This lease constitutes the entire agreement between the parties and may not be modified except in writing signed by both parties.

21. HARASSMENT. Tenant shall not do any acts to intentionally harass the Landlord or other tenants.

22. ATTORNEY'S FEES. In the event it becomes necessary to enforce this Agreement through the services of an attorney, Tenant shall be required to pay Landlord's attorney's fees.

23. SEVERABILITY. In the event any section of this Agreement shall be held to be invalid, all remaining provisions shall remain in full force and effect.

24. RECORDING. This lease shall not be recorded in any public records.

25. WAIVER. Any failure by Landlord to exercise any rights under this agreement shall not constitute a waiver of Landlord's rights.

26. ABANDONMENT. In the event Tenant abandons the property prior to the expiration of this lease, Landlord may relet the premises and hold Tenant liable for any costs, lost rent or damage to the premises. Landlord may dispose of any property abandoned by Tenant.

27. SUBORDINATION. Tenant's interest in the premises shall be subordinate to any encumbrances now or hereafter placed on the premises, to any advances made under such encumbrances, and to any extensions or renewals thereof. Tenant agrees to sign any documents indicating such subordination which may be required by lenders.

28. SURRENDER OF PREMISES. At the expiration of the term of this lease, Tenant shall immediately surrender the premises in as good condition as at the start of this lease. The Tenant shall turn over to Landlord all keys to the premises, including keys made by Tenant or Tenant's agents.

29. HOLDOVER BY TENANT. If Tenant fails to deliver possession of the premises to Landlord at the expiration of this lease, the tenancy shall still be governed by this lease on a month-to-month basis. If such holdover is without the consent of the Landlord, Tenant shall be liable for double the monthly rent for each month or fraction thereof.

30. DAMAGE TO PREMISES. In the event the premises are damaged or destroyed by fire or other casualty or are declared uninhabitable by a governmental authority, Landlord may terminate this lease or may repair the premises.

31. PEST CONTROL. Tenant agrees to be responsible for pest control and extermination services on the premises, and to keep the premises clean and sanitary to avoid such problems. Tenant shall notify Landlord immediately of any evidence of termites. Landlord shall not be responsible to provide living arrangements for Tenant in the event the premises must be vacated for termite or other pest control treatment.

32. LIENS. The estate of Landlord shall not be subject to any liens for improvements contracted by Tenant.

33. WATERBEDS. In the event Tenant uses a flotation type bedding device on the premises, Tenant shall maintain an insurance policy of at least $_____ to cover damages from such device and shall list Landlord as a named insured on said policy.

34. MISCELLANEOUS PROVISIONS. _____

_____

_____

_____

_____

WITNESS the hands and seals of the parties hereto as of this _____ day of _____, 20_____.

LANDLORD: TENANT:

_____   _____

_____   _____

APARTMENT RENTAL AGREEMENT—SET TERM

LANDLORD: _____   TENANT: _____

_____   _____

PROPERTY:_____

IN CONSIDERATION of the mutual covenants and agreements herein contained, Landlord hereby leases to Tenant and Tenant hereby leases from Landlord the above-described property together with any personal property listed on "Schedule A" attached hereto, under the following terms and conditions:

1. TERM. This lease shall be for a term of _____ beginning
_____, 20____ and ending _____, 20____.

2. RENT. The rent shall be $_____ per _____ and shall be due on or before the _____ day of each _____. In the event the full amount of rent is not received on the due date, a late charge of $_____ shall be due. In the event a check bounces or an eviction notice must be posted, Tenant agrees to pay a $15.00 charge.

3. PAYMENT. Payment must be received by Landlord on or before the due date at the following address: _____ or such place as designated by Landlord in writing. Tenant understands that this may require early mailing. In the event a check bounces, Landlord may require cash or certified funds.

4. DEFAULT. In the event Tenant defaults under any term of this lease, Landlord may recover possession as provided by law and seek monetary damages.

5. SECURITY. Tenant shall pay Landlord the sum of $_____ as security for the performance of this lease. Said amount shall not be used as rent.

6. UTILITIES. Tenant agrees to pay all utility charges on the property except: _____ _____.

7. MAINTENANCE. Tenant has examined the property, acknowledges it to be in good repair and agrees to inform Landlord promptly of any maintenance problems. Tenant agrees to keep the premises in clean and sanitary condition. In the event damage has been done by Tenant or Tenant's guests, either intentionally or negligently, Tenant shall pay for such repairs within ten days.

8. LOCKS. If Tenant adds or changes locks on the premises, Landlord shall be given copies of the keys. Landlord shall at all times have keys for access to the premises in case of emergencies.

9. ASSIGNMENT. Tenant may not assign this lease or sublet any part of the premises without Landlord's written consent, which consent shall be at Landlord's sole discretion.

10. USE. Tenant agrees to use the premises for residential purposes only and not for any illegal purpose or any purpose which will increase the rate of insurance. Tenant further agrees not to violate any zoning laws or subdivision restrictions or to engage in any activity which would injure the premises or constitute a nuisance to the neighbors or Landlord.

11. CONDOMINIUM. In the event the premises are a condominium unit, Tenant agrees to abide by all applicable rules and regulations. Maintenance and recreation fees are to be paid by _____. This lease is subject to the approval of the condominium association and Tenant agrees to pay any fee necessary for such approval.

12. LIABILITY. Tenant agrees to hold Landlord harmless from any and all claims for damages occurring on the premises, and to be solely responsible for insuring Tenant's own possessions on the premises.

13. ACCESS. Landlord reserves the right to enter the premises for the purposes of inspection, repair, or showing to prospective tenants or purchasers.

14. PETS. No pets shall be allowed on the premises except: _____ and there shall be a $_____ non-refundable pet deposit. Landlord reserves the right to revoke consent if pet becomes a nuisance.

15. OCCUPANCY. The premises shall not be occupied by more than _____ persons.

16. TENANT'S APPLIANCES. Tenant agrees not to use any heaters, fixtures or appliances drawing excessive current without the written consent of the Landlord.

17. PARKING. Tenant agrees that no parking is allowed on the premises except: _____ _____. Campers, trailers, boats, recreational vehicles or inoperable vehicles shall not be stored on the premises without the written consent of the Landlord.

18. FURNISHINGS. Any articles provided to Tenant and listed on attached schedule are to be returned in good condition at the termination of this lease.

19. ALTERATIONS AND IMPROVEMENTS. Tenant shall make no alterations or improvements to the premises (including paint) without the written consent of the Landlord and any such alterations or improvements shall become the property of the Landlord unless otherwise agreed to in writing.

20. ENTIRE AGREEMENT. This lease constitutes the entire agreement between the parties and may not be modified except in writing signed by both parties.

21. HARASSMENT. Tenant shall not do any acts to intentionally harass the Landlord or other tenants.

22. ATTORNEY'S FEES. In the event it becomes necessary to enforce this Agreement through the services of an attorney, Tenant shall be required to pay Landlord's attorney's fees.

23. SEVERABILITY. In the event any section of this Agreement shall be held to be invalid, all remaining provisions shall remain in full force and effect.

24. RECORDING. This lease shall not be recorded in any public records.

25. WAIVER. Any failure by Landlord to exercise any rights under this agreement shall not constitute a waiver of Landlord's rights.

26. ABANDONMENT. In the event Tenant abandons the property prior to the expiration of this lease, Landlord may relet the premises and hold Tenant liable for any costs, lost rent or damage to the premises. Landlord may dispose of any property abandoned by Tenant.

27. SUBORDINATION. Tenant's interest in the premises shall be subordinate to any encumbrances now or hereafter placed on the premises, to any advances made under such encumbrances, and to any extensions or renewals thereof. Tenant agrees to sign any documents indicating such subordination which may be required by lenders.

28. SURRENDER OF PREMISES. At the expiration of the term of this lease, Tenant shall immediately surrender the premises in as good condition as at the start of this lease. The Tenant shall turn over to Landlord all keys to the premises, including keys made by Tenant or Tenant's agents.

29. HOLDOVER BY TENANT. If Tenant fails to deliver possession of the premises to Landlord at the expiration of this lease, the tenancy shall still be governed by this lease on a month-to-month basis. If such holdover is without the consent of the Landlord, Tenant shall be liable for double the monthly rent for each month or fraction thereof.

30. DAMAGE TO PREMISES. In the event the premises are damaged or destroyed by fire or other casualty or are declared uninhabitable by a governmental authority, Landlord may terminate this lease or may repair the premises.

31. LIENS. The estate of Landlord shall not be subject to any liens for improvements contracted by Tenant.

32. WATERBEDS. In the event Tenant uses a flotation type bedding device on the premises, Tenant shall maintain an insurance policy of at least $_____ to cover damages from such device and shall list Landlord as a named insured on said policy.

33. MISCELLANEOUS PROVISIONS. _____

_____

_____

_____

_____

WITNESS the hands and seals of the parties hereto as of this _____ day of _____, 20_____.

LANDLORD: TENANT:

_____   _____

_____   _____

APARTMENT RENTAL AGREEMENT—MONTH-TO-MONTH

LANDLORD: _____   TENANT: _____

_____   _____

PROPERTY:_____

IN CONSIDERATION of the mutual covenants and agreements herein contained, Landlord hereby leases to Tenant and Tenant hereby leases from Landlord the above-described property together with any personal property listed on "Schedule A" attached hereto, under the following terms and conditions:

1. TERM. This rental agreement shall be for a month-to-month tenancy which may be cancelled by either party upon giving notice to the other party at least 30 days prior to the end of the month.

2. RENT. The rent shall be $_____ per _____ and shall be due on or before the _____ day of each _____. In the event the full amount of rent is not received on the due date, a late charge of $_____ shall be due. In the event a check bounces or an eviction notice must be posted, Tenant agrees to pay a $15.00 charge.

3. PAYMENT. Payment must be received by Landlord on or before the due date at the following address: _____ or such place as designated by Landlord in writing. Tenant understands that this may require early mailing. In the event a check bounces, Landlord may require cash or certified funds.

4. DEFAULT. In the event Tenant defaults under any term of this lease, Landlord may recover possession as provided by law and seek monetary damages.

5. SECURITY. Tenant shall pay Landlord the sum of $_____ as security for the performance of this lease. Said amount shall not be used as rent.

6. UTILITIES. Tenant agrees to pay all utility charges on the property except: _____ _____.

7. MAINTENANCE. Tenant has examined the property, acknowledges it to be in good repair and agrees to inform Landlord promptly of any maintenance problems. Tenant agrees to keep the premises in clean and sanitary condition. In the event damage has been done by Tenant or Tenant's guests, either intentionally or negligently, Tenant shall pay for such repairs within ten days.

8. LOCKS. If Tenant adds or changes locks on the premises, Landlord shall be given copies of the keys. Landlord shall at all times have keys for access to the premises in case of emergencies.

9. ASSIGNMENT. Tenant may not assign this lease or sublet any part of the premises without Landlord's written consent, which consent shall be at Landlord's sole discretion.

10. USE. Tenant agrees to use the premises for residential purposes only and not for any illegal purpose or any purpose which will increase the rate of insurance. Tenant further agrees not to violate any zoning laws or subdivision restrictions or to engage in any activity which would injure the premises or constitute a nuisance to the neighbors or Landlord.

11. CONDOMINIUM. In the event the premises are a condominium unit, Tenant agrees to abide by all applicable rules and regulations. Maintenance and recreation fees are to be paid by _____. This lease is subject to the approval of the condominium association, and Tenant agrees to pay any fee necessary for such approval.

12. LIABILITY. Tenant agrees to hold Landlord harmless from any and all claims for damages occurring on the premises, and to be solely responsible for insuring Tenant's own possessions on the premises.

13. ACCESS. Landlord reserves the right to enter the premises for the purposes of inspection, repair, or showing to prospective tenants or purchasers.

14. PETS. No pets shall be allowed on the premises except: _____ and there shall be a $_____ nonrefundable pet deposit. Landlord reserves the right to revoke consent if pet becomes a nuisance.

15. OCCUPANCY. The premises shall not be occupied by more than _____ persons.

16. TENANT'S APPLIANCES. Tenant agrees not to use any heaters, fixtures or appliances drawing excessive current without the written consent of the Landlord.

17. PARKING. Tenant agrees that no parking is allowed on the premises except: _____ _____. Campers, trailers, boats, recreational vehicles or inoperable vehicles shall not be stored on the premises without the written consent of the Landlord.

18. FURNISHINGS. Any articles provided to Tenant and listed on attached schedule are to be returned in good condition at the termination of this lease.

19. ALTERATIONS AND IMPROVEMENTS. Tenant shall make no alterations or improvements to the premises (including paint) without the written consent of the Landlord and any such alterations or improvements shall become the property of the Landlord unless otherwise agreed to in writing.

20. ENTIRE AGREEMENT. This lease constitutes the entire agreement between the parties and may not be modified except in writing signed by both parties.

21. HARASSMENT. Tenant shall not do any acts to intentionally harass the Landlord or other tenants.

22. ATTORNEY'S FEES. In the event it becomes necessary to enforce this Agreement through the services of an attorney, Tenant shall be required to pay Landlord's attorney's fees.

23. SEVERABILITY. In the event any section of this Agreement shall be held to be invalid, all remaining provisions shall remain in full force and effect.

24. RECORDING. This lease shall not be recorded in any public records.

25. WAIVER. Any failure by Landlord to exercise any rights under this agreement shall not constitute a waiver of Landlord's rights.

26. ABANDONMENT. In the event Tenant abandons the property prior to the expiration of this lease, Landlord may relet the premises and hold Tenant liable for any costs, lost rent or damage to the premises. Landlord may dispose of any property abandoned by Tenant.

27. SUBORDINATION. Tenant's interest in the premises shall be subordinate to any encumbrances now or hereafter placed on the premises, to any advances made under such encumbrances, and to any extensions or renewals thereof. Tenant agrees to sign any documents indicating such subordination which may be required by lenders.

28. SURRENDER OF PREMISES. At the expiration of the term of this lease, Tenant shall immediately surrender the premises in as good condition as at the start of this lease. The Tenant shall turn over to Landlord all keys to the premises, including keys made by Tenant or Tenant's agents.

29. HOLDOVER BY TENANT. If Tenant fails to deliver possession of the premises to Landlord at the expiration of this lease, the tenancy shall still be governed by this lease on a month-to-month basis. If such holdover is without the consent of the Landlord, Tenant shall be liable for double the monthly rent for each month or fraction thereof.

30. DAMAGE TO PREMISES. In the event the premises are damaged or destroyed by fire or other casualty or are declared uninhabitable by a governmental authority, Landlord may terminate this lease or may repair the premises.

31. LIENS. The estate of Landlord shall not be subject to any liens for improvements contracted by Tenant.

32. WATERBEDS. In the event Tenant uses a flotation type bedding device on the premises, Tenant shall maintain an insurance policy of at least $_____ to cover damages from such device and shall list Landlord as a named insured on said policy.

33. MISCELLANEOUS PROVISIONS. _____

_____

_____

_____

_____

WITNESS the hands and seals of the parties hereto as of this _____ day of _____,
20_____.

LANDLORD: TENANT:

_____   _____

_____   _____

PET AGREEMENT

THIS AGREEMENT is made pursuant to that certain Lease dated _____ between
_____ as Landlord and
_____ as Tenant.

In consideration of $_____ as non-refundable cleaning payment and $_____ as additional security deposit paid by Tenant to Landlord, Tenant is allowed to keep the following pet(s): _____ on the premises _____ under the following conditions:

1. In the event the pet produces a litter, Tenant may keep them at the premises no longer than one month past weaning.

2. Tenant shall not engage in any commercial pet-raising activities.

3. No pets other than those listed above shall be kept on the premises without the further written permission of the Landlord.

4. Tenant agrees at all times to keep the pet from becoming a nuisance to neighbors and/or other tenants. This includes controlling the barking of the pet, if necessary, and cleaning any animal waste on and about the premises.

5. In the event the pet causes destruction of the property, becomes a nuisance, or Tenant otherwise violates this agreement, Landlord may terminate the Lease according to _____ (state) law.

Date: _____

Landlord: Tenant:

_____   _____

_____   _____

This page intentionally left blank.

AMENDMENT TO LEASE AGREEMENT

For valuable consideration, the receipt and sufficiency of which is hereby acknowledged by each of the parties, this agreement amends a lease agreement (the Lease) between _____ (the Landlord) and _____ (the Tenant) dated _____, relating to property located at _____. This agreement is hereby incorporated into the Lease.

Except as changed by this amendment, the Lease shall continue in effect according to its terms. The amendments herein shall be effective on the date this document is executed by both parties.

Executed on _____, 20____.

Landlord: Tenant:

_____   _____

_____   _____

This page intentionally left blank.

LEASE ASSIGNMENT

This Lease Assignment is entered into by and among _____ (the Assignor), _____ (the Assignee), and _____ (the Landlord). For valuable consideration, it is agreed by the parties as follows:

1. The Landlord and the Assignor have entered into a lease agreement (the Lease) dated _____, concerning the premises described as: _____.

2. The Assignor hereby assigns and transfers to the Assignee all of Assignor's rights and delegates all of Assignor's duties under the Lease effective _____ (the Effective Date).

3. The Assignee hereby accepts such assignment of rights and delegation of duties and agrees to pay all rents promptly when due and perform all of Assignor's obligations under the Lease accruing on and after the Effective Date. The Assignee further agrees to indemnify and hold the Assignor harmless from any breach of Assignee's duties hereunder.

4.   ❏   The Assignor agrees to transfer possession of the leased premises to the Assignee on the Effective Date. All rents and obligations of the Assignor under the Lease accruing before the Effective Date shall have been paid or discharged.

      ❏   The Landlord hereby assents to the assignment of the Lease hereunder and as of the Effective Date hereby releases and discharges the Assignor from all duties and obligations under the Lease accruing after the Effective Date.

      ❏   The Landlord hereby assents to this lease assignment provided that the Landlord's assent shall not discharge the Assignor of any obligations under the Lease in the event of breach by the Assignee. The Landlord will give notice to the Assignor of any breach by the Assignee. If the Assignor pays all accrued rents and cures any other default of the Assignee, the Assignor may enforce the terms of the Lease and this Assignment against the Assignee, in the name of the Landlord, if necessary.

5. There shall be no further assignment of the Lease without the written consent of the Landlord.

6. This agreement shall be binding upon and inure to the benefit of the parties, their successors, assigns, and personal representatives.

This assignment was executed under seal on _____.

Assignor: Assignee:

_____   _____

_____   _____

Landlord:

_____

_____

This page intentionally left blank.

CONSENT TO SUBLEASE

FOR VALUABLE CONSIDERATION, the undersigned (the Landlord) hereby consents to the sublease of all or part of the premises located at _____

_____ which is the subject of a lease agreement between

Landlord and _____ (the Tenant), pursuant to an Agreement to Sublease

dated _____, 20_____, between the Tenant and _____,

as Subtenant, dated _____, 20_____.

This consent was signed by the Landlord on _____, 20_____.

Landlord: _____

This page intentionally left blank.

ROOMMATE AGREEMENT

The undersigned, intending to share a dwelling unit located at _____
_____, in consideration of the mutual promises contained in this
agreement, agree as follows:

1. They shall share the unit as follows: _____
_____
_____

2. Rent shall be paid as follows: _____
_____

3. Each party shall be responsible for his/her own long distance and toll charges on the telephone bill(s), regardless of whose name the bill is in.

4. The other utilities and fees shall be paid as follows: _____
_____
_____

5. No party is obligated to pay another party's share of the rent or other bills, but in the event one party finds it necessary to pay a bill for another party to stop eviction or termination of service, the party paying shall have the right to reimbursement in full, plus a $_____ charge. In the event the nonpaying party fails to reimburse such amounts, the paying party shall be entitled to interest at the highest legal rate, attorneys' fees, and court costs if legal action is necessary.

6. The parties also agree:

Smoking _____
Overnight guests _____

7. The parties agree to respect each other's privacy, to keep the shared areas reasonably clean, not to make unreasonable noise during normal sleeping hours, not to leave food where it would invite infestation, and to be courteous and considerate of the other's needs. They agree that if their guests do not follow these rules, such guests shall not be permitted in the unit. They further agree not to do anything that violates the lease and could cause eviction.

8. The parties further agree as follows: _____
_____
_____
_____

_____

_____

This page intentionally left blank.

NOTICE TO LANDLORD TO MAKE REPAIRS

To Landlord:

From Tenant:

Re: Rental Premises:

This is notice that the above-referenced rental premises are in need of repairs as follows:

Unless these are made by you, I shall enforce our legal remedies under state law, which may include, but not be limited to, making the repairs and deducting the cost from rent, or terminating the rental agreement.

_____

Tenant

This page intentionally left blank.

ANNUAL LETTER—CONTINUATION OF TENANCY

DATE:

TO:

Dear _____,

This letter is to remind you that your lease will expire on _____. Please advise us within _____ days as to whether you intend to renew your lease. If so, we will prepare a new lease for your signature(s).

If you do not intend to renew your lease, the keys should be delivered to us at the address below on or before the end of the lease, along with your forwarding address. We will inspect the premises for damages, deduct any amounts necessary for repairs, and refund any remaining balance as required by law.

If we have not heard from you as specified above, we will assume that you will be vacating the premises and will arrange for a new tenant to move in at the end of your term.

Sincerely,

_____

Address:

Phone:

This page intentionally left blank.

LETTER TO VACATING TENANT

DATE:

TO:

Dear _____,

This letter is to remind you that your ❏ lease ❏ oral rental agreement will expire on _____.
Please be advised that we do not intend to renew or extend it.

The keys should be delivered to us at the address below on or before the end of the lease, along with your forwarding
address. We will inspect the premises for damages, deduct any amounts necessary for repairs, and refund any remaining balance as required by law.

Sincerely,

_____

Address:

Phone:

This page intentionally left blank.

NOTICE OF INTENT TO VACATE AT END OF LEASE

To: _____

_____

_____

This letter is to inform you that I/we intend to move out at the end of the current lease, to wit, on _____, 20_____.

Please advise as to when and how my/our security deposit will be refunded.

Sincerely,

_____

_____

_____

This page intentionally left blank.

DEMAND FOR RETURN OF SECURITY DEPOSIT

To: _____

_____

_____

This letter is to demand return of my/our security deposit in the amount of $_____.

Please advise as to when and how my/our security deposit will be refunded.

Sincerely,

_____

_____

_____

This page intentionally left blank.

WAIVER AND ASSUMPTION OF RISK

I, _____, hereby voluntarily sign this Waiver and Assumption of Risk in favor of _____ (the Owner), fully waiving and releasing the Owner from any and all claims for personal injury, property damage, or death that may result from my use of the Owner's property or from my participation in the following activities (activities):

I sign this Waiver and Assumption of Risk in consideration of the opportunity to use the Owner property, or to participate in activities as described above.

I acknowledge and understand that there are dangers and risks associated with the activities described above, which have been fully explained to me. I fully assume the dangers and risks and agree to use my best judgment in engaging in those activities and to follow the safety instructions provided.

I am a competent adult, age _____, and I freely and voluntarily assume the risks associated with the activities described above.

_____   _____
Signed   Dated

_____
Name

_____   _____
Address   Telephone

_____
Witness

In case of emergency, please contact:

_____
Name

_____   _____
Address   Telephone

_____   _____
                                               Relationship

This page intentionally left blank.

DECLARATION OF HOMESTEAD

I, _____, hereby declare:

1.   I declare as homestead the premises located in _____
_____, more particularly described as follows:
_____
_____
_____
_____

2.   I am the homestead owner of the above-declared homestead.

3.   I own the following interest in the above-declared homestead:
_____

4.   The above-declared homestead is

   ❏   my principal dwelling

   ❏   the principal dwelling of my spouse and I am currently residing on that declared homestead.

   My spouse is _____.

Dated _____

_____

State of _____)
County of _____)

On _____, 20____, before me personally appeared _____, who are personally known to me or who provided _____ as identification, and signed the above document in my presence.

_____
Notary Public

My Commission expires:

Chapter 7:
Employment Forms

There are many instances when you may need to hire people to help you get things accomplished. You might need a caretaker for your children or house. You may need some major work done on your house. If you hire professionals, they will usually have their own forms and agreements. But, if your neighbor offers to work for you for a fee or if you hire someone who does not have a business set up, you may need your own forms to protect yourself legally.

Forms in Chapter:
- **Application for Employment**
- **Authorization to Release**
    Employment Information
- **Verification of Education**
- **Verification of Licensure**
- **Employment Eligibility Verification (I-9)**
- **Application for Employer**
    Identification Number (SS-4)
- **Employee's Withholding**
    Allowance Certificate (W-4)
- **Household Help Agreement**
- **Determination of Worker Status (SS-8)**
- **Independent Contractor Agreement**
- **Modification of Independent**
    Contractor Agreement
- **Termination of Independent**
    Contractor Agreement

Employees

The hiring of an employee, whether for a household or a business, is a risky endeavor. If the person you hire kills someone while driving, molests a neighborhood child, or injures a visitor to your home, you could be sued for millions of dollars in damages. There is also the risk of damage or injury to your home and family.

There are numerous governmental laws and regulations that cover hiring, and failure to comply can result in financial penalties. For example, if someone does not have the legal right to work in this country, you can be fined for hiring him or her.

For these reasons, you should thoroughly check the background of anyone you hire. An **APPLICATION FOR EMPLOYMENT** can be used to get references and other information. (see form 92, p.303.) While former employers may be afraid to say anything negative about a person, a glowing review can work well in the applicant's favor.

Background Checks

To check an applicant's background, you can use an **AUTHORIZATION TO RELEASE EMPLOYMENT INFORMATION**, **VERIFICATION OF EDUCATION**, and **VERIFICATION OF LICENSURE**. These forms are signed by the applicant and grant you permission to obtain the information you need. The **AUTHORIZATION TO RELEASE EMPLOYMENT INFORMATION** can be used to check on employees for any type of job. (see form 93, p.305.) The other two forms would only be necessary if the applicant's education or license was important to the job. (see form 94, p.307 and form 95, p.309.) However, you might check these things just to see if the employee was honest on the application.

To confirm an employee's legal status, you should use **FORM I-9**. (see form 96, p.311.) This shows you which documentation is adequate to check eligibility to work. If the applicant uses fake identification, you are not liable for hiring him or her, as long as you made an honest effort to be sure they produced the documentation required by law. This form should not be used until you have decided to hire a person.

Taxes

If you hire someone for more than a few hours work, you are required to register with the state and federal government to withhold taxes. Before you hire someone, you must obtain an employer identification number using **IRS FORM SS-4**. (see form 97, p.313.) Once you hire someone, you must have them complete **IRS FORM W-4** in order to calculate their withholding of income taxes. (see form 98, p.321.)

Most states have their own registration and reporting requirements. Contact your state department of revenue for forms and applications.

Employment Agreement

Whenever you hire an employee for household help, have a written agreement with them. This is useful for spelling out their rights and responsibilities. It also protects you from misunderstandings and liability. The included **HOUSEHOLD HELP AGREEMENT** is a basic form, but you can add additional terms under paragraph 15, such as additional duties or benefits that were promised. (see form 99, p.323.)

Independent Contractors

Independent contractor is a legal term for a person who works for you but is not your employee. You pay them to do a job, but they are an independent business that takes care of its own taxes and insurance.

You cannot just avoid all employment laws by calling your workers independent contractors. There are rules and regulations detailing when a person can and cannot be an independent contractor. The most important rule is that a person cannot be an independent contractor if you control how and when they do their work. If you just hire them to do a job and let them do it in their way at their time, then they can be considered independent contractors. But if you supervise, give them the tools to use, and tell them when to show up, most likely you will have to treat them as employees.

A list of factors to be considered follows. A *yes* answer to all or most of the following questions will likely mean that the person hired is an independent contractor rather than an employee. For more certainty, use **IRS FORM SS-8**. (see form 100, p.325.)

- ◆ Does the person hired exercise independent control over the details of the work, such as the methods used to complete the job?
- ◆ Is the person hired in a business different from that of the person hiring? (For example, a plumber is hired by a lawyer.)
- ◆ Does the person hired work as a specialist without supervision by the person hiring?
- ◆ Does the person hired supply his or her own tools?
- ◆ Is the person hired for only a short period of time rather than consistently over a relatively long period?
- ◆ Does the job require a relatively high degree of skill?
- ◆ Is the person paid *by the job* rather than *by the hour*?

Contractor Agreement

Contracts with independent contractors do not have to be in writing; however, having these in writing is often more important than having an employment agreement in writing. For one thing, an employment contract in writing is an opportunity to state clearly that you intend it to be an independent contractor arrangement. Also, since by definition you have relatively little control over the way an independent contractor does the work, the writing may be your last chance to influence important matters, like exactly what the job is and when it must be completed.

NOTE: *It is often tempting to use the word **employer** in these contracts; however, it is not appropriate since the independent contractor is not **employed** (and you do not want the IRS thinking otherwise).*

An **INDEPENDENT CONTRACTOR AGREEMENT** is included. (see form 101, p.329.) A sample of how to complete the form follows.

Sample: **Independent Contractor Agreement**

INDEPENDENT CONTRACTOR AGREEMENT

This agreement is entered into by and between ____Jon Dough____ (the "Company") and ____Victor Fixet_____ (the "Contractor"). It is agreed by the parties as follows:

1.The Contractor shall supply all of the labor and materials to perform the following work for the Company as an independent contractor:

   Painting all exterior painted surfaces of home at 123 Elm Street, Anytown, U.S.A. with Everlast Exterior paint, white for walls and Beige 304 for trim.

❏ The attached plans and specifications are to be followed and are hereby made a part of this Agreement.

2. The Contractor agrees to the following completion dates for portions of the work and final completion of the work:

<table>
<tr><td><u>Description of Work</u></td><td><u>Completion Date</u></td></tr>
</table>

Complete entire job by June 25, 2006.

3. The Contractor shall perform the work in a workmanlike manner, according to standard industry practices, unless other standards or requirements are set forth in any attached plans and specifications.

Changes to Contract

Occasionally it becomes necessary to change the terms of your agreement with an independent contractor or to terminate it altogether. For example, for the sample contract, if it rained the whole two weeks in which the party was to paint your house, it would have been impossible to complete the job. Therefore, you would probably want to modify the contract to change the completion date. Or, if the independent contractor broke his or her leg before completion, you would want to terminate the agreement unless he or she could get someone to complete it. A **MODIFICATION OF INDEPENDENT CONTRACTOR AGREEMENT** and a **TERMINATION OF INDEPENDENT CONTRACTOR AGREEMENT** can assist you in these situations. (see form 102, p.331 and form 103, p.333.)

APPLICATION FOR EMPLOYMENT

We consider applicants for all positions without regard to race, color, religion, sex, national origin, age, marital or veteran status, the presence of a non-job-related medical condition or handicap, or any other legally protected status. Proof of citizenship or immigration status will be required upon employment.

(PLEASE TYPE OR PRINT)

Position Applied For	Date of Application

Last Name	First Name	Middle Name or Initial

Is there any other information regarding your name that will be needed to check work or school records? ❑ Yes ❑ No

Address	*Number Street*	*City*	*State*	*Zip Code*

Telephone Number(s) [indicate home or work]	Social Security Number

Date Available:_____   Are you available: ❑ Full Time   ❑ Part Time   ❑ Weekends

Are you 18 years of age or older?   ❑ Yes   ❑ No

Have you been convicted of a felony within the past 7 years?   ❑ Yes   ❑ No

Conviction will not necessarily disqualify an applicant from employment.
If Yes, attach explanation.

Can you produce documents proving you are authorized to work in the United States? ❑ Yes   ❑ No

Education

	High School	Undergraduate	Graduate
School Name & Location			
Years Completed	1 2 3 4	1 2 3 4	1 2 3 4
Diploma / Degree			
Course of Study			

State any additional information you feel may be helpful to us in considering your application (such as any specialized training; skills; apprenticeships; honors received; professional, trade, business or civic organizations or activities; job-related military training or experience; foreign language abilities; etc.)

_____
_____
_____
_____

Employment Experience

Start with your present or last job. Include any job-related military service assignments and voluntary activities. You may exclude organizations which indicate race, color, religion, gender, national origin, handicap, or other protected status.

1.

Employer Name & Address	Dates Employed	Job Title/Duties
	Hourly Rate/Salary	
May we contact this employer? ☐ Yes ☐ No	Hours Per Week	
Employer Phone		
Supervisor		
Reason for Leaving		

2.

Employer Name & Address	Dates Employed	Job Title/Duties
	Hourly Rate/Salary	
Employer Phone	Hours Per Week	
Supervisor		
Reason for Leaving		

3.

Employer Name & Address	Dates Employed	Job Title/Duties
	Hourly Rate/Salary	
Employer Phone	Hours Per Week	
Supervisor		
Reason for Leaving		

References: Name   Occupation   Address   Phone #   Relationship   Years known

1. _____
2. _____
3. _____

If you need additional space, continue on a separate sheet of paper.

Applicant's Statement

I certify that the information given on this application is true and complete to the best of my knowledge. I authorize investigation of all statements contained in this application, and understand that false or misleading information given in my application or interview(s) may result in discharge.

I understand and acknowledge that, unless otherwise defined by applicable law, any employment relationship with this organization is "at will," which means that I may resign at any time and the employer may discharge me at any time with or without cause. I further understand that this "at will" employment relationship may not be changed orally, by any written document, or by conduct, unless such change is specifically acknowledged in writing by an authorized executive of this organization.

_____   _____

Signature of Applicant   Date

AUTHORIZATION TO RELEASE EMPLOYMENT INFORMATION

To:

The undersigned applicant hereby authorizes you to release records of his/her dates of employment, job title, salary, and reason for leaving your company to:

_____

_____

_____

_____

Applicant's signature

This page intentionally left blank.

VERIFICATION OF EDUCATION

To:

The undersigned applicant hereby authorizes you to release records verifying his/her education at your institution to:

_____

_____

_____

_____

Applicant's signature

This page intentionally left blank.

VERIFICATION OF LICENSURE

To:

The undersigned applicant hereby authorizes you to verify that he/she is licensed as a _____,
that such license has been valid since _____ and is still valid.

_____

_____

_____

_____

Applicant's signature

This page intentionally left blank.

U.S. Department of Justice
Immigration and Naturalization Service

OMB No. 1115-0136

Employment Eligibility Verification

INSTRUCTIONS
PLEASE READ ALL INSTRUCTIONS CAREFULLY BEFORE COMPLETING THIS FORM.

Anti-Discrimination Notice. It is illegal to discriminate against any individual (other than an alien not authorized to work in the U.S.) in hiring, discharging, or recruiting or referring for a fee because of that individual's national origin or citizenship status. It is illegal to discriminate against work eligible individuals. Employers **CANNOT** specify which document(s) they will accept from an employee. The refusal to hire an individual because of a future expiration date may also constitute illegal discrimination.

Section 1 - Employee.
All employees, citizens and noncitizens, hired after November 6, 1986, must complete Section 1 of this form at the time of hire, which is the actual beginning of employment. **The employer is responsible for ensuring that Section 1 is timely and properly completed.**

Preparer/Translator Certification. The Preparer/Translator Certification must be completed if Section 1 is prepared by a person other than the employee. A preparer/translator may be used only when the employee is unable to complete Section 1 on his/her own. However, the employee must still sign Section 1.

Section 2 - Employer.
For the purpose of completing this form, the term "employer" includes those recruiters and referrers for a fee who are agricultural associations, agricultural employers or farm labor contractors.

Employers must complete Section 2 by examining evidence of identity and employment eligibility within three (3) business days of the date employment begins. If employees are authorized to work, but are unable to present the required document(s) within three business days, they must present a receipt for the application of the document(s) within three business days and the actual document(s) within ninety (90) days. However, if employers hire individuals for a duration of less than three business days, Section 2 must be completed at the time employment begins. **Employers must record: 1)** document title; **2)** issuing authority; **3)** document number, **4)** expiration date, if any; and **5)** the date employment begins. Employers must sign and date the certification. Employees must present original documents. Employers may, but are not required to, photocopy the document(s) presented. These photocopies may only be used for the verification process and must be retained with the I-9. **However, employers are still responsible for completing the I-9.**

Section 3 - Updating and Reverification.
Employers must complete Section 3 when updating and/or reverifying the I-9. Employers must reverify employment eligibility of their employees on or before the expiration date recorded in Section 1. Employers **CANNOT** specify which document(s) they will accept from an employee.

- If an employee's name has changed at the time this form is being updated/ reverified, complete Block A.

- If an employee is rehired within three (3) years of the date this form was originally completed and the employee is still eligible to be employed on the same basis as previously indicated on this form (updating), complete Block B and the signature block.

- If an employee is rehired within three (3) years of the date this form was originally completed and the employee's work authorization has expired **or** if a current employee's work authorization is about to expire (reverification), complete Block B and:
  - examine any document that reflects that the employee is authorized to work in the U.S. (see List A or C),
  - record the document title, document number and expiration date (if any) in Block C, and complete the signature block.

Photocopying and Retaining Form I-9. A blank I-9 may be reproduced, provided both sides are copied. The Instructions must be available to all employees completing this form. Employers must retain completed I-9s for three (3) years after the date of hire or one (1) year after the date employment ends, whichever is later.

For more detailed information, you may refer to the INS Handbook for Employers, (Form M-274). You may obtain the handbook at your local INS office.

Privacy Act Notice. The authority for collecting this information is the Immigration Reform and Control Act of 1986, Pub. L. 99-603 (8 USC 1324a).

This information is for employers to verify the eligibility of individuals for employment to preclude the unlawful hiring, or recruiting or referring for a fee, of aliens who are not authorized to work in the United States.

This information will be used by employers as a record of their basis for determining eligibility of an employee to work in the United States. The form will be kept by the employer and made available for inspection by officials of the U.S. Immigration and Naturalization Service, the Department of Labor and the Office of Special Counsel for Immigration Related Unfair Employment Practices.

Submission of the information required in this form is voluntary. However, an individual may not begin employment unless this form is completed, since employers are subject to civil or criminal penalties if they do not comply with the Immigration Reform and Control Act of 1986.

Reporting Burden. We try to create forms and instructions that are accurate, can be easily understood and which impose the least possible burden on you to provide us with information. Often this is difficult because some immigration laws are very complex. Accordingly, the reporting burden for this collection of information is computed as follows: **1)** learning about this form, 5 minutes; **2)** completing the form, 5 minutes; and **3)** assembling and filing (recordkeeping) the form, 5 minutes, for an average of 15 minutes per response. If you have comments regarding the accuracy of this burden estimate, or suggestions for making this form simpler, you can write to the Immigration and Naturalization Service, HQPDI, 425 I Street, N.W., Room 4307r, Washington, DC 20536. OMB No. 1115-0136.

EMPLOYERS MUST RETAIN COMPLETED FORM I-9
PLEASE DO NOT MAIL COMPLETED FORM I-9 TO INS

Form I-9 (Rev. 11-21-91)N

U.S. Department of Justice
Immigration and Naturalization Service

OMB No. 1115-0136

Employment Eligibility Verification

Please read instructions carefully before completing this form. The instructions must be available during completion of this form. ANTI-DISCRIMINATION NOTICE: It is illegal to discriminate against work eligible individuals. Employers CANNOT specify which document(s) they will accept from an employee. The refusal to hire an individual because of a future expiration date may also constitute illegal discrimination.

Section 1. Employee Information and Verification. To be completed and signed by employee at the time employment begins.

Print Name: Last	First	Middle Initial	Maiden Name

Address (Street Name and Number)	Apt. #	Date of Birth (month/day/year)

City	State	Zip Code	Social Security #

I am aware that federal law provides for imprisonment and/or fines for false statements or use of false documents in connection with the completion of this form.	I attest, under penalty of perjury, that I am (check one of the following): ☐ A citizen or national of the United States ☐ A Lawful Permanent Resident (Alien # A ☐ An alien authorized to work until ___/___/___ (Alien # or Admission #)

Employee's Signature	Date (month/day/year)

Preparer and/or Translator Certification. (To be completed and signed if Section 1 is prepared by a person other than the employee.) I attest, under penalty of perjury, that I have assisted in the completion of this form and that to the best of my knowledge the information is true and correct.

Preparer's/Translator's Signature	Print Name

Address (Street Name and Number, City, State, Zip Code)	Date (month/day/year)

Section 2. Employer Review and Verification. To be completed and signed by employer. Examine one document from List A OR examine one document from List B and one from List C, as listed on the reverse of this form, and record the title, number and expiration date, if any, of the document(s)

List A	OR	List B	AND	List C
Document title:				
Issuing authority:				
Document #:				
Expiration Date (if any): ___/___/___		___/___/___		___/___/___
Document #:				
Expiration Date (if any): ___/___/___				

CERTIFICATION - I attest, under penalty of perjury, that I have examined the document(s) presented by the above-named employee, that the above-listed document(s) appear to be genuine and to relate to the employee named, that the employee began employment on (month/day/year) ___/___/___ and that to the best of my knowledge the employee is eligible to work in the United States. (State employment agencies may omit the date the employee began employment.)

Signature of Employer or Authorized Representative	Print Name	Title

Business or Organization Name	Address (Street Name and Number, City, State, Zip Code)	Date (month/day/year)

Section 3. Updating and Reverification. To be completed and signed by employer.

A. New Name (if applicable)	B. Date of rehire (month/day/year) (if applicable)

C. If employee's previous grant of work authorization has expired, provide the information below for the document that establishes current employment eligibility.

Document Title:_____ Document #: _____ Expiration Date (if any): ___/___/___

I attest, under penalty of perjury, that to the best of my knowledge, this employee is eligible to work in the United States, and if the employee presented document(s), the document(s) I have examined appear to be genuine and to relate to the individual.

Signature of Employer or Authorized Representative	Date (month/day/year)

Form 97   313

Form **SS-4**	**Application for Employer Identification Number**	EIN	

Form **SS-4**
(Rev. December 2001)
Department of the Treasury
Internal Revenue Service

Application for Employer Identification Number
(For use by employers, corporations, partnerships, trusts, estates, churches, government agencies, Indian tribal entities, certain individuals, and others.)
► See separate instructions for each line.   ► Keep a copy for your records.

EIN

OMB No. 1545-0003

Type or print clearly.

1 Legal name of entity (or individual) for whom the EIN is being requested

2 Trade name of business (if different from name on line 1)

3 Executor, trustee, "care of" name

4a Mailing address (room, apt., suite no. and street, or P.O. box)

5a Street address (if different) (Do not enter a P.O. box.)

4b City, state, and ZIP code

5b City, state, and ZIP code

6 County and state where principal business is located

7a Name of principal officer, general partner, grantor, owner, or trustor

7b SSN, ITIN, or EIN

8a **Type of entity** (check only one box)
☐ Sole proprietor (SSN) _____
☐ Partnership
☐ Corporation (enter form number to be filed) ► _____
☐ Personal service corp.
☐ Church or church-controlled organization
☐ Other nonprofit organization (specify) ► _____
☐ Other (specify) ►

☐ Estate (SSN of decedent) _____
☐ Plan administrator (SSN) _____
☐ Trust (SSN of grantor) _____
☐ National Guard   ☐ State/local government
☐ Farmers' cooperative ☐ Federal government/military
☐ REMIC   ☐ Indian tribal governments/enterprises
Group Exemption Number (GEN) ► _____

8b If a corporation, name the state or foreign country (if applicable) where incorporated

State

Foreign country

9 **Reason for applying** (check only one box)
☐ Started new business (specify type) ► _____
☐ Hired employees (Check the box and see line 12.)
☐ Compliance with IRS withholding regulations
☐ Other (specify) ►

☐ Banking purpose (specify purpose) ► _____
☐ Changed type of organization (specify new type) ► _____
☐ Purchased going business
☐ Created a trust (specify type) ► _____
☐ Created a pension plan (specify type) ► _____

10 Date business started or acquired (month, day, year)

11 Closing month of accounting year

12 First date wages or annuities were paid or will be paid (month, day, year). **Note:** If applicant is a withholding agent, enter date income will first be paid to nonresident alien. (month, day, year) . . . . ►

13 Highest number of employees expected in the next 12 months. **Note:** If the applicant does not expect to have any employees during the period, enter "-0-." . . . . ►

Agricultural	Household	Other

14 Check **one** box that best describes the principal activity of your business.
☐ Construction   ☐ Rental & leasing   ☐ Transportation & warehousing
☐ Real estate   ☐ Manufacturing   ☐ Finance & insurance
☐ Health care & social assistance   ☐ Wholesale–agent/broker
☐ Accommodation & food service   ☐ Wholesale–other   ☐ Retail
☐ Other (specify)

15 Indicate principal line of merchandise sold; specific construction work done; products produced; or services provided.

16a Has the applicant ever applied for an employer identification number for this or any other business? . . . . . ☐ Yes   ☐ No
Note: If "Yes," please complete lines 16b and 16c.

16b If you checked "Yes" on line 16a, give applicant's legal name and trade name shown on prior application if different from line 1 or 2 above.
Legal name ►   Trade name ►

16c Approximate date when, and city and state where, the application was filed. Enter previous employer identification number if known.
Approximate date when filed (mo., day, year)   City and state where filed   Previous EIN

Third Party Designee	Complete this section **only** if you want to authorize the named individual to receive the entity's EIN and answer questions about the completion of this form.	
	Designee's name	Designee's telephone number (include area code) ( )
	Address and ZIP code	Designee's fax number (include area code) ( )

Under penalties of perjury, I declare that I have examined this application, and to the best of my knowledge and belief, it is true, correct, and complete.

Applicant's telephone number (include area code) (   )

Name and title (type or print clearly) ►

Applicant's fax number (include area code) (   )

Signature ►   Date ►

For Privacy Act and Paperwork Reduction Act Notice, see separate instructions.   Cat. No. 16055N   Form **SS-4** (Rev. 12-2001)

Do I Need an EIN?

File Form SS-4 if the applicant entity does not already have an EIN but is required to show an EIN on any return, statement, or other document.[1] **See also the separate instructions for each line on Form SS-4.**

IF the applicant...	AND...	THEN...
Started a new business	Does not currently have (nor expect to have) employees	Complete lines 1, 2, 4a-6, 8a, and 9-16c.
Hired (or will hire) employees, including household employees	Does not already have an EIN	Complete lines 1, 2, 4a-6, 7a-b (if applicable), 8a, 8b (if applicable), and 9-16c.
Opened a bank account	Needs an EIN for banking purposes only	Complete lines 1-5b, 7a-b (if applicable), 8a, 9, and 16a-c.
Changed type of organization	Either the legal character of the organization or its ownership changed (e.g., you incorporate a sole proprietorship or form a partnership)[2]	Complete lines 1-16c (as applicable).
Purchased a going business[3]	Does not already have an EIN	Complete lines 1-16c (as applicable).
Created a trust	The trust is other than a grantor trust or an IRA trust[4]	Complete lines 1-16c (as applicable).
Created a pension plan as a plan administrator[5]	Needs an EIN for reporting purposes	Complete lines 1, 2, 4a-6, 8a, 9, and 16a-c.
Is a foreign person needing an EIN to comply with IRS withholding regulations	Needs an EIN to complete a Form W-8 (other than Form W-8ECI), avoid withholding on portfolio assets, or claim tax treaty benefits[6]	Complete lines 1-5b, 7a-b (SSN or ITIN optional), 8a-9, and 16a-c.
Is administering an estate	Needs an EIN to report estate income on Form 1041	Complete lines 1, 3, 4a-b, 8a, 9, and 16a-c.
Is a withholding agent for taxes on non-wage income paid to an alien (i.e., individual, corporation, or partnership, etc.)	Is an agent, broker, fiduciary, manager, tenant, or spouse who is required to file **Form 1042,** Annual Withholding Tax Return for U.S. Source Income of Foreign Persons	Complete lines 1, 2, 3 (if applicable), 4a-5b, 7a-b (if applicable), 8a, 9, and 16a-c.
Is a state or local agency	Serves as a tax reporting agent for public assistance recipients under Rev. Proc. 80-4, 1980-1 C.B. 581[7]	Complete lines 1, 2, 4a-5b, 8a, 9, and 16a-c.
Is a single-member LLC	Needs an EIN to file **Form 8832,** Classification Election, for filing employment tax returns, **or** for state reporting purposes[8]	Complete lines 1-16c (as applicable).
Is an S corporation	Needs an EIN to file **Form 2553,** Election by a Small Business Corporation[9]	Complete lines 1-16c (as applicable).

[1] For example, a sole proprietorship or self-employed farmer who establishes a qualified retirement plan, or is required to file excise, employment, alcohol, tobacco, or firearms returns, must have an EIN. **A partnership, corporation, REMIC (real estate mortgage investment conduit), nonprofit organization (church, club, etc.), or farmers' cooperative must use an EIN for any tax-related purpose even if the entity does not have employees.**

[2] However, **do not** apply for a new EIN if the existing entity only **(a)** changed its business name, **(b)** elected on Form 8832 to change the way it is taxed (or is covered by the default rules), or **(c)** terminated its partnership status because at least 50% of the total interests in partnership capital and profits were sold or exchanged within a 12-month period. (The EIN of the terminated partnership should continue to be used. See Regulations section 301.6109-1(d)(2)(iii).)

[3] Do not use the EIN of the prior business unless you became the "owner" of a corporation by acquiring its stock.

[4] However, IRA trusts that are required to file **Form 990-T,** Exempt Organization Business Income Tax Return, must have an EIN.

[5] A plan administrator is the person or group of persons specified as the administrator by the instrument under which the plan is operated.

[6] Entities applying to be a Qualified Intermediary (QI) need a QI-EIN even if they already have an EIN. **See Rev. Proc. 2000-12.**

[7] See also *Household employer* on page 4. (**Note:** State or local agencies may need an EIN for other reasons, e.g., hired employees.)

[8] Most LLCs **do not** need to file Form 8832. See **Limited liability company (LLC)** on page 4 for details on completing Form SS-4 for an LLC.

[9] An existing corporation that is electing or revoking S corporation status should use its previously-assigned EIN.

Instructions for Form SS-4

(Rev. September 2003)

For use with Form SS-4 (Rev. December 2001)
Application for Employer Identification Number.
Section references are to the Internal Revenue Code unless otherwise noted.

General Instructions

Use these instructions to complete **Form SS-4,** Application for Employer Identification Number. Also see **Do I Need an EIN?** on page 2 of Form SS-4.

Purpose of Form

Use Form SS-4 to apply for an employer identification number (EIN). An EIN is a nine-digit number (for example, 12-3456789) assigned to sole proprietors, corporations, partnerships, estates, trusts, and other entities for tax filing and reporting purposes. The information you provide on this form will establish your business tax account.

 *An EIN is for use in connection with your business activities only. Do **not** use your EIN in place of your social security number (SSN).*

Items To Note

Apply online. You can now apply for and receive an EIN online using the internet. See **How To Apply** below.

File only one Form SS-4. Generally, a sole proprietor should file only one Form SS-4 and needs only one EIN, regardless of the number of businesses operated as a sole proprietorship or trade names under which a business operates. However, if the proprietorship incorporates or enters into a partnership, a new EIN is required. Also, each corporation in an affiliated group must have its own EIN.

EIN applied for, but not received. If you do not have an EIN by the time a return is due, write "Applied For" and the date you applied in the space shown for the number. **Do not** show your SSN as an EIN on returns.

If you do not have an EIN by the time a tax deposit is due, send your payment to the Internal Revenue Service Center for your filing area as shown in the instructions for the form that you are filing. Make your check or money order payable to the "United States Treasury" and show your name (as shown on Form SS-4), address, type of tax, period covered, and date you applied for an EIN.

How To Apply

You can apply for an EIN online, by telephone, by fax, or by mail depending on how soon you need to use the EIN. Use only one method for each entity so you do not receive more than one EIN for an entity.

Online. You can receive your EIN by internet and use it immediately to file a return or make a payment. Go to the

IRS website at **www.irs.gov/businesses** and click on **Employer ID Numbers** under **topics.**

Telephone. You can receive your EIN by telephone and use it immediately to file a return or make a payment. Call the IRS at **1-800-829-4933.** (International applicants must call 215-516-6999.) The hours of operation are 7:00 a.m. to 10:00 p.m. The person making the call must be authorized to sign the form or be an authorized designee. See **Signature** and **Third Party Designee** on page 6. Also see the **TIP** below.

If you are applying by telephone, it will be helpful to complete Form SS-4 before contacting the IRS. An IRS representative will use the information from the Form SS-4 to establish your account and assign you an EIN. Write the number you are given on the upper right corner of the form and sign and date it. Keep this copy for your records.

If requested by an IRS representative, mail or fax (facsimile) the signed Form SS-4 (including any Third Party Designee authorization) within 24 hours to the IRS address provided by the IRS representative.

 *Taxpayer representatives can apply for an EIN on behalf of their client and request that the EIN be faxed to their **client** on the same day. **Note:** By using this procedure, you are authorizing the IRS to fax the EIN without a cover sheet.*

Fax. Under the Fax-TIN program, you can receive your EIN by fax within 4 business days. Complete and fax Form SS-4 to the IRS using the Fax-TIN number listed on page 2 for your state. A long-distance charge to callers outside of the local calling area will apply. Fax-TIN numbers can only be used to apply for an EIN. **The numbers may change without notice.** Fax-TIN is available 24 hours a day, 7 days a week.

Be sure to provide your fax number so the IRS can fax the EIN back to you. **Note:** By using this procedure, you are authorizing the IRS to fax the EIN without a cover sheet.

Mail. Complete Form SS-4 at least 4 to 5 weeks before you will need an EIN. Sign and date the application and mail it to the service center address for your state. You will receive your EIN in the mail in approximately 4 weeks. See also **Third Party Designee** on page 6.

Call 1-800-829-4933 to verify a number or to ask about the status of an application by mail.

Where To Fax or File

If your principal business, office or agency, or legal residence in the case of an individual, is located in:	Call the Fax-TIN number shown or file with the "Internal Revenue Service Center" at:
Connecticut, Delaware, District of Columbia, Florida, Georgia, Maine, Maryland, Massachusetts, New Hampshire, New Jersey, New York, North Carolina, Ohio, Pennsylvania, Rhode Island, South Carolina, Vermont, Virginia, West Virginia	Attn: EIN Operation P. O. Box 9003 Holtsville, NY 11742-9003 Fax-TIN 631-447-8960
Illinois, Indiana, Kentucky, Michigan	Attn: EIN Operation Cincinnati, OH 45999 Fax-TIN 859-669-5760
Alabama, Alaska, Arizona, Arkansas, California, Colorado, Hawaii, Idaho, Iowa, Kansas, Louisiana, Minnesota, Mississippi, Missouri, Montana, Nebraska, Nevada, New Mexico, North Dakota, Oklahoma, Oregon, Puerto Rico, South Dakota, Tennessee, Texas, Utah, Washington, Wisconsin, Wyoming	Attn: EIN Operation Philadelphia, PA 19255 Fax-TIN 215-516-3990
If you have no legal residence, principal place of business, or principal office or agency in any state:	Attn: EIN Operation Philadelphia, PA 19255 Telephone 215-516-6999 Fax-TIN 215-516-3990

How To Get Forms and Publications

Phone. You can order forms, instructions, and publications by phone 24 hours a day, 7 days a week. Call 1-800-TAX-FORM (1-800-829-3676). You should receive your order or notification of its status within 10 workdays.

Personal computer. With your personal computer and modem, you can get the forms and information you need using the IRS website at **www.irs.gov** or File Transfer Protocol at **ftp.irs.gov.**

CD-ROM. For small businesses, return preparers, or others who may frequently need tax forms or publications, a CD-ROM containing over 2,000 tax products (including many prior year forms) can be purchased from the National Technical Information Service (NTIS).

To order **Pub. 1796,** Federal Tax Products on CD-ROM, call **1-877-CDFORMS** (1-877-233-6767) toll free or connect to **www.irs.gov/cdorders.**

Tax Help for Your Business

IRS-sponsored Small Business Workshops provide information about your Federal and state tax obligations.

For information about workshops in your area, call 1-800-829-4933.

Related Forms and Publications

The following **forms** and **instructions** may be useful to filers of Form SS-4:

- **Form 990-T,** Exempt Organization Business Income Tax Return
- **Instructions for Form 990-T**
- **Schedule C (Form 1040),** Profit or Loss From Business
- **Schedule F (Form 1040),** Profit or Loss From Farming
- **Instructions for Form 1041 and Schedules A, B, D, G, I, J, and K-1,** U.S. Income Tax Return for Estates and Trusts
- **Form 1042,** Annual Withholding Tax Return for U.S. Source Income of Foreign Persons
- **Instructions for Form 1065,** U.S. Return of Partnership Income
- **Instructions for Form 1066,** U.S. Real Estate Mortgage Investment Conduit (REMIC) Income Tax Return
- **Instructions for Forms 1120 and 1120-A**
- **Form 2553,** Election by a Small Business Corporation
- **Form 2848,** Power of Attorney and Declaration of Representative
- **Form 8821,** Tax Information Authorization
- **Form 8832,** Entity Classification Election
  For more **information** about filing Form SS-4 and related issues, see:
- **Circular A,** Agricultural Employer's Tax Guide (Pub. 51)
- **Circular E,** Employer's Tax Guide (Pub. 15)
- **Pub. 538,** Accounting Periods and Methods
- **Pub. 542,** Corporations
- **Pub. 557,** Exempt Status for Your Organization
- **Pub. 583,** Starting a Business and Keeping Records
- **Pub. 966,** Electronic Choices for Paying ALL Your Federal Taxes
- **Pub. 1635,** Understanding Your EIN
- **Package 1023,** Application for Recognition of Exemption Under Section 501(c)(3) of the Internal Revenue Code
- **Package 1024,** Application for Recognition of Exemption Under Section 501(a)

Specific Instructions

Print or type all entries on Form SS-4. Follow the instructions for each line to expedite processing and to avoid unnecessary IRS requests for additional information. Enter "N/A" (nonapplicable) on the lines that do not apply.

Line 1—Legal name of entity (or individual) for whom the EIN is being requested. Enter the legal name of the entity (or individual) applying for the EIN exactly as it appears on the social security card, charter, or other applicable legal document.

Individuals. Enter your first name, middle initial, and last name. If you are a sole proprietor, enter your individual name, not your business name. Enter your business name on line 2. Do not use abbreviations or nicknames on line 1.

Trusts. Enter the name of the trust.

Estate of a decedent. Enter the name of the estate.

Partnerships. Enter the legal name of the partnership as it appears in the partnership agreement.

Corporations. Enter the corporate name as it appears in the corporation charter or other legal document creating it.

Plan administrators. Enter the name of the plan administrator. A plan administrator who already has an EIN should use that number.

Line 2—Trade name of business. Enter the trade name of the business if different from the legal name. The trade name is the "doing business as " (DBA) name.

*Use the full legal name shown on line 1 on all tax returns filed for the entity. (However, if you enter a trade name on line 2 and choose to use the trade name instead of the legal name, enter the trade name on **all returns** you file.) To prevent processing delays and errors, **always** use the legal name only (or the trade name only) on **all** tax returns.*

Line 3—Executor, trustee, "care of" name. Trusts enter the name of the trustee. Estates enter the name of the executor, administrator, or other fiduciary. If the entity applying has a designated person to receive tax information, enter that person's name as the "care of" person. Enter the individual's first name, middle initial, and last name.

Lines 4a-b—Mailing address. Enter the mailing address for the entity's correspondence. If line 3 is completed, enter the address for the executor, trustee or "care of" person. Generally, this address will be used on all tax returns.

*File **Form 8822,** Change of Address, to report any subsequent changes to the entity's mailing address.*

Lines 5a-b—Street address. Provide the entity's physical address **only** if different from its mailing address shown in lines 4a-b. **Do not** enter a P.O. box number here.

Line 6—County and state where principal business is located. Enter the entity's primary **physical** location.

Lines 7a-b—Name of principal officer, general partner, grantor, owner, or trustor. Enter the first name, middle initial, last name, and SSN of **(a)** the principal officer if the business is a corporation, **(b)** a general partner if a partnership, **(c)** the owner of an entity that is disregarded as separate from its owner (disregarded entities owned by a corporation enter the corporation's name and EIN), or **(d)** a grantor, owner, or trustor if a trust.

If the person in question is an **alien individual** with a previously assigned individual taxpayer identification number (ITIN), enter the ITIN in the space provided and submit a copy of an official identifying document. If

necessary, complete **Form W-7,** Application for IRS Individual Taxpayer Identification Number, to obtain an ITIN.

You are **required** to enter an SSN, ITIN, or EIN unless the only reason you are applying for an EIN is to make an entity classification election (see Regulations sections 301.7701-1 through 301.7701-3) and you are a nonresident alien with no effectively connected income from sources within the United States.

Line 8a—Type of entity. Check the box that best describes the type of entity applying for the EIN. If you are an alien individual with an ITIN previously assigned to you, enter the ITIN in place of a requested SSN.

*This is not an election for a tax classification of an entity. See **Limited liability company (LLC)** on page 4.*

Other. If not specifically listed, check the "Other" box, enter the type of entity and the type of return, if any, that will be filed (for example, "Common Trust Fund, Form 1065" or "Created a Pension Plan"). Do not enter "N/A." If you are an alien individual applying for an EIN, see the **Lines 7a-b** instructions above.

● **Household employer.** If you are an individual, check the "Other" box and enter "Household Employer" and your SSN. If you are a state or local agency serving as a tax reporting agent for public assistance recipients who become household employers, check the "Other" box and enter "Household Employer Agent." If you are a trust that qualifies as a household employer, you do not need a separate EIN for reporting tax information relating to household employees; use the EIN of the trust.

● **QSub.** For a qualified subchapter S subsidiary (QSub) check the "Other" box and specify "QSub."

● **Withholding agent.** If you are a withholding agent required to file Form 1042, check the "Other" box and enter "Withholding Agent."

Sole proprietor. Check this box if you file Schedule C, C-EZ, or F (Form 1040) and have a qualified plan, or are required to file excise, employment, alcohol, tobacco, or firearms returns, or are a payer of gambling winnings. Enter your SSN (or ITIN) in the space provided. If you are a nonresident alien with no effectively connected income from sources within the United States, you do not need to enter an SSN or ITIN.

Corporation. This box is for any corporation **other than a personal service corporation.** If you check this box, enter the income tax form number to be filed by the entity in the space provided.

*If you entered "1120S" after the "Corporation" checkbox, the corporation **must** file Form 2553 **no later than the 15th day of the 3rd month of the tax year the election is to take effect.** Until Form 2553 has been received and approved, you will be considered a Form 1120 filer. See the Instructions for Form 2553.*

Personal service corp. Check this box if the entity is a personal service corporation. An entity is a personal service corporation for a tax year only if:

- The principal activity of the entity during the testing period (prior tax year) for the tax year is the performance of personal services substantially by employee-owners, and
- The employee-owners own at least 10% of the fair market value of the outstanding stock in the entity on the last day of the testing period.

Personal services include performance of services in such fields as health, law, accounting, or consulting. For more information about personal service corporations, see the Instructions for Forms 1120 and 1120-A and Pub. 542.

Other nonprofit organization. Check this box if the nonprofit organization is other than a church or church-controlled organization and specify the type of nonprofit organization (for example, an educational organization).

 If the organization also seeks tax-exempt status, you must file either Package 1023 or Package 1024. See Pub. 557 for more information.

If the organization is covered by a group exemption letter, enter the four-digit **group exemption number (GEN).** (Do not confuse the GEN with the nine-digit EIN.) If you do not know the GEN, contact the parent organization. Get Pub. 557 for more information about group exemption numbers.

Plan administrator. If the plan administrator is an individual, enter the plan administrator's SSN in the space provided.

REMIC. Check this box if the entity has elected to be treated as a real estate mortgage investment conduit (REMIC). See the Instructions for Form 1066 for more information.

Limited liability company (LLC). An LLC is an entity organized under the laws of a state or foreign country as a limited liability company. For Federal tax purposes, an LLC may be treated as a partnership or corporation or be disregarded as an entity separate from its owner.

By **default,** a domestic LLC with only one member is **disregarded** as an entity separate from its owner and must include all of its income and expenses on the owner's tax return (e.g., **Schedule C (Form 1040)**). Also by default, a domestic LLC with two or more members is treated as a partnership. A domestic LLC may file Form 8832 to avoid either default classification and elect to be classified as an association taxable as a corporation. For more information on entity classifications (including the rules for foreign entities), see the instructions for Form 8832.

 Do not *file Form 8832 if the LLC accepts the default classifications above.* **However, if the LLC will be electing S Corporation status, it must timely file both Form 8832 and Form 2553.**

Complete Form SS-4 for LLCs as follows:
- A single-member domestic LLC that accepts the default classification (above) does not need an EIN and generally should not file Form SS-4. Generally, the LLC should use the name and EIN of its **owner** for all Federal tax purposes. However, the reporting and payment of employment taxes for employees of the LLC may be made using the name and EIN of **either** the owner or the LLC as explained in Notice 99-6. You can find Notice 99-6 on page 12 of Internal Revenue Bulletin 1999-3 at **www.irs.gov/pub/irs-irbs/irb99-03.pdf.** (**Note:** If the LLC applicant indicates in box 13 that it has employees or expects to have employees, the owner (whether an individual or other entity) of a single-member domestic LLC will also be assigned its own EIN (if it does not already have one) even if the LLC will be filing the employment tax returns.)
- A single-member, domestic LLC that accepts the default classification (above) and wants an EIN for filing employment tax returns (see above) or non-Federal purposes, such as a state requirement, must check the "Other" box and write "Disregarded Entity" or, when applicable, "Disregarded Entity—Sole Proprietorship" in the space provided.
- A multi-member, domestic LLC that accepts the default classification (above) must check the "Partnership" box.
- A domestic LLC that will be filing Form 8832 to elect corporate status must check the "Corporation" box and write in "Single-Member" or "Multi-Member" immediately below the "form number" entry line.

Line 9—Reason for applying. Check only **one** box. Do not enter "N/A."

Started new business. Check this box if you are starting a new business that requires an EIN. If you check this box, enter the type of business being started. **Do not** apply if you already have an EIN and are only adding another place of business.

Hired employees. Check this box if the existing business is requesting an EIN because it has hired or is hiring employees and is therefore required to file employment tax returns. **Do not** apply if you already have an EIN and are only hiring employees. For information on employment taxes (e.g., for family members), see Circular E.

 You may be required to make electronic deposits of all depository taxes (such as employment tax, excise tax, and corporate income tax) using the Electronic Federal Tax Payment System (EFTPS). See section 11, Depositing Taxes, of Circular E and Pub. 966.

Created a pension plan. Check this box if you have created a pension plan and need an EIN for reporting purposes. Also, enter the type of plan in the space provided.

 Check this box if you are applying for a trust EIN when a new pension plan is established. In addition, check the "Other" box in line 8a and write "Created a Pension Plan" in the space provided.

Banking purpose. Check this box if you are requesting an EIN for banking purposes only, and enter the banking purpose (for example, a bowling league for depositing dues or an investment club for dividend and interest reporting).

Changed type of organization. Check this box if the business is changing its type of organization. For example, the business was a sole proprietorship and has been incorporated or has become a partnership. If you check this box, specify in the space provided (including available space immediately below) the type of change made. For example, "From Sole Proprietorship to Partnership."

Purchased going business. Check this box if you purchased an existing business. **Do not** use the former owner's EIN unless you became the "owner" of a corporation by acquiring its stock.

Created a trust. Check this box if you created a trust, and enter the type of trust created. For example, indicate if the trust is a nonexempt charitable trust or a split-interest trust.

Exception. Do **not** file this form for certain grantor-type trusts. The trustee does not need an EIN for the trust if the trustee furnishes the name and TIN of the grantor/owner and the address of the trust to all payors. See the Instructions for Form 1041 for more information.

 Do not check this box if you are applying for a trust EIN when a new pension plan is established. Check "Created a pension plan."

Other. Check this box if you are requesting an EIN for any other reason; and enter the reason. For example, a newly-formed state government entity should enter "Newly-Formed State Government Entity" in the space provided.

Line 10—Date business started or acquired. If you are starting a new business, enter the starting date of the business. If the business you acquired is already operating, enter the date you acquired the business. If you are changing the form of ownership of your business, enter the date the new ownership entity began. Trusts should enter the date the trust was legally created. Estates should enter the date of death of the decedent whose name appears on line 1 or the date when the estate was legally funded.

Line 11—Closing month of accounting year. Enter the last month of your accounting year or tax year. An accounting or tax year is usually 12 consecutive months, either a calendar year or a fiscal year (including a period of 52 or 53 weeks). A calendar year is 12 consecutive months ending on December 31. A fiscal year is either 12 consecutive months ending on the last day of any month other than December or a 52-53 week year. For more information on accounting periods, see Pub. 538.

Individuals. Your tax year generally will be a calendar year.

Partnerships. Partnerships must adopt one of the following tax years:
• The tax year of the majority of its partners,
• The tax year common to all of its principal partners,
• The tax year that results in the least aggregate deferral of income, or
• In certain cases, some other tax year.

See the Instructions for Form 1065 for more information.

REMICs. REMICs must have a calendar year as their tax year.

Personal service corporations. A personal service corporation generally must adopt a calendar year unless:
• It can establish a business purpose for having a different tax year, or
• It elects under section 444 to have a tax year other than a calendar year.

Trusts. Generally, a trust must adopt a calendar year except for the following:
• Tax-exempt trusts,
• Charitable trusts, and
• Grantor-owned trusts.

Line 12—First date wages or annuities were paid or will be paid. If the business has or will have employees, enter the date on which the business began or will begin to pay wages. If the business does not plan to have employees, enter "N/A."

Withholding agent. Enter the date you began or will begin to pay income (including annuities) to a nonresident alien. This also applies to individuals who are required to file Form 1042 to report alimony paid to a nonresident alien.

Line 13—Highest number of employees expected in the next 12 months. Complete each box by entering the number (including zero ("-0-")) of "Agricultural," "Household," or "Other" employees expected by the applicant in the next 12 months. For a definition of agricultural labor (farmwork), see Circular A.

Lines 14 and 15. Check the **one** box in line 14 that best describes the principal activity of the applicant's business. Check the "Other" box (and specify the applicant's principal activity) if none of the listed boxes applies.

Use line 15 to describe the applicant's principal line of business in more detail. For example, if you checked the "Construction" box in line 14, enter additional detail such as "General contractor for residential buildings" in line 15.

Construction. Check this box if the applicant is engaged in erecting buildings or other structures, (e.g., streets, highways, bridges, tunnels). The term "Construction" also includes special trade contractors, (e.g., plumbing, HVAC, electrical, carpentry, concrete, excavation, etc. contractors).

Real estate. Check this box if the applicant is engaged in renting or leasing real estate to others; managing, selling, buying or renting real estate for others; or providing related real estate services (e.g., appraisal services).

Rental and leasing. Check this box if the applicant is engaged in providing tangible goods such as autos, computers, consumer goods, or industrial machinery and equipment to customers in return for a periodic rental or lease payment.

Manufacturing. Check this box if the applicant is engaged in the mechanical, physical, or chemical transformation of materials, substances, or components into new products. The assembling of component parts of manufactured products is also considered to be manufacturing.

Transportation & warehousing. Check this box if the applicant provides transportation of passengers or cargo; warehousing or storage of goods; scenic or sight-seeing transportation; or support activities related to these modes of transportation.

Finance & insurance. Check this box if the applicant is engaged in transactions involving the creation, liquidation, or change of ownership of financial assets and/or facilitating such financial transactions; underwriting annuities/insurance policies; facilitating such underwriting by selling insurance policies; or by providing other insurance or employee-benefit related services.

Health care and social assistance. Check this box if the applicant is engaged in providing physical, medical, or psychiatric care using licensed health care professionals or providing social assistance activities such as youth centers, adoption agencies, individual/family services, temporary shelters, etc.

Accommodation & food services. Check this box if the applicant is engaged in providing customers with lodging, meal preparation, snacks, or beverages for immediate consumption.

Wholesale–agent/broker. Check this box if the applicant is engaged in arranging for the purchase or sale of goods owned by others or purchasing goods on a commission basis for goods traded in the wholesale market, usually between businesses.

Wholesale–other. Check this box if the applicant is engaged in selling goods in the wholesale market generally to other businesses for resale on their own account.

Retail. Check this box if the applicant is engaged in selling merchandise to the general public from a fixed store; by direct, mail-order, or electronic sales; or by using vending machines.

Other. Check this box if the applicant is engaged in an activity not described above. Describe the applicant's principal business activity in the space provided.

Lines 16a-c. Check the applicable box in line 16a to indicate whether or not the entity (or individual) applying for an EIN was issued one previously. Complete lines 16b and 16c **only** if the "Yes" box in line 16a is checked. If the applicant previously applied for **more than one** EIN, write "See Attached" in the empty space in line 16a and attach a separate sheet providing the line 16b and 16c information for each EIN previously requested.

Third Party Designee. Complete this section **only** if you want to authorize the named individual to receive the entity's EIN and answer questions about the completion of Form SS-4. The designee's authority terminates at the time the EIN is assigned and released to the designee. **You must complete the signature area for the authorization to be valid.**

Signature. When required, the application must be signed by **(a)** the individual, if the applicant is an individual, **(b)** the president, vice president, or other principal officer, if the applicant is a corporation, **(c)** a responsible and duly authorized member or officer having knowledge of its affairs, if the applicant is a partnership, government entity, or other unincorporated organization, or **(d)** the fiduciary, if the applicant is a trust or an estate. Foreign applicants may have any duly-authorized person, (e.g., division manager), sign Form SS-4.

Privacy Act and Paperwork Reduction Act Notice. We ask for the information on this form to carry out the Internal Revenue laws of the United States. We need it to comply with section 6109 and the regulations thereunder which generally require the inclusion of an employer identification number (EIN) on certain returns, statements, or other documents filed with the Internal Revenue Service. If your entity is required to obtain an EIN, you are required to provide all of the information requested on this form. Information on this form may be used to determine which Federal tax returns you are required to file and to provide you with related forms and publications.

We disclose this form to the Social Security Administration for their use in determining compliance with applicable laws. We may give this information to the Department of Justice for use in civil and criminal litigation, and to the cities, states, and the District of Columbia for use in administering their tax laws. We may also disclose this information to Federal and state agencies to enforce Federal nontax criminal laws and to combat terrorism.

We will be unable to issue an EIN to you unless you provide all of the requested information which applies to your entity. Providing false information could subject you to penalties.

You are not required to provide the information requested on a form that is subject to the Paperwork Reduction Act unless the form displays a valid OMB control number. Books or records relating to a form or its instructions must be retained as long as their contents may become material in the administration of any Internal Revenue law. Generally, tax returns and return information are confidential, as required by section 6103.

The time needed to complete and file this form will vary depending on individual circumstances. The estimated average time is:

Recordkeeping	6 min.
Learning about the law or the form	22 min.
Preparing the form	46 min.
Copying, assembling, and sending the form to the IRS	20 min.

If you have comments concerning the accuracy of these time estimates or suggestions for making this form simpler, we would be happy to hear from you. You can write to the Tax Products Coordinating Committee, Western Area Distribution Center, Rancho Cordova, CA 95743-0001. **Do not** send the form to this address. Instead, see **How To Apply** on page 1.

Form W-4 (2005)

Purpose. Complete Form W-4 so that your employer can withhold the correct federal income tax from your pay. Because your tax situation may change, you may want to refigure your withholding each year.

Exemption from withholding. If you are exempt, complete only lines 1, 2, 3, 4, and 7 and sign the form to validate it. Your exemption for 2005 expires February 16, 2006. See Pub. 505, Tax Withholding and Estimated Tax.

Note. You cannot claim exemption from withholding if (a) your income exceeds $800 and includes more than $250 of unearned income (for example, interest and dividends) and (b) another person can claim you as a dependent on their tax return.

Basic instructions. If you are not exempt, complete the **Personal Allowances Worksheet** below. The worksheets on page 2 adjust your withholding allowances based on itemized deductions, certain credits, adjustments to income, or two-

earner/two-job situations. Complete all worksheets that apply. However, you may claim fewer (or zero) allowances.

Head of household. Generally, you may claim head of household filing status on your tax return only if you are unmarried and pay more than 50% of the costs of keeping up a home for yourself and your dependent(s) or other qualifying individuals. See line **E** below.

Tax credits. You can take projected tax credits into account in figuring your allowable number of withholding allowances. Credits for child or dependent care expenses and the child tax credit may be claimed using the **Personal Allowances Worksheet** below. See Pub. 919, How Do I Adjust My Tax Withholding? for information on converting your other credits into withholding allowances.

Nonwage income. If you have a large amount of nonwage income, such as interest or dividends, consider making estimated tax payments using Form 1040-ES, Estimated Tax for Individuals. Otherwise, you may owe additional tax.

Two earners/two jobs. If you have a working spouse or more than one job, figure the total number of allowances you are entitled to claim on all jobs using worksheets from only one Form W-4. Your withholding usually will be most accurate when all allowances are claimed on the Form W-4 for the highest paying job and zero allowances are claimed on the others.

Nonresident alien. If you are a nonresident alien, see the Instructions for Form 8233 before completing this Form W-4.

Check your withholding. After your Form W-4 takes effect, use Pub. 919 to see how the dollar amount you are having withheld compares to your projected total tax for 2005. See Pub. 919, especially if your earnings exceed $125,000 (Single) or $175,000 (Married).

Recent name change? If your name on line 1 differs from that shown on your social security card, call 1-800-772-1213 to initiate a name change and obtain a social security card showing your correct name.

Personal Allowances Worksheet (Keep for your records.)

A Enter "1" for **yourself** if no one else can claim you as a dependent . . . . **A** _____

B Enter "1" if:
- You are single and have only one job; or
- You are married, have only one job, and your spouse does not work; or
- Your wages from a second job or your spouse's wages (or the total of both) are $1,000 or less.

. . . **B** _____

C Enter "1" for your **spouse**. But, you may choose to enter "-0-" if you are married and have either a working spouse or more than one job. (Entering "-0-" may help you avoid having too little tax withheld.) . . . . **C** _____

D Enter number of **dependents** (other than your spouse or yourself) you will claim on your tax return . . . . **D** _____

E Enter "1" if you will file as **head of household** on your tax return (see conditions under **Head of household** above) . . **E** _____

F Enter "1" if you have at least $1,500 of **child or dependent care expenses** for which you plan to claim a credit . . . **F** _____
(**Note.** Do **not** include child support payments. See **Pub. 503,** Child and Dependent Care Expenses, for details.)

G **Child Tax Credit** (including additional child tax credit):
- If your total income will be less than $54,000 ($79,000 if married), enter "2" for each eligible child.
- If your total income will be between $54,000 and $04,000 ($79,000 and $119,000 if married), enter "1" for each eligible child plus "1" **additional** if you have four or more eligible children. **G** _____

H Add lines A through G and enter total here. (**Note.** This may be different from the number of exemptions you claim on your tax return.) ▶ **H** _____

For accuracy, complete all worksheets that apply.
- If you plan to **itemize or claim adjustments to income** and want to reduce your withholding, see the **Deductions and Adjustments Worksheet** on page 2.
- If you have **more than one job** or are **married and you and your spouse both work** and the combined earnings from all jobs exceed $35,000 ($25,000 if married) see the **Two-Earner/Two-Job Worksheet** on page 2 to avoid having too little tax withheld.
- If **neither** of the above situations applies, **stop here** and enter the number from line H on line 5 of Form W-4 below.

- Cut here and give Form W-4 to your employer. Keep the top part for your records. - - - - - - - - - - - -

Form **W-4** Department of the Treasury Internal Revenue Service	**Employee's Withholding Allowance Certificate** ▶ Whether you are entitled to claim a certain number of allowances or exemption from withholding is subject to review by the IRS. Your employer may be required to send a copy of this form to the IRS.	OMB No. 1545-0010 20**05**

1 Type or print your first name and middle initial	Last name		**2** Your social security number
Home address (number and street or rural route)		**3** ☐ Single ☐ Married ☐ Married, but withhold at higher Single rate. **Note.** If married, but legally separated, or spouse is a nonresident alien, check the "Single" box.	
City or town, state, and ZIP code		**4** If your last name differs from that shown on your social security card, check here. You must call 1-800-772-1213 for a new card. ▶ ☐	

5 Total number of allowances you are claiming (from line **H** above **or** from the applicable worksheet on page 2)   **5** _____

6 Additional amount, if any, you want withheld from each paycheck . . . .   **6** $ _____

7 I claim exemption from withholding for 2005, and I certify that I meet **both** of the following conditions for exemption.
- Last year I had a right to a refund of **all** federal income tax withheld because I had **no tax liability** and
- This year I expect a refund of **all** federal income tax withheld because I expect to have **no tax liability**.

If you meet both conditions, write "Exempt" here . . . . ▶ **7** _____

Under penalties of perjury, I declare that I have examined this certificate and to the best of my knowledge and belief, it is true, correct, and complete.

Employee's signature
(Form is not valid unless you sign it.) ▶ _____   Date ▶ _____

8 Employer's name and address (Employer: Complete lines 8 and 10 only if sending to the IRS.)	**9** Office code (optional)	**10** Employer identification number (EIN)

For Privacy Act and Paperwork Reduction Act Notice, see page 2.   Cat. No. 10220Q   Form **W-4** (2005)

Deductions and Adjustments Worksheet

Note. Use this worksheet *only* if you plan to itemize deductions, claim certain credits, or claim adjustments to income on your 2005 tax return.

1	Enter an estimate of your 2005 itemized deductions. These include qualifying home mortgage interest, charitable contributions, state and local taxes, medical expenses in excess of 7.5% of your income, and miscellaneous deductions. (For 2005, you may have to reduce your itemized deductions if your income is over $145,950 ($72,975 if married filing separately). See *Worksheet 3* in Pub. 919 for details.)	**1**	$
2	Enter: { $10,000 if married filing jointly or qualifying widow(er) / $ 7,300 if head of household / $ 5,000 if single or married filing separately }	**2**	$
3	**Subtract** line 2 from line 1. If line 2 is greater than line 1, enter "-0-"	**3**	$
4	Enter an estimate of your 2005 adjustments to income, including alimony, deductible IRA contributions, and student loan interest	**4**	$
5	**Add** lines 3 and 4 and enter the total. (Include any amount for credits from *Worksheet 7* in Pub. 919) ..	**5**	$
6	Enter an estimate of your 2005 nonwage income (such as dividends or interest)	**6**	$
7	**Subtract** line 6 from line 5. Enter the result, but not less than "-0-"	**7**	$
8	**Divide** the amount on line 7 by $3,200 and enter the result here. Drop any fraction	**8**	
9	Enter the number from the **Personal Allowances Worksheet,** line H, page 1	**9**	
10	**Add** lines 8 and 9 and enter the total here. If you plan to use the **Two-Earner/Two-Job Worksheet,** also enter this total on line 1 below. Otherwise, **stop here** and enter this total on Form W-4, line 5, page 1 ..	**10**	

Two-Earner/Two-Job Worksheet (See *Two earners/two jobs* on page 1.)

Note. Use this worksheet *only* if the instructions under line H on page 1 direct you here.

1	Enter the number from line H, page 1 (or from line 10 above if you used the **Deductions and Adjustments Worksheet**)	**1**	
2	Find the number in **Table 1** below that applies to the **LOWEST** paying job and enter it here	**2**	
3	If line 1 is **more than or equal to** line 2, subtract line 2 from line 1. Enter the result here (if zero, enter "-0-") and on Form W-4, line 5, page 1. **Do not** use the rest of this worksheet	**3**	

Note. If line 1 is *less than* line 2, enter "-0-" on Form W-4, line 5, page 1. Complete lines 4–9 below to calculate the additional withholding amount necessary to avoid a year-end tax bill.

4	Enter the number from line 2 of this worksheet	**4**	
5	Enter the number from line 1 of this worksheet	**5**	
6	**Subtract** line 5 from line 4	**6**	
7	Find the amount in **Table 2** below that applies to the **HIGHEST** paying job and enter it here	**7**	$
8	**Multiply** line 7 by line 6 and enter the result here. This is the additional annual withholding needed . ..	**8**	$
9	**Divide** line 8 by the number of pay periods remaining in 2005. For example, divide by 26 if you are paid every two weeks and you complete this form in December 2004. Enter the result here and on Form W-4, line 6, page 1. This is the additional amount to be withheld from each paycheck	**9**	$

Table 1: Two-Earner/Two-Job Worksheet

Married Filing Jointly						All Others	
If wages from **HIGHEST** paying job are—	AND, wages from **LOWEST** paying job are—	Enter on line 2 above	If wages from **HIGHEST** paying job are—	AND, wages from **LOWEST** paying job are—	Enter on line 2 above	If wages from **LOWEST** paying job are—	Enter on line 2 above
$0 - $40,000	$0 - $4,000	0	$40,001 and over	30,001 - 36,000	6	$0 - $6,000	0
	4,001 - 8,000	1		36,001 - 45,000	7	6,001 - 12,000	1
	8,001 - 18,000	2		45,001 - 50,000	8	12,001 - 18,000	2
	18,001 and over	3		50,001 - 60,000	9	18,001 - 24,000	3
				60,001 - 65,000	10	24,001 - 31,000	4
$40,001 and over	$0 - $4,000	0		65,001 - 75,000	11	31,001 - 45,000	5
	4,001 - 8,000	1		75,001 - 90,000	12	45,001 - 60,000	6
	8,001 - 18,000	2		90,001 - 100,000	13	60,001 - 75,000	7
	18,001 - 22,000	3		100,001 - 115,000	14	75,001 - 80,000	8
	22,001 - 25,000	4		115,001 and over	15	80,001 - 100,000	9
	25,001 - 30,000	5				100,001 and over	10

Table 2: Two-Earner/Two-Job Worksheet

Married Filing Jointly		All Others	
If wages from **HIGHEST** paying job are—	Enter on line 7 above	If wages from **HIGHEST** paying job are—	Enter on line 7 above
$0 - $60,000	$480	$0 - $30,000	$480
60,001 - 110,000	800	30,001 - 70,000	800
110,001 - 160,000	900	70,001 - 140,000	900
160,001 - 280,000	1,060	140,001 - 320,000	1,060
280,001 and over	1,120	320,001 and over	1,120

Privacy Act and Paperwork Reduction Act Notice. We ask for the information on this form to carry out the Internal Revenue laws of the United States. The Internal Revenue Code requires this information under sections 3402(f)(2)(A) and 6109 and their regulations. Failure to provide a properly completed form will result in your being treated as a single person who claims no withholding allowances; providing fraudulent information may also subject you to penalties. Routine uses of this information include giving it to the Department of Justice for civil and criminal litigation, to cities, states, and the District of Columbia for use in administering their tax laws, and using it in the National Directory of New Hires. We may also disclose this information to other countries under a tax treaty, to federal and state agencies to enforce federal nontax criminal laws, or to federal law enforcement and intelligence agencies to combat terrorism.

You are not required to provide the information requested on a form that is subject to

the Paperwork Reduction Act unless the form displays a valid OMB control number. Books or records relating to a form or its instructions must be retained as long as their contents may become material in the administration of any Internal Revenue law. Generally, tax returns and return information are confidential, as required by Code section 6103.

The time needed to complete this form will vary depending on individual circumstances. The estimated average time is: Recordkeeping, 45 min.; Learning about the law or the form, 12 min.; Preparing the form, 58 min. If you have comments concerning the accuracy of these time estimates or suggestions for making this form simpler, we would be happy to hear from you. You can write to: Internal Revenue Service, Tax Products Coordinating Committee, SE:W:CAR:MP:T:T:SP, 1111 Constitution Ave. NW, IR-6406, Washington, DC 20224. **Do not** send Form W-4 to this address. Instead, give it to your employer.

 Printed on recycled paper

HOUSEHOLD HELP AGREEMENT

This agreement is between _____ (Employer) and

_____ (Employee) as follows:

1. Employee is being hired to provide household help including, but not limited to, the following:

    ❏ Child care   ❏ Interior cleaning   ❏ Food preparation
    ❏ Gardening   ❏ Exterior cleaning   ❏ Laundry
    ❏ Shopping   ❏ Transportation

2. The employment is agreed by both parties to be "at will," meaning it can be terminated by either party at any time. Employee represents that no verbal promises to the contrary have been made.

3. The first _____ days of employment shall be probationary for both sides. If Employee's work is not satisfactory, or Employee is not satisfied with the job, the employment shall end at the end of this period.

4. Employee's hours may be adjusted from time to time. Initially, Employee's hours shall be: _____. Employee shall be entitled to the following breaks and holidays: _____ _____ _____ _____ Employee _____ be paid for holidays.

5. Employee's initial compensation shall be as follows: _____ _____.

6. Employee shall not have the power to bind Employer in any contracts.

7. Employee agrees not to divulge any information of a personal nature about Employer or Employer's family to anyone and not to publish any such information in any manner.

8. Employee agrees not to drink alcohol or take any illegal drugs during working hours, and not to smoke in Employer's home or vehicles.

9. Employee shall not permit anyone to come onto Employer's property without Employer's express consent.

10. Employee agrees at all times to perform his/her duties to the best of his/her ability. Employee will not perform work for anyone else while on duty for Employer.

11. If Employee notices any dangerous condition on the property of Employer, Employee agrees to immediately bring it to the attention of Employer.

12. This agreement shall be governed by the laws of the state of _____.

13. This agreement constitutes the entire agreement between the parties. No representations or promises have been made.

14. The company and employee agree that any disputes between them will be submitted to binding arbitration, rather than taken to court, and the costs of said arbitration shall be decided by the arbitrator. Each party specifically waives the right to take such disputes to court.

15. The parties agree to the following additional terms: ❑   None

Dated: _____

Employee: Employer:

_____   _____

Form **SS-8**
(Rev. June 2003)

Department of the Treasury
Internal Revenue Service

Determination of Worker Status
for Purposes of Federal Employment Taxes
and Income Tax Withholding

OMB No. 1545-0004

Name of firm (or person) for whom the worker performed services	Worker's name

Firm's address (include street address, apt. or suite no., city, state, and ZIP code)	Worker's address (include street address, apt. or suite no., city, state, and ZIP code)

Trade name	Telephone number (include area code) ( )	Worker's social security number

Telephone number (include area code) ( )	Firm's employer identification number	Worker's employer identification number (if any)

If the worker is paid by a firm other than the one listed on this form for these services, enter the name, address, and employer identification number of the payer.

Important Information Needed To Process Your Request

We must have your permission to disclose your name and the information on this form and any attachments to other parties involved with this request. **Do we have your permission to disclose this information?** . . . . ☐ **Yes**   ☐ **No**
If you answered "No" or did not mark a box, we will not process your request and will not issue a determination.

You must answer ALL items OR mark them "Unknown" or "Does not apply." If you need more space, attach another sheet.

A   This form is being completed by: ☐ Firm   ☐ Worker; for services performed _____ to _____ .
                                                           (beginning date)   (ending date)

B   Explain your reason(s) for filing this form (e.g., you received a bill from the IRS, you believe you received a Form 1099 or Form W-2 erroneously, you are unable to get worker's compensation benefits, you were audited or are being audited by the IRS). -----------------------

C   Total number of workers who performed or are performing the same or similar services _____ .

D   How did the worker obtain the job?   ☐ Application   ☐ Bid   ☐ Employment Agency   ☐ Other (specify) _____ .

E   Attach copies of all supporting documentation (contracts, invoices, memos, Forms W-2, Forms 1099, IRS closing agreements, IRS rulings, etc.). In addition, please inform us of any current or past litigation concerning the worker's status. If no income reporting forms (Form 1099-MISC or W-2) were furnished to the worker, enter the amount of income earned for the year(s) at issue $ _____ .

F   Describe the firm's business. -----------------------

G   Describe the work done by the worker and provide the worker's job title. -----------------------

H   Explain why you believe the worker is an employee or an independent contractor. -----------------------

I   Did the worker perform services for the firm before getting this position? . . . . ☐ **Yes**   ☐ **No**   ☐ **N/A**
     If "Yes," what were the dates of the prior service? -----------------------
     If "Yes," explain the differences, if any, between the current and prior service. -----------------------

J   If the work is done under a written agreement between the firm and the worker, attach a copy (preferably signed by both parties). Describe the terms and conditions of the work arrangement. -----------------------

---

For Privacy Act and Paperwork Reduction Act Notice, see page 5.   Cat. No. 16106T   Form **SS-8** (Rev. 6-2003)

Part I   Behavioral Control

1   What specific training and/or instruction is the worker given by the firm? ....

2   How does the worker receive work assignments? ....

3   Who determines the methods by which the assignments are performed? ....

4   Who is the worker required to contact if problems or complaints arise and who is responsible for their resolution? ....

5   What types of reports are required from the worker? Attach examples. ....

6   Describe the worker's daily routine (i.e., schedule, hours, etc.). ....

7   At what location(s) does the worker perform services (e.g., firm's premises, own shop or office, home, customer's location, etc.)? ....

8   Describe any meetings the worker is required to attend and any penalties for not attending (e.g., sales meetings, monthly meetings, staff meetings, etc.). ....

9   Is the worker required to provide the services personally? . . . . ☐ **Yes**   ☐ **No**

10   If substitutes or helpers are needed, who hires them? ....

11   If the worker hires the substitutes or helpers, is approval required? . . . . ☐ **Yes**   ☐ **No**
        If "Yes," by whom? ....

12   Who pays the substitutes or helpers? ....

13   Is the worker reimbursed if the worker pays the substitutes or helpers? . . . . ☐ **Yes**   ☐ **No**
        If "Yes," by whom?

Part II   Financial Control

1   List the supplies, equipment, materials, and property provided by each party:
        The firm ....
        The worker ....
        Other party ....

2   Does the worker lease equipment? . . . . ☐ **Yes**   ☐ **No**
        If "Yes," what are the terms of the lease? (Attach a copy or explanatory statement.) ....

3   What expenses are incurred by the worker in the performance of services for the firm? ....

4   Specify which, if any, expenses are reimbursed by:
        The firm ....
        Other party ....

5   Type of pay the worker receives: ☐ Salary   ☐ Commission   ☐ Hourly Wage   ☐ Piece Work
        ☐ Lump Sum   ☐ Other (specify) ....
        If type of pay is commission, and the firm guarantees a minimum amount of pay, specify amount $ _____ .

6   Is the worker allowed a drawing account for advances? . . . . ☐ **Yes**   ☐ **No**
        If "Yes," how often? ....
        Specify any restrictions. ....

7   Whom does the customer pay? . . . . ☐ Firm   ☐ Worker
        If worker, does the worker pay the total amount to the firm? ☐ **Yes**   ☐ **No**   If "No," explain. ....

8   Does the firm carry worker's compensation insurance on the worker? . . . . ☐ **Yes**   ☐ **No**

9   What economic loss or financial risk, if any, can the worker incur beyond the normal loss of salary (e.g., loss or damage of equipment, material, etc.)? ....

Part III Relationship of the Worker and Firm

1 List the benefits available to the worker (e.g., paid vacations, sick pay, pensions, bonuses). ....

2 Can the relationship be terminated by either party without incurring liability or penalty? . . . . ☐ **Yes** ☐ **No**
     If "No," explain your answer. ....

3 Does the worker perform similar services for others? . . . . ☐ **Yes** ☐ **No**
     If "Yes," is the worker required to get approval from the firm? . . . . ☐ **Yes** ☐ **No**

4 Describe any agreements prohibiting competition between the worker and the firm while the worker is performing services or during any later period. Attach any available documentation. ....

5 Is the worker a member of a union? . . . . ☐ **Yes** ☐ **No**

6 What type of advertising, if any, does the worker do (e.g., a business listing in a directory, business cards, etc.)? Provide copies, if applicable.
     ....

7 If the worker assembles or processes a product at home, who provides the materials and instructions or pattern? ....
     ....

8 What does the worker do with the finished product (e.g., return it to the firm, provide it to another party, or sell it)? ....
     ....

9 How does the firm represent the worker to its customers (e.g., employee, partner, representative, or contractor)? ....

10 If the worker no longer performs services for the firm, how did the relationship end? ....
     ....

Part IV For Service Providers or Salespersons— Complete this part if the worker provided a service directly to customers or is a salesperson.

1 What are the worker's responsibilities in soliciting new customers? ....
     ....

2 Who provides the worker with leads to prospective customers? ....

3 Describe any reporting requirements pertaining to the leads. ....
     ....

4 What terms and conditions of sale, if any, are required by the firm? ....

5 Are orders submitted to and subject to approval by the firm? . . . . ☐ **Yes** ☐ **No**

6 Who determines the worker's territory? ....

7 Did the worker pay for the privilege of serving customers on the route or in the territory? . . . . ☐ **Yes** ☐ **No**
     If "Yes," whom did the worker pay? ....
     If "Yes," how much did the worker pay? . . . . $ _____ .

8 Where does the worker sell the product (e.g., in a home, retail establishment, etc.)? ....
     ....

9 List the product and/or services distributed by the worker (e.g., meat, vegetables, fruit, bakery products, beverages, or laundry or dry cleaning services). If more than one type of product and/or service is distributed, specify the principal one. ....
     ....

10 Does the worker sell life insurance full time? . . . . ☐ **Yes** ☐ **No**

11 Does the worker sell other types of insurance for the firm? . . . . ☐ **Yes** ☐ **No**
     If "Yes," enter the percentage of the worker's total working time spent in selling other types of insurance. . . . _____%

12 If the worker solicits orders from wholesalers, retailers, contractors, or operators of hotels, restaurants, or other similar establishments, enter the percentage of the worker's time spent in the solicitation. . . . . _____%

13 Is the merchandise purchased by the customers for resale or use in their business operations? . . . . ☐ **Yes** ☐ **No**
     Describe the merchandise and state whether it is equipment installed on the customers' premises. ....
     ....

Part V Signature (see page 4)

Under penalties of perjury, I declare that I have examined this request, including accompanying documents, and to the best of my knowledge and belief, the facts presented are true, correct, and complete.

Signature ▶ _____   Title ▶ _____   Date ▶ _____
              (Type or print name below)

This page intentionally left blank.

INDEPENDENT CONTRACTOR AGREEMENT

This indemnification agreement is entered into by and between _____ (the Company) and _____ (the Contractor). It is agreed by the parties as follows:

1.   The Contractor shall supply all of the labor and materials to perform the following work for the Company as an independent contractor:

❏ The attached plans and specifications are to be followed and are hereby made a part of this Agreement.

2.   The Contractor agrees to the following completion dates for portions of the work and final completion of the work:

Description of Work   Completion Date

3.   The Contractor shall perform the work in a workmanlike manner, according to standard industry practices, unless other standards or requirements are set forth in any attached plans and specifications.

4.   The Company shall pay the Contractor the sum of $_____, in full payment for the work as set forth in this Agreement, to be paid as follows:

5.   Any additional work or services shall be agreed to in writing, signed by both parties.

6.   The Contractor shall obtain and maintain any licenses or permits necessary for the work to be performed. The Contractor shall obtain and maintain any required insurance, including but not limited to workers' compensation insurance, to cover the Contractor's employees and agents.

7.   The Contractor shall be responsible for the payment of any subcontractors and shall obtain lien releases from subcontractors as may be necessary. The Contractor agrees to indemnify and hold harmless the Company from any claims or liability arising out of the work performed by the Contractor under this Agreement.

8.   Time is of the essence of this Agreement.

9.   This Agreement shall be governed by the laws of _____.

10.   If any part of this agreement is adjudged invalid, illegal, or unenforceable, the remaining parts shall not be affected and shall remain in full force and effect.

11.   This Agreement shall be binding upon the parties and upon their heirs, executors, personal representatives, administrators, and assigns. No person shall have a right or cause of action arising out of or resulting from this Agreement, except those who are parties to it and their successors in interest.

12.   This instrument, including any attached exhibits and addenda, constitutes the entire agreement of the parties. No representations or promises have been made except those that are set out in this agreement. This Agreement may not be modified except in writing signed by all the parties.

IN WITNESS WHEREOF the parties have signed this agreement under seal on _____.

Company: Contractor:

_____   _____

_____   _____

MODIFICATION OF INDEPENDENT CONTRACTOR AGREEMENT

For valuable consideration, the receipt and sufficiency of which is acknowledged by each of the parties, this agreement amends an Independent Contractor Agreement, dated _____, 20___, between _____ and _____, relating to _____. This amendment is hereby incorporated into the Contract.

Except as changed by this amendment, the Independent Contractor Agreement shall continue in effect according to its terms. The amendments herein shall be effective on the date this document is executed by all parties.

IN WITNESS WHEREOF the parties have signed this agreement under seal on _____.

_____   _____

_____   _____

This page intentionally left blank.

TERMINATION OF INDEPENDENT CONTRACTOR AGREEMENT

For valuable consideration, the receipt and sufficiency of which is acknowledged by each of the parties to that certain Independent Contractor Agreement, dated _____, 20_____, between _____ and _____, relating to _____, hereby agree that said Independent Contractor Agreement shall be terminated by mutual agreement, and that each party releases the other from any and all claims thereunder.

IN WITNESS WHEREOF the parties have signed this termination under seal on _____, 20____.

_____

_____

Chapter 8:
Miscellaneous Forms

This chapter explains several useful forms that do not fit into the categories of the previous chapters *or* can be used in matters covered by several chapters.

> ### *Forms in Chapter:*
> - **Affidavit**
> - **Arbitration Agreement**
> - **Mediation Agreement**
> - **Covenant Not to Sue**
> - **Accident Worksheet**
> - **General Release**
> - **Specific Release**
> - **Mutual Release**
> - **Request for Information**
>   **under the Freedom of Information Act**
> - **Mailing List Name Removal**
> - **Request to Stop Telephone Solicitations**

Affidavit

An *affidavit* is a form in which a person swears something is true or that certain facts occurred. There are limitations on how an affidavit can be used. Because a person in court has a right to confront witnesses, an affidavit cannot be used in court to substitute a live witness. However, it can be used outside of court in negotiations. For example, if you get three people to sign an affidavit that your neighbor was constantly teasing your dog, this may convince your neighbor's attorney not to file a dog bite case against you. An **AFFIDAVIT** form is included, and a sample is shown below. (see form 104, p.345.)

Sample: **Affidavit**

AFFIDAVIT

The undersigned, being first duly sworn, deposes and says:

I live at 125 Elm Street, Anytown, Iowa across the street from Jon Dough and I have observed on many occasions Billy Williams throwing rocks at and taunting Jon Dough's dog Fifi. I have never seen Fifi attack Billy Williams without provocation.

This affidavit was executed by me on ___May 1, 2006_____.

[Notary omitted to save space.]

Dispute Resolution

Going to court is expensive, slow, and risky. In recent years, various means of *alternative dispute resolution* have become popular. Used correctly, the alternative dispute resolution procedures of *arbitration* and *mediation* can be much more efficient than litigation at settling disputes between parties who cannot come to an agreement on their own. These days there are trained arbitrators, mediators, and arbitration and mediation organizations in most areas. You can locate them through your lawyer or by calling your local or state bar association.

Arbitration

An *arbitrator* is a person who, like an umpire or a judge, has the power to decide. The disputants, either by themselves or with the assistance of lawyers, present their arguments to the arbitrator, agreeing in advance to abide by his or her decision. It is a kind of private court system in which the parties get to choose the judge and make their own rules about procedure and evidence.

The following samples are clauses to be inserted in a contract if the parties agree that any disputes to arise will be arbitrated. The first provides for arbitration under the rules of an organization that provides arbitration services. There are many such organizations. The most prominent one is the *American Arbitration Association*. It provides services around the country. The second sample provides for arbitrators to be appointed by the parties without being overseen by such an organization.

Sample Contract Clause: **Arbitration of Disputes (organization rules)**

The parties agree that any controversy, claim, or dispute arising out of or related to this agreement or any breach of this agreement shall be submitted to arbitration by and according to the applicable rules of the American Arbitration Association. The judgment upon an award rendered by the arbitrator may be entered in any court having jurisdiction.

Sample Contract Clause: **Arbitration of Disputes (arbitrator selected by parties)**

The parties agree that any controversy, claim, or dispute arising out of or related to this agreement or any breach of this agreement shall be submitted to arbitration. Such arbitration shall take place in _____Denver_____, _____Colorado_____ or at such other place as may be agreed upon by the parties. The parties shall attempt to agree on one arbitrator. If they are unable to so agree, then each party shall appoint one arbitrator and those appointed shall appoint a third arbitrator. The expenses of arbitration shall be divided equally by the parties. The prevailing party shall be entitled to reasonable attorneys' fees. The arbitrators shall conclusively decide all issues of law and fact related to the arbitrated dispute. Judgment upon an award rendered by the arbitrator may be entered in any court having jurisdiction.

If, after a dispute has arisen, you and the other party wish to submit to arbitration, you can use an **ARBITRATION AGREEMENT**. (see form 105, p.347.)

Sample: **Arbitration Agreement**

ARBITRATION AGREEMENT

This Arbitration Agreement is made this _____12th_____ day of _____October_____, _____2005_____, by and between _____Western Distributors, Inc_____. and _____Mountain Packaging_____, who agree as follows:

1.   The parties agree that any controversy, claim, or dispute arising out of or related to:

the contract executed by and between the parties on March 3, 2005

shall be submitted to arbitration. Such arbitration shall take place at _____7635 Red Rocks Hwy., Denver, CO_____ or at such other place as may be agreed upon by the parties.

2.   The parties shall attempt to agree on one arbitrator. If they are unable to so agree, then each party shall appoint one arbitrator and those appointed shall appoint a third arbitrator.

continued...

---

3.   The expenses of arbitration shall be divided equally by the parties.

4.   The arbitrators shall conclusively decide all issues of law and fact related to the arbitrated dispute. Judgment upon an award rendered by the arbitrator may be entered in any court having jurisdiction.

5.   The prevailing party ☒ shall ❑ shall not be entitled to reasonable attorneys' fees.

Mediation

A *mediator* has no power to decide disputes. A mediator is a neutral party who acts as a *go between* to help the parties reach their own compromises and agreements. You might think that a mediator would be useless. If the parties cannot agree by themselves, why would they suddenly be able to do so with the help of a mediator who has no power to make decisions? Nevertheless, it frequently works. It also has an advantage over both litigation and arbitration. In court or arbitration, you put the results in the hands of outsiders. The judge or arbitrator gets to fill in the terms any way he or she wants. In mediation, the only people who can decide are the parties themselves. They keep complete control over the process.

If you are in a dispute with another party, you both may decide that mediation could be helpful and sign a **MEDIATION AGREEMENT**. (see form 106, p.349.) The sample below presumes that the parties can agree on a mediator. This is usually easy to do since the mediator has no decision making power. Besides, if you cannot even agree on a mediator, mediation probably will not be successful.

Sample: **Mediation Agreement**

MEDIATION AGREEMENT

The undersigned parties are engaged in a dispute regarding <u>the contract between the parties dated February 12, 2006</u>. We hereby agree to submit such dispute to mediation by <u>Neighborhood Mediation Services</u> and that all matters resolved in mediation shall be reduced to a binding written agreement signed by the parties. The costs of mediation shall be borne equally by the parties.

Dated: <u>August 8, 2006</u>.

Covenant Not to Sue

There is a difference between agreeing that one person has no further claim of liability against another and promising that, although there may be a claim, the person will not bring a lawsuit based on it. The former is a *release.* The latter is a **Covenant Not to Sue.** Once a claim has been released, it no longer exists and (unless there has been fraud involved) cannot be revived. But if you promise not to sue on a claim, the claim does not go away. You have just promised not to try to enforce it. If the promise not to sue goes away, the claim is still there, ready to be enforced.

If a claimant receives cash in an agreed settlement of the claim, it is appropriate to give a release. There will never be any need to enforce a debt that has been fully paid. If you only have a promise to pay something in the future, such as a promissory note, then maybe a **Covenant Not to Sue** is appropriate. (see form 107, p.351.) The claimant promises not to bring a lawsuit on the claim as long as the note is not in default.

Sample: **Covenant Not to Sue**

COVENANT NOT TO SUE

This agreement is made by and between _____Jon Dough_____ (the "Covenantor"), for [~~itself~~/himself/~~herself~~] and for [~~its~~/his/~~her~~] heirs, legal representatives and assigns, and ____Mary Smith____ (the "Covenantee").

1.   In exchange for the Covenantor's covenant herein, the Covenantee __promises and agrees to pay all of the Covenantor's medical bills and $50 per day for lost wages arising out of injuries Covenantor received on July 4, 2005 at the Covenantee's premises__.

2.   In exchange for the consideration stated in paragraph 1 above, the receipt and sufficiency of which is hereby acknowledged by the Covenantor, the Covenantor covenants with the Covenantee never to institute any suit or action at law or in equity against the Covenantee by reason of any claim the Covenantor now has or may hereafter acquire related to: __injuries Covenantor received on July 4, 2006 at the Covenantee's premises__.

This agreement was executed by the parties under seal on __August 15, 2006__.

Accidents

Whenever you are involved in any type of accident, you should write down as much information about the event as soon as possible. You may think the event is etched in your memory and you will never forget it, but details will quickly fade away. You should write down as many details as you can think of, even if you do not think they are important at the time. The **ACCIDENT WORKSHEET** will help you gather and remember key information about your accident. (see form 108, p.353.)

Discharging Liability (After It Arises)

A *liability* is a debt owed. Like other debts, liabilities of *tort* (*personal injury*) or liabilities of contract can be discharged in various ways, including the payment of money or promise to pay money. The first sample is a **GENERAL RELEASE** from all liabilities that the person released may owe to the signer. (see form 109, p.357.)

The second sample is a **SPECIFIC RELEASE** and is limited to matters related to a specific event or contract. (see form 110, p.359.)

In the third sample, the parties release each other from liabilities, making it a **MUTUAL RELEASE**. (see form 111, p.361.)

Sample: **General Release**

GENERAL RELEASE

In exchange for the sum of $10.00 and other valuable consideration, the receipt and sufficiency of which is hereby acknowledged, the undersigned hereby forever releases, discharges, and acquits _____Jon Dough_____, and [~~its~~/his/~~her~~] successors, assigns, heirs, and personal representatives, from any and all claims, actions, suits, agreements, or liabilities in favor of or owed to the undersigned, existing at any time up to the date of this release.

IN WITNESS WHEREOF, the undersigned has executed this release under seal on _May 8,_ _____2006_____.

Sample: **Specific Release**

SPECIFIC RELEASE

In exchange for the sum of $10.00 and other valuable consideration, the receipt and sufficiency of which is hereby acknowledged, the undersigned hereby forever releases, discharges, and acquits ___Scrupulous Corporation___ , and [its/~~his/her~~] successors, assigns, heirs, and personal representatives, from any and all claims, actions, suits, agreements, or liabilities arising out of or related to:

any and all injuries and damages sustained by the undersigned, pursuant to the undersigned slipping and falling at the premises of Scrupulous Corporation on July 4, 2003.

IN WITNESS WHEREOF, the undersigned has executed this release under seal on ___August 28, 2006___ .

Sample: **Mutual Release**

MUTUAL RELEASE

In exchange for the sum of $10.00 and other valuable consideration, the receipt and sufficiency of which is hereby acknowledged, the undersigned hereby forever release, discharge, and acquit each other, and their successors, assigns, heirs, and personal representatives, from any and all claims, actions, suits, agreements, or liabilities arising out of or related to: ___the contract executed by and between the parties on March 3, 2003___ .

IN WITNESS WHEREOF, the undersigned have executed this release under seal and by authority of their respective boards of directors as of ___October 27, 2006___ .

Freedom of Information Act Request

The laws of the federal government and most states give you a right to obtain information held by government agencies. While a few matters are exempt for purposes of national security, most other information is available. To obtain information, you must usually make a written request. In some cases, there is a small fee for copies of the information. This should not exceed the actual cost of producing these forms.

A **REQUEST FOR INFORMATION UNDER THE FREEDOM OF INFORMATION ACT** can be used to request information under the federal *Freedom of Information Act*. (see form 112, p.363.) For obtaining state information, you can adapt the form using the law for your state.

State-by-State
Freedom of Information/Open Records Laws

Alabama	Open Records Statute	Ala. Code § 36-12-40
Alaska	Public Records Act	Alaska Stat. §§40.25.120, -.220
Arizona	Public Records Law	Ariz. Rev. Stat. § 39-121
Arkansas	Ark. Freedom of Infrmtn Act	Ark. Code Ann. § 25-19-103
California	Public Records Act	Cal. Gov't Code § 6250
Colorado	Open Records Act	Colo. Rev. Stat. § 24-72-203
Connecticut	Freedom of Information Act	Conn. Gen. Stat. § 1-200
Delaware	Freedom of Information Act	Del. Code Ann. Tit. 29, § 10002
D.C.	Freedom of Information Act	D.C. Dode Ann. §§ 2-502, 2-539
Florida	Sunshine Law	Fla. Stat. Ch. 119.011
Georgia	Open Records Act	Ga. Code Ann. § 50-18-70
Hawaii	Uniform Info. Practices Act	Haw. Rev. Stat. § 92F-3
Idaho	Open Records Act	Idaho Code § 9-337
Illinois	Freedom of Information Act	5 ILCS 140/1
Indiana	Access to Public Records Act	Ind. Code § 5-14-3-2
Iowa	Open Records Act	Iowa Code § 22.1
Kansas	Open Records Act	Kan. Stat. Ann. § 45-217
Kentucky	Open Records Act	Ky. Rev. Stat. Ann. § 61.870(2)
Louisiana	Public Records Act	La. Rev. Stat. Ann.§ 44:1
Maine	Freedom of Access Act	Me. Rev. Stat. Ann. Tit. 1, § 402
Maryland	Public Information Act	Md. Code Ann., State Gov't § 10-611
Massachusetts	Public Records Law	Mass.Gen. Laws Ann. Ch.4, § 7, Cl. 26
Michigan	Freedom of Information Act	Mich. Comp. Laws Ann. § 15.232
Minnesota	Gov't Data Practices Act	Minn. Stat. § 13.01
Mississippi	Public Records Act	Miss. Code Ann. § 25-61-1
Missouri	Sunshine Law	Mo. Rev. Stat. § 610.010
Montana	Public Records Act	Mont. Code Ann. § 2-6-110(1)
Nebraska	Open Records Law	Neb. Rev. Stat. § 84-712.01
Nevada	Open Records Law	Nev. Rev. Stat. § 239.010
New Hampshire	Right to Know Law	N.H. Rev. Stat. Ann. § 91-A:4
New Jersey	Right to Know Law	N.J. Stat. Ann. § 47:1A-1.1
New Mexico	Public Records Act	N.M. Stat. Ann. § 14-2-6
New York	Freedom of Information Law	N.Y. Pub. Off. Law § 86
North Carolina	Public Records Law	N.C. Gen. Stat. § 132-1
North Dakota	Open Records Statute	N.D. Cent. Code § 44-04-18
Ohio	State laws	Ohio Rev. Code § 149.011(G)
Oklahoma	Open Records Act	Okla. Stat. Tit. 51, § 24A.3
Oregon	Public Records Law	Ore. Rev. Stat. § 192.410
Pennsylvania	Open Records Law	Pa. Cons. Stat. Ann. Tit. 65, § 66.1
Rhode Island	Access to Public Records Act	R.I. Gen. Laws § 38-2-1
South Carolina	Freedom of Information Act	S.C. Code Ann. § 30-4-20

South Dakota	Open Records Statute	S.D. Codified Laws Ann. § 1-27-1
Tennessee	Public Records Act	Tenn. Code Ann. § 10-7-503
Texas	Open Records Act	Tex. Gov't Code Ann. § 552.002
Utah	Gov't Records Access and Management Act	Utah Code Ann. § 63-2-103
Vermont	Access to Public Records Law	Vt. Stat. Ann. Tit.1, § 317(b)
Virginia	Freedom of Information Act	Va. Code Ann. § 2.2-3701
Washington	Public Records Law	Wash.Rev. Code § 40.14.010
West Virginia	Freedom of Information Act	W.Va. Code § 29B-1-1
Wisconsin	Open Records Statute	Wis. Stat. § 19.32
Wyoming	Public Records Act	Wyo. Stat. § 16-4-201

Unwanted Solicitations

Most people today are bombarded with unwanted telemarketing calls and unwanted junk mail. The federal government, as well as most state legislatures, has taken action to reduce the amount of these types of annoyances. If you have access to the Internet and a valid email address, you can sign up on the *National Do Not Call Registry* at **http://donotcall.gov**. By following the directions online, you can put an end to many of those annoying calls. If you do not have a valid email address, you can call 888-382-1222 to register.

For junk mail or unwanted solicitations, use the MAILING LIST NAME REMOVAL. (see form 113, p.365.) Most companies will honor your request, but it may take more than one submission to the organization in order to accomplish the removal of your name.

One exception to the do not call law is that companies with whom you have a business relationship can still call you. This means that if you place an order with a company, they can call you endlessly with special offers. When they call you should ask to be put on their do not call list. If this does not work, or if you prefer not to talk with them at all, you can send them a notice that you do not wish to be called. Use the REQUEST TO STOP TELEPHONE SOLICITATIONS to do this. (see form 114, p.367.)

AFFIDAVIT

The undersigned, being first duly sworn, deposes and says:

This affidavit was executed by me on _____, 20_____.

_____

STATE OF   )
COUNTY OF   )

I certify that _____ ,who ❑ is personally known to me to be the person whose name is subscribed to the foregoing instrument ❑ produced _____ as identification, personally appeared before me on _____, and ❑ acknowledged the execution of the foregoing instrument ❑ acknowledged that (s)he is (Assistant) Secretary of _____ and that by authority duly given and as the act of the corporation, the foregoing instrument was signed in its name by its (Vice) President, sealed with its corporate seal and attested by him/her as its (Assistant) Secretary.

_____
Notary Public

My commission expires:

This page intentionally left blank.

ARBITRATION AGREEMENT

This Arbitration Agreement is made this _____ day of _____, 20_____, by and between
_____ and _____,
who agree as follows:

1.   The parties agree that any controversy, claim, or dispute arising out of or related to:

shall be submitted to arbitration. Such arbitration shall take place at_____
_____ or at such other place as may be
agreed upon by the parties.

2.   The parties shall attempt to agree on one arbitrator. If they are unable to so agree, then each party shall appoint one arbitrator, and those appointed shall appoint a third arbitrator.

3.   The expenses of arbitration shall be divided equally by the parties.

4.   The arbitrators shall conclusively decide all issues of law and fact related to the arbitrated dispute. Judgment upon an award rendered by the arbitrator may be entered in any court having jurisdiction.

5.   The prevailing party ❏ shall ❏ shall not be entitled to reasonable attorneys' fees.

_____   _____

_____   _____

This page intentionally left blank.

MEDIATION AGREEMENT

This Mediation Agreement is made this _____ day of _____, 20_____, by and between _____ and _____, who agree as follows:

1. The parties agree that any controversy, claim, or dispute arising out of or related to:

shall be submitted to mediation. Such mediation shall take place at _____ _____ or at such other place as may be agreed upon by the parties.

2. The parties have agreed to use _____ as mediator.

3. The expenses of mediation shall be divided equally by the parties.

_____   _____

_____   _____

This page intentionally left blank.

COVENANT NOT TO SUE

This agreement is made by and between _____
(the Covenantor), for [itself/himself/herself] and for its/his/her heirs, legal representatives, and assigns, and
_____ (the Covenantee).

1. In exchange for the Covenantor's covenant herein, the Covenantee _____
_____
_____
_____
_____.

2. In exchange for the consideration stated in paragraph 1 above, the receipt and sufficiency of which is hereby
acknowledged by the Covenantor, the Covenantor covenants with the Covenantee never to institute any suit or
action at law or in equity against the Covenantee by reason of any claim the Covenantor now has or may hereafter
acquire related to: _____
_____
_____.

This agreement was executed by the parties under seal on _____, 20____.

Covenantor: Covenantee:

_____   _____

_____   _____

This page intentionally left blank.

ACCIDENT WORKSHEET

Date of accident _____, 20_____ Time _____

Place of accident _____

Weather (if outdoors) _____

Description of accident _____

_____

_____

Parties Involved

Name _____

Address _____

City, state, zip _____

Day phone _____

Evening phone _____

Cell phone _____

Pager _____

Insurance Company _____

Address _____

City, state, zip _____

Phone _____

Claim No. _____

Adjuster's name _____

Adjuster's phone _____

Name _____

Address _____

City, state, zip _____

Day phone _____

Evening phone _____

Cell phone _____

Pager _____

Insurance Company _____

Address _____

City, state, zip _____

Phone _____

Claim No. _____

Adjuster's name _____

Adjuster's phone _____

Witnesses

Name _____

Address _____

City, state, zip _____

Day phone _____

Evening phone _____

Cell phone _____

Pager _____

What witness saw _____

_____

Name _____

Address _____

City, state, zip _____

Day phone _____

Evening phone _____

Cell phone _____

Pager _____

What witness saw _____

_____

Repair Estimates:

Amount $_____ Date _____, 20_____

Name _____

Address _____

City, state, zip _____

Phone _____

Amount $_____ Date _____, 20_____

Name _____

Address _____

City, state, zip _____

Phone _____

Amount $_____ Date _____, 20_____

Name _____

Address _____

City, state, zip _____

Phone _____

Medical Treatments

Provider _____

Address _____

City, state, zip _____

Phone _____

Date _____, 20_____ Treatment _____

Cost $_____ Prognosis _____

Provider _____

Address _____

City, state, zip _____

Phone _____

Date _____, 20_____ Treatment _____

Cost $_____ Prognosis _____

Provider _____

Address _____

City, state, zip _____

Phone _____

Date _____, 20_____ Treatment _____

Cost $_____ Prognosis _____

GENERAL RELEASE

In exchange for the sum of $10.00 and other valuable consideration, the receipt and sufficiency of which is hereby acknowledged, the undersigned corporation hereby forever releases, discharges, and acquits _____, and [its/his/her] successors, assigns, heirs, and personal representatives, from any and all claims, actions, suits, agreements, or liabilities in favor of or owed to the undersigned, existing at any time up to the date of this release.

IN WITNESS WHEREOF, the undersigned has executed this release under seal on _____.

_____

This page intentionally left blank.

SPECIFIC RELEASE

In exchange for the sum of $10.00 and other valuable consideration, the receipt and sufficiency of which is hereby acknowledged, the undersigned hereby forever releases, discharges and acquits _____, and [its/his/her] successors, assigns, heirs, and personal representatives, from any and all claims, actions, suits, agreements, or liabilities arising out of or related to:

IN WITNESS WHEREOF, the undersigned has executed this release under seal on _____.

_____

This page intentionally left blank.

MUTUAL RELEASE

In exchange for the sum of $10.00 and other valuable consideration, the receipt and sufficiency of which is hereby acknowledged, the undersigned hereby forever release, discharge, and acquit each other, and their successors, assigns, heirs, and personal representatives, from any and all claims, actions, suits, agreements, or liabilities arising out of or related to:

IN WITNESS WHEREOF, the undersigned have executed this release under seal on _____.

_____   _____

_____   _____

This page intentionally left blank.

REQUEST FOR INFORMATION UNDER THE FREEDOM OF INFORMATION ACT

To:

Under the Freedom of Information Act, I request any and all information you have regarding the following:

In the event that the cost for such information exceeds $_____, please advise me in advance of what material will be included and what the cost will be.

Thank you,

_____

[print name]

_____

_____

[address]

_____

This page intentionally left blank.

MAILING LIST NAME REMOVAL

Date:

To:

To whom it may concern:

I have received unsolicited mail from your firm and I wish that such mailings be discontinued. Please remove my name and address from any and all lists you maintain. Do not provide my name and address to any other parties.

My name and address are as follows:

[print or attach label]

Thank you,

_____

This page intentionally left blank.

REQUEST TO STOP TELEPHONE SOLICITATIONS

To: _____

   _____

   _____

This letter is to request that my phone number, _____-_____-_____, be put on your DO NOT CALL list. I do not wish to receive any phone calls from your firm for any reason.

If any further phone calls are made, I shall pursue my remedies as provided by law.

Sincerely,

_____

Index

limited partnership, 15
Living Trust, 99, 101, 119
living will, 102, 139
loans, 95, 149, 154, 155, 198, 199, 219, 224
    default, 155
Louisiana Partnership Act, 14

M

Mailing List Name Removal, 343, 365
marital agreement, 33, 51
Marital Settlement Agreement, 34, 63
Mediation Agreement, 338, 349
mediators, 336, 338
Modification of Independent Contractor
    Agreement, 301, 331
mortgage, 198, 224
    documents, 224
    execution, 224
    payment tables, 149
    recording, 224
mutual funds, 99
Mutual Release, 340, 341, 361

N

name change, 34
National Do Not Call Registry, 343
notary, 1, 16, 97
notice, 224, 232
Notice of Assignment of a Contract, 7
Notice of Breach, 9
Notice of Change of Name, 34
Notice of Death of Debtor, 155, 193
Notice of Death to Social Security
    Administration, 103, 145
Notice of Intent to Vacate at End of Lease,
    232
Notice of Lost Credit Card, 153, 179
Notice of Name Change, 57
Notice to Landlord to Make Repairs, 231, 283
Notice to Vacate at the End of Lease, 289

O

Official Mail Forwarding Change of Address
    Order, 36, 75
Option Agreement, 224, 247
optionee, 224

optionor, 224
options, 224
oral contracts, 3, 4
owner, 223

P

palimony, 31
parental responsibility, 35
partial performance, 3
partnership, 223
passport, 37
pension, 33
personal representative, 96
Pet Agreement, 226, 273
Pet Care Agreement, 35, 73
power of attorney, 101, 102
premarital agreement, 29, 32, 33, 45
probate, 95, 96, 97, 98, 99
promissory notes, 12, 13, 149, 150, 151, 198,
    224, 339
    negotiable, 150
    secured, 151
Promissory Note—Amortized with
    Guarantee, 161
Promissory Note—Lump Payment, 159
Promissory Note—payable on demand, 163
property, 2, 13, 29, 30, 32, 33, 34, 35, 95, 96,
    97, 98, 100, 101, 151, 155, 195, 196, 197,
    198, 199, 219, 220, 221, 223, 224, 225, 226,
    232, 233
    community, 101
    joint, 30, 33, 34, 98
    maintenance, 231
    marital, 33, 34
    separate, 30
    settlement agreement, 29
Protect Your Family from Lead in Your
    Home, 225

Q

Quitclaim Deed, 223, 241

R

radon testing, 226
real estate, 98, 99, 101, 196, 219, 220, 221,
    224, 225
    local requirements, 221

V

W

About the Authors

Mark Warda received his J.D. from the University of Illinois in Champaign. Licensed in Florida, he has written or coauthored over sixty self-help law books, including *How to Form Your Own Corporation in Florida* and *How to Make Your Own Will*.

James C. Ray received his law degree from the Duke Law School. Formerly a partner in the Raleigh office of LeBeouf, Lamb, Greene & MacRae, Mr. Ray is now a visiting lecturer in business law at North Carolina State University. He is also a member of the faculty of the legal assistants' program at Meredith College in Raleigh.